Nginx HTTP Server

Fourth Edition

Harness the power of Nginx to make the most of your
infrastructure and serve pages faster than ever before

Martin Fjordvald
Clement Nedelcu

BIRMINGHAM - MUMBAI

Nginx HTTP Server
Fourth Edition

Commissioning Editor: Vijin Boricha
Acquisition Editor: Shrilekha Inani
Content Development Editor: Sharon Raj
Technical Editor: Vishal K. Mewada
Copy Editor: Safis Editing
Project Coordinator: Virginia Dias
Proofreader: Safis Editing
Indexer: Pratik Shirodkar
Production Coordinator: Shantanu Zagade

First published: July 2010
Second edition: July 2013
Third edition: November 2015
Fourth edition: February 2018

Production reference: 1120218

Published by Packt Publishing Ltd.
Livery Place
35 Livery Street
Birmingham
B3 2PB, UK.

ISBN 978-1-78862-355-1

www.packtpub.com

To my wife Richole Huang, for her love, patience, and understanding throughout our marriage.

`mapt.io`

Mapt is an online digital library that gives you full access to over 5,000 books and videos, as well as industry leading tools to help you plan your personal development and advance your career. For more information, please visit our website.

Why subscribe?

- Spend less time learning and more time coding with practical eBooks and Videos from over 4,000 industry professionals

- Improve your learning with Skill Plans built especially for you

- Get a free eBook or video every month

- Mapt is fully searchable

- Copy and paste, print, and bookmark content

PacktPub.com

Did you know that Packt offers eBook versions of every book published, with PDF and ePub files available? You can upgrade to the eBook version at `www.PacktPub.com` and as a print book customer, you are entitled to a discount on the eBook copy. Get in touch with us at `service@packtpub.com` for more details.

At `www.PacktPub.com`, you can also read a collection of free technical articles, sign up for a range of free newsletters, and receive exclusive discounts and offers on Packt books and eBooks.

Contributors

About the authors

Martin Fjordvald is a 29-year-old Danish entrepreneur who started his company straight out of high school. Backed by a popular website, he became a jack of all trades having to deal with the business, programming, and marketing side of his business. The popularity of his website grew and so did the performance requirements of his code and servers.

He got involved with the community project to document Nginx early on and has written several blog posts and wiki articles detailing how Nginx works.

Special thanks to the entire Packt team for their patience during the course of writing this book.

Clement Nedelcu was born in France and studied at UK, French, and Chinese universities. After teaching computer science, programming, and systems administration at several eastern Chinese universities, he worked as a technology consultant in France, specialized in the web and .NET software development as well as Linux server administration. Since 2005, he has also been administering a major network of websites in his spare time, which allowed him to discover Nginx. Clement now works as CTO. for a Hong-Kong-based company developing management software for schools.

About the reviewer

Amet Umerov works as a Linux system engineer with promising start-up. InsideDNA, which provides cloud-based genomics and data analytics to the biotechnology sector working on oncology drugs.

Amet develops computing platforms for reproducible research in bioinformatics.

Specifically, he builds and supports highly parallel, scalable, and stable computing environments for compute-intense analytics. He uses Nginx as the frontend for web applications and load balancers for Docker environments.

> *I would like to express my gratitude to my family, friends, and colleagues.*

Packt is searching for authors like you

If you're interested in becoming an author for Packt, please visit `authors.packtpub.com` and apply today. We have worked with thousands of developers and tech professionals, just like you, to help them share their insight with the global tech community. You can make a general application, apply for a specific hot topic that we are recruiting an author for, or submit your own idea.

Table of Contents

Preface

It is a well-known fact that the web server market has a long-established leader: Apache. According to recent surveys, as of October 2015, almost 35 percent of the World Wide Web is served by this 20-year-old open source application. However, for the past few years, the same reports reveal the rise of a new competitor: Nginx, a lightweight HTTP server originating from Russia—pronounced engine X. There have been many questions surrounding this young web server. What is the reason causing so many server administrators to switch to Nginx since the beginning of year 2009? Is this tiny piece of software mature enough to run my high-traffic website? To begin with, Nginx is not as young as one might think. Originally started in 2002, the project was first carried out by a standalone developer, Igor Sysoev, for the needs of an extremely high-traffic Russian website, namely Rambler, which received as of September 2008 over 500 million HTTP requests per day. The application is now used to serve some of the most popular websites on the web, such as Reddit, Wikipedia, WordPress, Dropbox, and many more. Nginx has proven to be a very efficient, lightweight yet powerful web server. Throughout this book, you will discover many features of Nginx and progressively understand why so many administrators have decided to place their trust in this new HTTP server, often at the expense of Apache.

There are many aspects in which Nginx is more efficient than its competitors, first and foremost, speed: making use of asynchronous sockets, Nginx does not spawn processes as many times as it receives requests. One process per core suffices to handle thousands of connections, allowing a much lighter CPU load and memory consumption. Second, ease of use: configuration files are much simpler to read and tweak than with other web server solutions, such as Apache. A couple of lines are enough to set up a complete virtual host configuration. Last but not least, modularity: not only is Nginx a completely open source project released under a BSD-like license, but it also comes with a powerful plug-in system—referred to as modules. A large variety of modules are included with the original distribution archive, and many third-party ones can be downloaded online. All in all, Nginx combines speed, efficiency, and power, providing you the perfect ingredients for a successful web server; it appears to be the best Apache alternative as of today.

Who this book is for

By covering both the early setup stages and advanced topics, this book suits web administrators who are interested in ways to optimize their infrastructure, whether you are looking into replacing your existing web server software or integrating a new tool to cooperate with applications that are already up and running. If you, your visitors, and your operating system have been disappointed by Apache, this book is exactly what you need.

What this book covers

Chapter 1, *Downloading and Installing Nginx*, will guide you through the early setup stages of downloading and configuring your own build of the program.

Chapter 2, *Basic Nginx Configuration*, covers the essential aspects of the Nginx configuration structure and syntax.

Chapter 3, *HTTP Configuration*, takes you through the configuration of the HTTP server components enabling you to serve a first simple static site.

Chapter 4, *Module Configuration*, provides an in-depth explanation of the large variety of modules available with the standard Nginx package.

Chapter 5, *PHP and Python with Nginx*, is a comprehensive guide to setting up backend programs for serving dynamic content through Nginx.

Chapter 6, *Nginx as an Application Server*, describes how Nginx fits into the modern web of microservices and complex SaaS applications.

Chapter 7, *Apache and Nginx Together*, describes how both server applications can cooperate on the same architecture to improve existing websites and services.

Chapter 8, *From Apache to Nginx*, provides key information toward fully switching your server or web infrastructure from Apache to Nginx.

Chapter 9, *Introduction to Load Balancing and Optimization*, provides useful leads for server administrators that manage sites under heavy load.

Chapter 10, *Case Studies*, offers a practical approach to several real-life examples that include some of the most common tasks performed with Nginx.

`Chapter 11`, *Troubleshooting*, covers the most common issues encountered while setting up Nginx or during production stages.

To get the most out of this book

Although Nginx is available for Windows since version 0.7.52, it is common knowledge that Linux- or BSD-based distributions are preferred for hosting production sites. During the various processes described in this book, we will thus assume that you are hosting your website on a Linux operating system, such as Debian, Ubuntu, CentOS, or other well-known distributions.

Conventions used

There are a number of text conventions used throughout this book.

`CodeInText`: Indicates code words in text, database table names, folder names, filenames, file extensions, pathnames, dummy URLs, user input, and Twitter handles. Here is an example: "The rewrite and HTTP core modules of Nginx use PCRE for the syntax of their regular expressions, as we will discover in later chapters. You will need to install two packages—`pcre` and `pcre-devel`"

A block of code is set as follows:

```
[nginx]
name=nginx repo
baseurl=http://nginx.org/packages/OS/OSRELEASE/$basearch/
gpgcheck=0
enabled=1
```

When we wish to draw your attention to a particular part of a code block, the relevant lines or items are set in bold:

```
[nginx]
name=nginx repo
baseurl=http://nginx.org/packages/OS/OSRELEASE/$basearch/
gpgcheck=0
enabled=1
```

Any command-line input or output is written as follows:

```
apt-cache search nginx
apt-cache show PACKAGE_NAME
apt-get install PACKAGE_NAME
```

Bold: Indicates a new term, an important word, or words that you see onscreen. For example, words in menus or dialog boxes appear in the text like this. Here is an example: "Select **System info** from the **Administration** panel."

 Warnings or important notes appear like this.

 Tips and tricks appear like this.

Get in touch

Feedback from our readers is always welcome.

General feedback: Email feedback@packtpub.com and mention the book title in the subject of your message. If you have questions about any aspect of this book, please email us at questions@packtpub.com.

Errata: Although we have taken every care to ensure the accuracy of our content, mistakes do happen. If you have found a mistake in this book, we would be grateful if you would report this to us. Please visit www.packtpub.com/submit-errata, selecting your book, clicking on the Errata Submission Form link, and entering the details.

Piracy: If you come across any illegal copies of our works in any form on the Internet, we would be grateful if you would provide us with the location address or website name. Please contact us at copyright@packtpub.com with a link to the material.

If you are interested in becoming an author: If there is a topic that you have expertise in and you are interested in either writing or contributing to a book, please visit authors.packtpub.com.

Reviews

Please leave a review. Once you have read and used this book, why not leave a review on the site that you purchased it from? Potential readers can then see and use your unbiased opinion to make purchase decisions, we at Packt can understand what you think about our products, and our authors can see your feedback on their book. Thank you!

For more information about Packt, please visit packtpub.com.

1
Downloading and Installing Nginx

In this first chapter, we will proceed with the necessary steps towards establishing a functional setup of Nginx. This moment is crucial for the smooth functioning of your web server—there are some required libraries and tools for installing the web server, some parameters that you will have to decide upon when compiling the binaries, and there may also be some configuration changes to perform on your system.

This chapter covers the following:

- Installing via package managers
- Downloading and installing the prerequisites for compiling Nginx binaries
- Downloading a suitable version of the Nginx source code
- Configuring Nginx compile-time options
- Controlling the application with an `init` script
- Configuring the system to launch Nginx automatically on startup
- A quick overview of the possibilities offered by the Nginx Plus platform

Installing via package managers

The quickest, and easiest, way to install Nginx is to simply use your OS-provided version. Most of the time, these are kept fairly updated; however, for some Linux distributions focusing on stability, you may only have older versions of Nginx available. Sometimes, your Linux distribution may provide multiple versions of Nginx with different compile flags.

In general, before embarking on a more complex journey, we should check if we can use the easy solution. For a Debian-based operating system, we first find the Nginx compiles available then get the info for the one we want:

```
apt-cache search nginx
apt-cache show PACKAGE_NAME
apt-get install PACKAGE_NAME
```

For Red Hat Linux-based operating systems, we need to enable the EPEL repo first and then do the same:

```
yum install epel-release
yum search nginx
yum info PACKAGE_NAME
yum install PACKAGE_NAME
```

If the version provided is current enough, then you're ready to configure Nginx in the next chapter.

If the version provided by your distribution is too old, then Nginx provides packages for RHEL/CentOS distributions as well as Debian/Ubuntu distributions.

Nginx provided packages

To set up a `yum` repository for RHEL/CentOS, create a file named `/etc/yum.repos.d/nginx.repo` with the following contents:

```
[nginx]
name=nginx repo
baseurl=http://nginx.org/packages/OS/OSRELEASE/$basearch/
gpgcheck=0
enabled=1
```

Replace `OS` with `rhel` or `centos`, depending on the distribution used, and `OSRELEASE` with 6 or 7, for versions 6.x or 7.x, respectively. Afterwards, Nginx can now be installed with yum:

```
yum install nginx
```

For Debian-based distributions, we need to first use their signing key to authenticate the package signatures. Download the following file first from `http://nginx.org/keys/nginx_signing.key`.

Then run the following command:

```
sudo apt-key add nginx_signing.key
```

With the key added, we can now add the Nginx repository to our `sources.list` found in `/etc/apt/sources.list`. For Debian, we add the following lines:

```
deb http://nginx.org/packages/debian/ codename nginx
deb-src http://nginx.org/packages/debian/ codename nginx
```

Where `codename` is either `jessie` or `stretch` depending on your version of Debian. For Ubuntu, we use the following dependencies:

```
deb http://nginx.org/packages/ubuntu/ codename nginx
deb-src http://nginx.org/packages/ubuntu/ codename nginx
```

Where `codename` is one of `trusty`, `xenial`, or `zesty` depending on your version of Ubuntu. Finally, we can install Nginx with the `apt-get` command option:

```
apt-get update
apt-get install nginx
```

Compiling from source

There are situations where compiling Nginx from source is preferable. It gives us the most flexibility regarding modules, so we can customize better for our intended usage. For example, we could compile a very lean version for embedded hardware.

Additionally, we can make sure we use the latest version of Nginx and have all new features available to us. Keep in mind, though, that when installing software from source you are responsible for keeping it updated. Nginx, just like every other piece of software, sometimes finds security issues that it needs to address. An OS package is much easier to update than a source install, but so long as you're aware of the need to maintain it yourself, there is absolutely no problem.

Depending on the optional modules that you select at compile time, you will perhaps need different prerequisites. We will guide you through the process of installing the most common ones, such as GCC, PCRE, zlib, and OpenSSL.

GNU Compiler Collection

Nginx is a program written in C, so you will first need to install a compiler tool such as the **GNU Compiler Collection** (**GCC**) on your system. GCC may already be present on your system, but if that is not the case you will have to install it before going any further.

 GCC is a collection of free open source compilers for various languages – C, C++, Java, Ada, FORTRAN, and so on. It is the most commonly used compiler suite in the Linux world, and Windows versions are also available. A vast number of processors are supported, such as x86, AMD64, PowerPC, ARM, MIPS, and more.

First, make sure it isn't already installed on your system:

```
[alex@example.com ~]$ gcc
```

If you get the following output, it means that GCC is correctly installed on your system and you can skip to the next section:

```
gcc: no input files
```

If you receive the following message, you will have to proceed with the installation of the compiler:

```
~bash: gcc: command not found
```

GCC can be installed using the default repositories of your package manager. Depending on your distribution, the package manager will be `vary-yum` for a Red Hat Linux-based distribution, `apt` for Debian and Ubuntu, `yast` for SuSE Linux, and so on. Here is the typical way to proceed with the download and installation of the GCC package:

```
[root@example.com ~]# yum groupinstall "Development Tools"
```

If you use `apt-get`, execute the following command:

```
[root@example.com ~]# apt-get install build-essentials
```

If you use another package manager with a different syntax, you will probably find the documentation with the `man` utility. Either way, your package manager should be able to download and install GCC correctly, after having resolved dependencies automatically. Note that this command will not only install GCC, it also proceeds with downloading and installing all common requirements for building applications from source, such as code headers and other compilation tools.

The PCRE library

The **Perl Compatible Regular Expression** (**PCRE**) library is required for compiling Nginx. The rewrite and HTTP core modules of Nginx use PCRE for the syntax of their regular expressions, as we will discover in later chapters. You will need to install two packages—pcre and pcre-devel. The first one provides the compiled version of the library, whereas the second one provides development headers and sources for compiling projects, which are required in our case.

Here are some example commands that you can run in order to install both the packages.

Using yum, execute the following command:

```
[root@example.com ~]# yum install pcre pcre-devel
```

Or you can install all PCRE-related packages using the following command:

```
[root@example.com ~]# yum install pcre*
```

If you use apt-get, use the following command:

```
[root@example.com ~]# apt-get install libpcre3 libpcre3-dev
```

If these packages are already installed on your system, you will receive a message saying something like nothing to do; in other words, the package manager did not install or update any component:

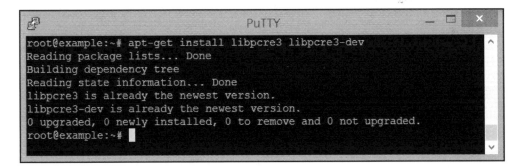

 Both components are already present on the system.

The zlib library

The `zlib` library provides developers with compression algorithms. It is required for the use of `.gzip` compression in various modules of Nginx. Again, you can use your package manager to install this component as it is part of the default repositories. Similar to PCRE, you will need both the library and its `source-zlib` and `zlib-devel`.

Using `yum`, execute the following command:

```
[root@example.com ~]# yum install zlib zlib-devel
```

Using `apt-get`, execute the following command:

```
[root@example.com ~]# apt-get install zlib1g zlib1g-dev
```

These packages install quickly and have no known dependency issues.

OpenSSL

> *The OpenSSL project is a collaborative effort to develop a robust, commercial-grade, full-featured, and open source toolkit implementing the Secure Sockets Layer (SSL v2/v3) and Transport Layer Security (TLS v1) protocols as well as a full-strength general purpose cryptography library. The project is managed by a worldwide community of volunteers that use the internet to communicate, plan, and develop the OpenSSL toolkit and its related documentation. For more information, visit http://www.openssl.org.*

The OpenSSL library will be used by Nginx to serve secure web pages. We thus need to install the library and its development package. The process remains the same here – you install `openssl` and `openssl-devel`:

```
[root@example.com ~]# yum install openssl openssl-devel
```

Using `apt-get`, execute the following command:

```
[root@example.com ~]# apt-get install openssl libssl-dev
```

 Please be aware of the laws and regulations in your own country. Some countries do not allow the use of strong cryptography. The author, publisher, and the developers of the OpenSSL and Nginx projects will not be held liable for any violations or law infringements on your part.

Now that you have installed all of the prerequisites, you are ready to download and compile the Nginx source code.

Downloading Nginx

This approach to the download process will lead us to discover the various resources at the disposal of server administrators, websites, communities, and wikis all relating to Nginx. We will also quickly discuss the different version branches available to you, and eventually select the most appropriate one for your setup.

Websites and resources

Although Nginx is a relatively new and growing project, there are already a good number of resources available on the **World Wide Web** (**WWW**) and an active community of administrators and developers.

The official website, which is at `http://nginx.org/`, currently serves as an official documentation reference, and provides links from which to download the latest version of the application source code and binaries. A wiki is also available at `https://www.nginx.com/resources/wiki/` and offers a wide selection of additional resources such as installation guides for various operating systems, tutorials related to the different modules of Nginx, and more.

There are several ways to get help if you should need it. If you have a specific question, try posting on the Nginx forum—`https://forum.nginx.org/`. An active community of users will answer your questions in no time. Additionally, the Nginx mailing list, which is relayed on the Nginx forum, will also prove to be an excellent resource for any question you may have. And if you need direct assistance, there is always a group of regulars helping each other out on the IRC channel `#Nginx` on irc.freenode.net.

Another interesting source of information is the blogosphere. A simple query on your favorite search engine should return a good number of blog articles documenting Nginx, its configuration, and modules:

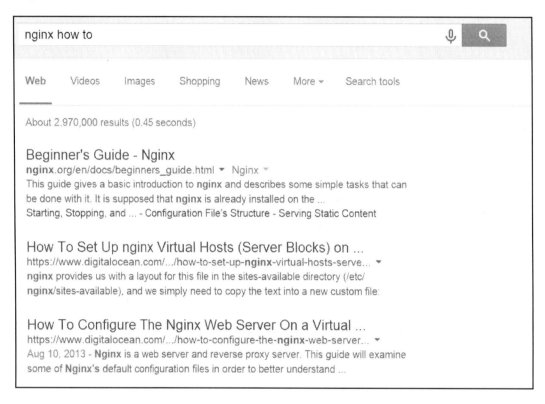

Personal websites and blogs documenting Nginx

It's now time to head over to the official website and get started with downloading the source code for compiling and installing Nginx. Before you do so, let us have a quick summary of the available versions and the features that come with them.

Version branches

Igor Sysoev, a talented Russian developer and server administrator, initiated this open source project back in 2002. Between the first release in 2004 and the current version, the market share of Nginx has been growing steadily. It now serves nearly 15% of websites on the internet, according to a June 2015 `https://www.netcraft.com/` survey. The features are numerous and render the application both powerful and flexible at the same time.

There are currently three version branches on the project:

- **Stable version**: This version is usually recommended, as it is approved by both developers and users, but is usually a little behind the mainline version.
- **Mainline version**: This is the latest version available for download and comes with the newest developments and bug fixes. It was formerly known as the **development version**. Although it is generally solid enough to be installed on production servers, there is a small chance that you will run into the occasional bug. As such, if you favor stability over novelty, going for the stable version is recommended.
- **Legacy version**: If, for some reason, you are interested in looking at the older versions, you will find several of them.

A recurrent question regarding mainline versions is "*Are they stable enough to be used on production servers?*" Cliff Wells, the original founder and maintainer of the Nginx wiki `https://www.nginx.com/resources/wiki/`, believes so – "*I generally use and recommend the latest development version. It's only bit me once!*" Early adopters rarely report critical problems. It is up to you to select the version you will be using on your server, knowing that the instructions given in this book should be valid regardless of the release as the Nginx developers have decided to maintain overall backwards compatibility in new versions. You can find more information on version changes, new additions, and bug fixes in the dedicated change log page on the official website.

Features

As of the mainline version 1.13.8, Nginx offers an impressive variety of features, which, contrary to what the title of this book indicates, are not all related to serving HTTP content. Here is a list of the main features of the web branch, quoted from the official website `http://nginx.org/`:

- Serving static and index files, auto indexing; open file descriptor cache; accelerated reverse proxying with caching; load balancing and fault tolerance.
- Accelerated support with caching of FastCGI, uWSGI, SCGI, and memcached servers; load balancing and fault tolerance; modular architecture. Filters include gzipping, byte ranges, chunked responses, XSLT, SSI, and image transformation filter. Multiple SSI inclusions within a single page can be processed in parallel if they are handled by proxies or FastCGI/uWSGI/SCGI servers.
- SSL and TLS SNI support.

Nginx can also be used as a mail proxy server, although this aspect is not closely documented in the book:

- User redirection to IMAP/POP3 backend using an external HTTP authentication server
- User authentication using an external HTTP authentication server and connection redirection to an internal SMTP backend
- Authentication methods:
  - **POP3**: USER/PASS, APOP, AUTH LOGIN/PLAIN/CRAM-MD5
  - **IMAP**: LOGIN, AUTH LOGIN/PLAIN/CRAM-MD5
  - **SMTP**: AUTH LOGIN/PLAIN/CRAM-MD5
  - SSL support
  - STARTTLS and STLS support

Nginx is compatible with most computer architectures and operating systems—Windows, Linux, Mac OS, FreeBSD, and Solaris. The application runs fine on 32- and 64-bit architectures.

Downloading and extracting

Once you have made your choice as to which version you will be using, head over to `http://nginx.org/` and find the URL of the file you wish to download. Position yourself in your `home` directory, which will contain the source code to be compiled, and download the file using `wget`:

```
[alex@example.com ~]$ mkdir src && cd src
[alex@example.com src]$ wget http://nginx.org/download/nginx-1.13.8.tar.gz
```

We will be using version 1.13.8, the latest stable version as of February, 2018. Once downloaded, extract the archive contents in the current folder:

```
[alex@example.com src]$ tar zxf nginx-1.13.8.tar.gz
```

You have successfully downloaded and extracted Nginx. Now, the next step will be to configure the compilation process in order to obtain a binary that perfectly fits your operating system.

Configure options

There are usually three steps when building an application from source—configuration, compilation, and installation. The configuration step allows you to select a number of options that will not be editable after the program is built, as it has a direct impact on the project binaries. Consequently, it is a very important stage that you need to follow carefully if you want to avoid surprises later, such as the lack of a specific module or files being located in a random folder.

The process consists of appending certain switches to the configure script that comes with the source code. We will discover the three types of switches that you can activate; but let us first study the easiest way to proceed.

The easy way

If, for some reason, you do not want to bother with the configuration step, such as for testing purposes or simply because you will be recompiling the application in the future, you may simply use the configure command with no switches. Execute the following three commands to build and install a working version of Nginx:

```
[alex@example.com nginx-1.13.8]# ./configure
```

Running this command should initiate a long procedure of verifications to ensure that your system contains all of the necessary components. If the configuration process fails, please make sure you check the prerequisites section again, as it is the most common cause of errors. For information about why the command failed, you may also refer to the `objs/autoconf.err` file, which provides a more detailed report:

```
[alex@example.com nginx-1.13.8]# make
```

The `make` command will compile the application. This step should not cause any errors as long as the configuration went fine:

```
[root@example.com nginx-1.13.8]# make install
```

This last step will copy the compiled files as well as other resources to the installation directory, by default `/usr/local/nginx`. You may need to be logged in as `root` to perform this operation depending on permissions granted to the `/usr/local` directory.

Again, if you build the application without configuring it, you take the risk of missing out on a lot of features, such as the optional modules and others that we are about to discover.

Path options

When running the `configure` command, you are offered the chance to enable some switches that let you specify the directory or file paths for a variety of elements. Please note that the options offered by the configuration switches may change according to the version you downloaded. The following options listed are valid with the stable version, as of release 1.13.8. If you use another version, run the `./configure --help` command to list the available switches for your setup.

Using a switch typically consists of appending some text to the command line. For instance, using the `--conf-path` switch:

```
[alex@example.com nginx-1.13.8]# ./configure --conf-
path=/etc/nginx/nginx.conf
```

Here is an exhaustive list of the configuration switches for configuring paths:

Switch	Usage	Default value
`--prefix=...`	The base folder in which Nginx will be installed.	`/usr/local/nginx` If you configure other switches using relative paths, they will connect to the base folder. For example; specifying `--conf-path=conf/nginx.conf` will result in your configuration file being found at `/usr/local/nginx/conf/nginx.conf`.
`--sbin-path=...`	The path where the Nginx binary file should be installed.	`<prefix>/sbin/nginx`.
`--conf-path=...`	The path of the main configuration file.	`<prefix>/conf/nginx.conf`.

Switch	Usage	Default value
`--error-log-path=...`	The location of your error log. Error logs can be configured very accurately in the configuration files. This path only applies in case you do not specify any error logging directive in your configuration.	`<prefix>/logs/error.log`.
`--pid-path=...`	The path of the Nginx PID file. You can specify the PID file path in the configuration file. If that's not the case, the value you specify for this switch will be used.	`<prefix>/logs/nginx.pid`. The PID file is a simple text file containing the process identifier. It is placed in a well-defined location so that other applications can easily find the PID of a running program.
`--lock-path=...`	The location of the lock file. Again, it can be specified in the configuration file, but if it isn't, this value will be used.	`<prefix>/logs/nginx.lock`. The lock file allows other applications to determine whether or not the program is running. In the case of Nginx, it is used to make sure that the process is not started twice.

Switch	Usage	Default value
`--with-perl_modules_path=...`	Defines the path to the Perl modules. This switch must be defined if you want to include additional Perl modules.	NA
`--with-perl=...`	Path to the Perl binary file; used for executing Perl scripts. This path must be set if you want to allow execution of Perl scripts.	NA
`--http-log-path=...`	Defines the location of access logs. This path is used only if the access log directive is unspecified in the configuration files.	`<prefix>/logs/access.log.`
`--http-client-body-temp-path=...`	Directory used for storing temporary files generated by client requests.	`<prefix>/client_body_temp.`
`--http-proxy-temp-path=...`	Location of the temporary files used by the proxy.	`<prefix>/proxy_temp.`

Switch	Usage	Default value
`--http-fastcgi-temp-path=...` `--http-uwsgi-temp-path=...` `--http-scgi-temp-path=...`	Location of the temporary files used by the HTTP FastCGI, uWSGI, and SCGI modules.	Respectively `<prefix>/fastcgi_temp`,`<prefix>/uwsgi_temp`, and `<prefix>/scgi_temp`.
`--builddir=...`	Location of the application build.	NA

Prerequisite options

Prerequisites come in the form of libraries and binaries. You should by now have them all installed on your system. Yet, even though they are present on your system, there may be occasions where the configuration script cannot locate them. The reasons might be diverse, for example, if they were installed in non-standard directories. In order to solve such problems, you are given the option to specify the path for prerequisites using the following switches. Miscellaneous prerequisite-related options are grouped together.

Compiler options	Usage
`--with-cc=...`	Specifies an alternate location for the C compiler.
`--with-cpp=...`	Specifies an alternate location for the C preprocessor.
`--with-cc-opt=...`	Defines additional options to be passed to the C compiler command line.
`--with-ld-opt=...`	Defines additional options to be passed to the C linker command line.
`--with-cpu-opt=...`	Specifies a different target processor architecture, from these values: `pentium`, `pentiumpro`, `pentium3`, `pentium4`, `athlon`, `opteron`, `sparc32`, `sparc64`, and `ppc64`.
`--with-compat`	Enables dynamic module compatibility. Should be enabled if planning to use dynamic modules.

PCRE options	Usage
--without-pcre	PCRE option disables usage of the PCRE library. This setting is not recommended, as it will remove support for regular expressions, consequently disabling the rewrite module.
--with-pcre	Forces usage of the PCRE library.
--with-pcre=...	Allows you to specify the path of the PCRE library source code.
--with-pcre-opt=...	Additional options for building the PCRE library.
--with-pcre-jit=...	Build PCRE with JIT compilation support.

zlib options	Usage
--with-zlib=...	Specifies the path to the zlib library sources.
--with-zlib-opt=...	Additional options for building the zlib library.
--with-zlib-asm=...	Uses assembler optimizations for these target architectures, pentium, pentiumpro.

OpenSSL options	Usage
--with-openssl=...	Specifies the path of OpenSSL library sources.
--with-openssl-opt=...	Additional options for building the OpenSSL library.

Libatomic	Usage
--with-libatomic=...	Forces usage of the libatomic_ops library on systems other than x86, amd64, and sparc. This library allows Nginx to perform atomic operations directly instead of resorting to lock files. Depending on your system, it may result in a decrease in SEGFAULT errors and possibly a higher request serving rate.
--with-libatomic=...	Specifies the path of the Libatomic library sources.

Module options

Modules, which will be detailed in *Chapter 3, HTTP Configuration*, and further, need to be selected before compiling the application. Some are enabled by default and some need to be enabled manually, as you will see in the following table.

Modules enabled by default

The following switches allow you to disable modules that are enabled by default:

Modules enabled by default	Description
`--without-http_charset_module`	Disables the charset module for re-encoding web pages.
`--without-http_gzip_module`	Disables the gzip compression module.
`--without-http_ssi_module`	Disables the server-side include module.
`--without-http_userid_module`	Disables the user ID module providing user identification via cookies.
`--without-http_access_module`	Disables the access module allowing access configuration for IP address ranges.
`--without-http_auth_basic_module`	Disables the basic authentication module.
`--without-mirror`	Disables the mirror module, used for creating mirror requests to alternative backends.
`--without-http_autoindex_module`	Disables the automatic index module.
`--without-http_geo_module`	Disables the geo module allowing you to define variables depending on IP address ranges.
`--without-http_map_module`	Disables the map module that allows you to declare map blocks.

Modules enabled by default	Description
`--without-http_split_clients_module`	Disables the split clients module, which can be used for A/B testing.
`--without-http_referer_module`	Disables the referer control module.
`--without-http_rewrite_module`	Disables the rewrite module.
`--without-http_proxy_module`	Disables the proxy module for transferring requests to other servers.

`--without-http_fastcgi_module`
`--without-http_uwsgi_module`
`--without-http_scgi_module`
	Disables the FastCGI, uWSGI, or SCGI modules for interacting with respectively FastCGI, uWSGI, or SCGI processes.

`--without-http_memcached_module`	Disables the memcached module for interacting with the memcache daemon.
`--without-http_limit_conn_module`	Disables the limit connections module for restricting resource usage according to defined zones.
`--without-http_limit_req_module`	Disables the limit requests module allowing you to limit the amount of requests per user.
`--without-http_empty_gif_module`	Disables the empty gif module that serves a blank GIF image from memory.
`--without-http_browser_module`	Disables the browser module that interprets the user agent string.
`--without-http_upstream_hash_module`	Disables the upstream hash module providing the hash directive in upstream blocks.
`--without-http_upstream_ip_hash_module`	Disables the upstream IP hash module providing the `ip_hash` directive in upstream blocks.

Modules enabled by default	Description
`--without-http_upstream_least_conn_module`	Disables the upstream least—conn module providing the `least_conn` directive in upstream blocks.
`--without-http_upstream_keepalive_module`	Disables the upstream keepalive module.
`--without-http_upstream_zone_module`	Disables the upstream shared memory zone module.

Modules disabled by default

The following switches allow you to enable modules that are disabled by default:

Modules disabled by default	Description
`--with-http_ssl_module`	Enables the SSL module for serving pages using HTTPS.
`--with-http_v2`	Enables support for HTTP/2.
`--with-http_realip_module`	Enables the realip module, for reading the real IP address from the request header data.
`--with-http_addition_module`	Enables the addition module which lets you append or prepend data to the response body.
`--with-http_xslt_module`	Enables the xslt module for applying XSL transformations to XML documents. You will need to install the `libxml2` and `libxslt` libraries on your system if you wish to compile these modules. You can pass this setting to the dynamic flag to compile as a dynamic module.
`--with-http_image_filter_module`	Enables the image_filter module, which lets you apply modifications to images. You will need to install the `libgd` library on your system if you wish to compile this module. You can pass it the dynamic flag to compile as the dynamic module.

Modules disabled by default	Description
--with-http_geoip_module	Enables the geoip module for achieving geographic localization using MaxMind's GeoIP binary database. You will need to install the `libgeoip` library on your system if you wish to compile this module. You can pass it the dynamic flag to compile as dynamic module.
--with-http_sub_module	Enables the substitution (sub) module for replacing text in web pages.
--with-http_dav_module	Enables the WebDAV module (distributed authoring and versioning via the web).
--with-http_flv_module	Enables the FLV module for special handling of `.flv` (**flash video**) files.
--with-http_mp4_module	Enables the MP4 module for special handling of `.mp4` video files.
--with-http_gzip_static_module	Enables the gzip static module for sending pre-compressed files.
--with-http_auth_request_module	Enables the auth_request module. This module allows you to delegate the HTTP authentication mechanism to a back-end server via a subrequest. The status code of the response can be stored in a variable.
--with-http_random_index_module	Enables the random_index module for picking a random file as the directory index.
--with-http_secure_link_module	Enables the secure_link module to check the presence of a keyword in the URL.
--with-http_stub_status_module	Enables the stub status module, which generates a server statistics and information page.
--with-google_perftools_module	Enables the Google performance tools module.
--with-http_degradation_module	Enables the degradation module, which controls the behavior of your server depending on current resource usage.

Modules disabled by default	Description
--with-http_perl_module	Enables the perl module allowing you to insert Perl code directly into your Nginx configuration files, and to make Perl calls from SSI.
--with-http_gunzip_module	Enables the gunzip module, which offers to decompress a gzip-encoded response from a back-end server before forwarding it to the client.

Miscellaneous options

Other options are available in the configuration script, for example, regarding the streaming modules, the mail server proxy feature, or event management.

Streaming server options	Usage
--with-stream	Enables the stream module for proxying data streams over TCP/UDP.
--with-mail_ssl_module	Enables SSL support for the mail server proxy. It is disabled by default.
--without-mail_pop3_module	Disables the POP3 module for the mail server proxy. It is enabled by default when the mail server proxy module is enabled.
--without-mail_imap_module	Disables the IMAP4 module for the mail server proxy. It is enabled by default when the mail server proxy module is enabled.
--without-mail_smtp_module	Disables the SMTP module for the mail server proxy. It is enabled by default when the mail server proxy module is enabled.

Mail server options	Usage
`--with-mail`	Mail server proxy option enables mail the server proxy module. Supports POP3, IMAP4, SMTP. It is disabled by default.
`--with-mail_ssl_module`	Enables SSL support for the mail server proxy. It is disabled by default.
`--without-mail_pop3_module`	Disables the POP3 module for the mail server proxy. It is enabled by default when the mail server proxy module is enabled.
`--without-mail_imap_module`	Disables the IMAP4 module for the mail server proxy. It is enabled by default when the mail server proxy module is enabled.
`--without-mail_smtp_module`	Disables the SMTP module for the mail server proxy. It is enabled by default when the mail server proxy module is enabled.

Event management (allows you to select an event notification system for the Nginx sequencer. For advanced users only)	Usage
`--with-rtsig_module`	Enables the rtsig module to use `rtsig` as the event notification mechanism.
`--with-select_module`	Enables the select module to use select as the event notification mechanism. By default, this module is enabled unless a better method is found on the system:`kqueue`, `epoll`, `rtsig`, or `poll`.
`--without-select_module`	Disables the select module.
`--with-poll_module`	Enables the poll module to use poll as the event notification mechanism. By default, this module is enabled if available, unless a better method is found on the `system-kqueue`, `epoll`, or `rtsig`.
`--without-poll_module`	Disables the poll module.

User and group options	Usage
--user=...	Default user account for starting the Nginx worker processes. This setting is used only if you omit to specify the user directive in the configuration file.
--group=...	Default user group for starting the Nginx worker processes. This setting is used only if you omit to specify the group directive in the configuration file.

--without-http	Disables the HTTP server.
--without-http-cache	Disables HTTP caching features.
--add-module=PATH	Adds a third-party module to the compile process by specifying its path. This switch can be repeated indefinitely if you wish to compile multiple modules.
--with-debug	Enables additional debugging information to be logged.
--with-file-aio	Enables support for Asynchronous IO Disk Operations or AIOs.
--build=name	Optionally set a name for this compile of Nginx. Can be used for internal identification.

Configuration examples

Here are a few examples of configuration commands that may be used for various cases. In these examples, the path switches were omitted as they are specific to each system and leaving the default values may simply function correctly.

Be aware that these configurations do not include additional third-party modules. Please refer to *Chapter 5, PHP and Python with Nginx*, for more information about installing add-ons.

About the prefix switch

During the configuration, you should take particular care over the `--prefix` switch. Many of the future configuration directives (which we will cover in further chapters) will be based on the path you select at this point. While it is not a an insoluble problem since absolute paths can still be employed, you should know that the prefix cannot be changed once the binaries have been compiled.

There is also another issue that you may run into if you plan to keep up with the times and update Nginx as new versions are released. The default prefix (if you do not override the setting by using the `--prefix` switch) is `/usr/local/nginx`. This path does not include the version number. Consequently, when you upgrade Nginx, if you do not specify a different prefix, the new install files will override the previous ones, which, among other problems, could potentially erase your currently running binaries.

It is thus recommended you use a different prefix for each version you will be using:

```
./configure --prefix=/usr/local/nginx-1.13.8
```

Additionally, to make future changes simpler, you may create a symbolic link `/usr/local/nginx` pointing to `/usr/local/nginx-1.13.8`. Once you upgrade, you can update the link to make it point to `/usr/local/nginx-newer.version`. This will allow the `init` script to always make use of the latest installed version of Nginx.

Regular HTTP and HTTPS servers

The first example describes a situation where the most important features and modules for serving HTTP and HTTPS content are enabled, and mail-related options are disabled:

```
./configure --user=www-data --group=www-data --with-http_ssl_module --with-http_realip_module
```

As you can see, the command is rather simple and most switches were left out. The reason is that the default configuration is rather efficient and most of the important modules are enabled. You will only need to include the `http_ssl` module for serving HTTPS content and optionally, the `realip` module for retrieving your visitors' IP addresses in case you are running Nginx as a backend server.

All modules enabled

The next situation: the entire package. All modules are enabled and it is up to you whether you want to use them or not at runtime:

```
./configure --user=www-data --group=www-data --with-http_ssl_module --with-
http_realip_module --with-http_addition_module --with-http_xslt_module --
with-http_image_filter_module --with-http_geoip_module --with-
http_sub_module --with-http_dav_module --with-http_flv_module --with-
http_mp4_module --with-http_gzip_static_module --with-
http_random_index_module --with-http_secure_link_module --with-
http_stub_status_module --with-http_perl_module --with-
http_degradation_module --with-http_gunzip_module --with-
http_auth_request_module
```

This configuration opens up a wide range of possible configuration options. *Chapter 3, HTTP Configuration*, to *Chapter 6, Apache and Nginx Together*, provide more detailed information on module configuration.

With this setup, all optional modules are enabled, thus requiring additional libraries to be installed: `libgeoip` for the GeoIP module, `libgd` for the image filter module, `libxml2`, and `libxslt` for the XSLT module. You may install those prerequisites using your system package manager , for instance by running `yum install libxml2` or `apt-get install libxml2`.

Mail server proxy

This last build configuration is somewhat special as it is dedicated to enabling mail server proxy features—a darker and less documented side of Nginx. The related features and modules are all enabled:

```
./configure --user=www-data --group=www-data --with-mail --with-
mail_ssl_module
```

If you wish to completely disable the HTTP serving features and only dedicate Nginx to mail proxying, you may add the `--without-http` switch.

In the previously listed commands, the user and group used for running the Nginx worker processes will be www-data, which implies that this user and group must exist on your system.

Build configuration issues

In some cases, the configure command may fail – after a long list of checks, you may receive a few error messages on your terminal. In most (if not all) cases, these errors are related to missing prerequisites or unspecified paths.

In such cases, proceed with the following verifications carefully to make sure you have all it takes to compile the application, and optionally consult the objs/autoconf.err file for more details about the compilation problem. This file is generated during the configure process and will tell you exactly which part of the process failed.

Make sure you installed the prerequisites

There are basically four main prerequisites: GCC, PCRE, zlib, and OpenSSL. The last three are libraries that must be installed in two packages: the library itself and its development sources. Make sure you have installed both for each of them. Please refer to the prerequisites section at the beginning of this chapter. Note that other prerequisites, such as LibXML2 or LibXSLT, might be required for enabling extra modules (for example, in the case of the HTTP XSLT module).

If you are positive that all of the prerequisites were installed correctly, perhaps the issue comes from the fact that the configure script is unable to locate the prerequisite files. In that case, make sure that you include the configuration switches related to file paths, as described earlier.

For example, the following switch allows you to specify the location of the OpenSSL library files:

```
./configure [...] --with-openssl=/usr/lib64
```

The OpenSSL library file will be looked for in the specified folder.

Directories exist and are writable

Always remember to check the obvious; everyone makes even the simplest of mistakes sooner or later. Make sure the directory you placed the Nginx files in has *read* and *write* permissions for the user running the configuration and compilation scripts. Also ensure that all paths specified in the configure script switches are existing, valid paths.

Compiling and installing

The configuration process is of the utmost importance—it generates a `makefile` for the application depending on the selected switches and performs a long list of requirement checks on your system. Once the `configure` script is successfully executed, you can proceed with compiling Nginx.

Compiling the project equates to executing the `make` command in the project source directory:

```
[alex@example.com nginx-1.13.8]$ make
```

A successful build should result in a final message appearing: `make[1]: leaving directory` followed by the project source path.

Again, problems might occur at compile time. Most of these problems can originate in missing prerequisites or invalid paths specified. If this occurs, run the `configure` command again and triple-check the switches and all of the prerequisite options. It may also occur that you downloaded a too recent version of the prerequisites that might not be backwards-compatible. In such cases, the best option is to visit the official website of the missing component and download an older version.

If the compilation process was successful, you are ready for the next step: installing the application. The following command must be executed with `root` privileges:

```
[root@example.com nginx-1.13.8]# make install
```

The `make install` command executes the `install` section of the `makefile`. In other words, it performs a few simple operations, such as copying binaries and configuration files to the specified install folder. It also creates directories for storing log and HTML files, if these do not already exist. The `make install` step is not generally a source of problems, unless your system encounters an exceptional error, such as a lack of storage space or memory.

You might require `root` privileges for installing the application in the `/usr/local/` folder, depending on the folder permissions.

Controlling the Nginx service

At this stage, you should have successfully built and installed Nginx. The default location for the output files is `/usr/local/nginx`, so we will be basing future examples on this.

Daemons and services

The next step is obviously to execute Nginx. However, before doing so, it's important to understand the nature of this application. There are two types of computer application—those that require immediate user input, thus running in the foreground, and those that do not, thus running in the background. Nginx is of the latter type, often referred to as daemon. Daemon names usually come with a trailing `d` and a couple of examples can be mentioned here—`httpd` the HTTP server daemon is the name given to Apache under several Linux distributions, named the nameserver daemon, or `cron` the task scheduler—although, as you will notice, it is not the case for Nginx. When started from the command line, a daemon immediately returns the prompt window, and in most cases, does not even bother outputting data to the terminal.

Consequently, when starting Nginx you will not see any text appear on the screen and the prompt will return immediately. While this might seem startling, it is on the contrary a good sign. It means the daemon was started correctly and the configuration did not contain any errors.

User and group

It is of the utmost importance to understand the process architecture of Nginx and particularly the user and groups its various processes run under. A very common source of troubles when setting up Nginx is invalid file access permissions—due to a user or group misconfiguration, you often end up getting `403 Forbidden` HTTP errors because Nginx cannot access the requested files.

There are two levels of processes with possibly different permission sets:

- **Nginx master process**: This should be started as `root`. In most Unix-like systems, processes started with the `root` account are allowed to open TCP sockets on any port, whereas other users can only open listening sockets on a port above `1024`. If you do not start Nginx as `root`, standard ports such as `80` or `443` will not be accessible.

 The user directive that allows you to specify a different user and group for the worker processes will not be taken into consideration for the master process.

- **Nginx worker processes**: These are automatically spawned by the master process under the account you specified in the configuration file with the user directive (detailed in *Chapter 2, Basic Nginx Configuration*). The configuration setting takes precedence over the configuration switch you may have specified at compile time. If you did not specify any of those, the worker processes will be started as user nobody, and the group will be nobody (or nogroup depending on your OS).

Nginx command-line switches

The Nginx binary accepts command-line arguments for performing various operations, among which is controlling background processes. To get a full list of commands, you may invoke the help screen using the following commands:

```
[alex@example.com ~]$ cd /usr/local/nginx/sbin
[alex@example.com sbin]$ ./nginx -h
```

The next few sections will describe the purpose of these switches. Some allow you to control the daemon, some let you perform various operations on the application configuration.

Starting and stopping the daemon

You can start Nginx by running the Nginx binary without any switches. If the daemon is already running, a message will show up indicating that a socket is already listening on the specified port:

```
[emerg]: bind() to 0.0.0.0:80 failed (98: Address already in use) [...]
[emerg]: still could not bind().
```

Beyond this point, you may control the daemon by stopping it, restarting it, or simply reloading its configuration. Controlling is done by sending signals to the process using the `nginx -s` command:

Command	Description
`nginx -s stop`	Stops the daemon immediately (using the TERM signal)
`nginx -s quit`	Stops the daemon gracefully (using the QUIT signal)
`nginx -s reopen`	Reopens log files
`nginx -s reload`	Reloads the configuration

When starting the daemon, stopping it, or performing any of the preceding operations, the configuration file is first parsed and verified. If the configuration is invalid, whatever command you have submitted will *fail*, even when trying to stop the daemon. In other words, in some cases you will not be able to even stop Nginx if the configuration file is invalid.

An alternate way to terminate the process, in desperate cases only, is to use the `kill` or `killall` commands with `root` privileges:

```
[root@example.com ~]# killall nginx
```

Testing the configuration

As you can imagine, this tiny bit of detail might become an important issue if you constantly tweak your configuration. The slightest mistake in any of the configuration files can result in a loss of control over the service—you are then unable to stop it via regular `init` control commands, and obviously, it will refuse to start again.

In consequence, the following command will be useful to you in many occasions. It allows you to check the syntax, validity, and integrity of your configuration:

```
[alex@example.com ~]$ /usr/local/nginx/sbin/nginx -t
```

The `-t` switch stands for **test configuration**. Nginx will parse the configuration anew and let you know whether it is valid or not. A valid configuration file does not necessarily mean Nginx will start though as there might be additional problems such as socket issues, invalid paths, or incorrect access permissions.

Obviously, manipulating your configuration files while your server is in production is a dangerous thing to do and should be avoided when possible. The best practice, in this case, is to place your new configuration into a separate temporary file and run the test on that file. Nginx makes it possible by offering the -c switch:

```
[alex@example.com sbin]$ ./nginx -t -c /home/alex/test.conf
```

This command will parse /home/alex/test.conf and make sure it is a valid Nginx configuration file. When you are done, after making sure that your new file is valid, proceed to replacing your current configuration file and reload the server configuration:

```
[alex@example.com sbin]$ cp -i /home/alex/test.conf
usr/local/nginx/conf/nginx.conf
cp: erase 'nginx.conf' ? yes
[alex@example.com sbin]$ ./nginx -s reload
```

Other switches

Another switch that might come in handy in many situations is -V. Not only does it tell you the current Nginx build version, but more importantly it also reminds you about the arguments that you used during the configuration step – in other words, the command switches that you passed to the configure script before compilation:

```
[alex@example.com sbin]$ ./nginx -V
nginx version: nginx/1.13.8 (Ubuntu)
built by gcc 4.8.4 (Ubuntu 4.8.4-2ubuntu1~14.04)
TLS SNI support enabled
configure arguments: --with-http_ssl_module
```

In this case, Nginx was configured with the --with-http_ssl_module switch only.

Why is this so important? Well, if you ever try to use a module that was not included with the configure script during the precompilation process, the directive enabling the module will result in a configuration error. Your first reaction will be to wonder where the syntax error comes from. Your second reaction will be to wonder if you even built the module in the first place! Running nginx -V will answer this question.

Additionally, the -g option lets you specify additional configuration directives, in case they were not included in the configuration file:

```
[alex@example.com sbin]$ ./nginx -g "timer_resolution 200ms";
```

Adding Nginx as a system service

In this section, we will create a script that will transform the Nginx daemon into an actual system service. This will result in mainly two outcomes—the daemon will be controllable using standard commands, and more importantly, it will automatically be launched on system startup and stopped on system shutdown.

System V scripts

Most Linux-based operating systems to date use a System-V style *init daemon*. In other words, their start up process is managed by a daemon called `init`, which functions in a way that is inherited from the old **System V** Unix-based operating system.

This daemon functions on the principle of *runlevels*, which represent the state of the computer. Here is a table representing the various runlevels and their signification:

Runlevel	State
0	System is halted
1	Single-user mode (rescue mode)
2	Multiuser mode, without NFS support
3	Full multiuser mode
4	Not used
5	Graphical interface mode
6	System reboot

You can manually initiate a runlevel transition: use the `telinit 0` command to shut down your computer or `telinit 6` to reboot it.

For each runlevel transition, a set of services are executed. This is the key concept to understand here: when your computer is stopped, its runlevel is 0. When you turn it on, there will be a transition from runlevel 0 to the default computer start up runlevel. The default start up runlevel is defined by your own system configuration (in the `/etc/inittab` file) and the default value depends on the distribution you are using: Debian and Ubuntu use runlevel 2, Red Hat and Fedora use runlevel 3 or 5, CentOS and Gentoo use runlevel 3, and so on, as the list is long.

So let us summarize. When you start your computer running CentOS, it operates a transition from runlevel 0 to runlevel 3. That transition consists of starting all services that are scheduled for runlevel 3. The question is—how to schedule a service to be started at a specific runlevel?

/etc					
Name	Ext	Size	Changed	Rights	Owner
rc0.d			15/01/2015 18:16:55	rwxr-xr-x	root
rc1.d			15/01/2015 18:16:55	rwxr-xr-x	root
rc2.d			15/01/2015 18:16:55	rwxr-xr-x	root
rc3.d			15/01/2015 18:16:55	rwxr-xr-x	root
rc4.d			15/01/2015 18:16:55	rwxr-xr-x	root
rc5.d			15/01/2015 18:16:55	rwxr-xr-x	root
rc6.d			15/01/2015 18:16:55	rwxr-xr-x	root
rcS.d			15/01/2015 16:37:38	rwxr-xr-x	root

For each runlevel, there is a directory containing scripts to be executed. If you enter these directories (`rc0.d`, `rc1.d`, to `rc6.d`) you will not find actual files, but rather symbolic links referring to scripts located in the `init.d` directory. Service startup scripts will indeed be placed in `init.d`, and links will be created by tools placing them in the proper directories.

About init scripts

An init script, also known as the service start up script or even SysV script, is a shell script respecting a certain standard. The script will control a daemon application by responding to commands such as start, stop, and others, which are triggered at two levels. Firstly, when the computer starts, if the service is scheduled to be started for the system runlevel, the init daemon will run the script with the start argument. The other possibility for you is to manually execute the script by calling it from the shell:

```
[root@example.com ~]# service httpd start
```

Or if your system does not come with the service command:

```
[root@example.com ~]# /etc/init.d/httpd start
```

The script must accept at least the start, stop, restart, force-reload, and status commands as they will be used by the system to respectively start up, shut down, restart, forcefully reload the service, or inquire its status. However, for enlarging your field of action as a system administrator, it is often interesting to provide further options, such as a reload argument to reload the service configuration or a try-restart argument to stop and start the service again.

Since service httpd start and /etc/init.d/httpd start essentially do the same thing, with the exception that the second command will work on all operating systems, we will make no further mention of the service command and will exclusively use the /etc/init.d/ method.

Init script for older Debian-based distributions

We will thus create a shell script for starting and stopping our Nginx daemon and also restarting and reloading it. The purpose here is not to discuss Linux shell script programming, so we will merely provide the source code of an existing init script, along with some comments to help you understand it.

Due to differences in the format of the init scripts from one distribution to another, we will here discover two separate scripts: this first one is meant for older Debian-based distributions before they were switched to Systemd.

First, create a file called `nginx` with the text editor of your choice, and save it in the `/etc/init.d/` directory (on some systems, `/etc/init.d/` is actually a symbolic link to `/etc/rc.d/init.d/`). In the file you just created, copy the following script carefully. Make sure that you change the paths to make them correspond to your actual setup.

You will need `root` permissions to save the script into the `init.d` directory.

 The complete `init` script for Debian-based distributions can be found in the code bundle.

Init script for SystemD-based distributions

Due to the system tools, shell programming functions, and specific formatting that it requires, the previously described script is only compatible with older Debian-based distributions. If your server is operated by a SystemD-based distribution such as CentOS, Fedora, newer Debian-based and many more, you will need an entirely different script.

 The complete `init` script for SystemD-based distributions can be found in the code bundle.

Installing the script

Placing the file in the `init.d` directory does not complete our work. There are additional steps that will be required for enabling the service. First of all, you need to make the script executable. So far, it is only a piece of text that the system refuses to run. Granting executable permissions on the script is done with the `chmod` command:

```
[root@example.com ~]# chmod +x /etc/init.d/nginx
```

 If you created the file as the `root` user, you will need to be logged in as `root` to change the file permissions.

At this point, you should already be able to start the service using `service nginx start` or `/etc/init.d/nginx start`, as well as stopping, restarting, or reloading the service.

The last step here will be to make it so the script is automatically started at the proper runlevels. Unfortunately, doing this entirely depends on what operating system you are using. We will cover the two most popular families – Debian, Ubuntu, or other Debian-based distributions and Red Hat/Fedora/CentOS, or other Red Hat-derived systems.

Debian-based distributions

For the Debian based distribution, a simple command will enable the `init` script for the system runlevel:

```
[root@example.com ~]# update-rc.d -f nginx defaults
```

This command will create links in the default system `runlevel` folders. For the reboot and shutdown runlevels, the script will be executed with the `stop` argument; for all other runlevels, the script will be executed with `start`. You can now restart your system and see your Nginx service being launched during the boot sequence.

Red Hat-based distributions

For the Red Hat-based systems family, the command differs, but you get an additional tool for managing system startup. Adding the service can be done via the following command:

```
[root@example.com ~]# chkconfig nginx on
```

Once that is done, you can then verify the runlevels for the service:

```
[root@example.com ~]# chkconfig --list nginx
Nginx   0:off   1:off   2:on   3:off   4:on   5:on   6:off
```

Another tool will be useful to you for managing system services, namely, `ntsysv`. It lists all services scheduled to be executed on system startup and allows you to enable or disable them at will:

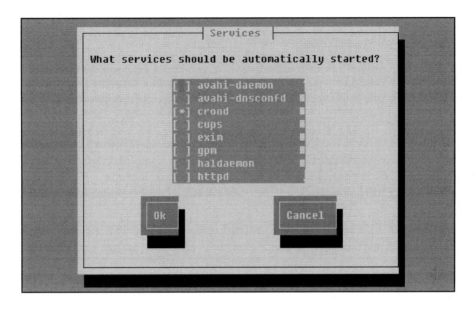

 ntsysv requires root privileges to be executed. Prior to using ntsysv, you must first run the chkconfig nginx on command, otherwise nginx will not appear in the list of services.

Nginx Plus

As of mid-2013 NGINX, Inc. the company behind the Nginx project also offers a paid subscription called Nginx Plus. The announcement came as a surprise for the open source community but several companies quickly jumped on the bandwagon and reported amazing improvements in terms of performance and scalability.

Nginx, Inc., the high performance web company, today announced the availability of NGINX Plus, a fully-supported version of the popular NGINX open source software complete with advanced features and offered with professional services. The product is developed and supported by the core engineering team at Nginx Inc., and is available immediately on a subscription basis.

As business requirements continue to evolve rapidly, such as the shift to mobile and the explosion of dynamic content on the Web, CIO's are continuously looking for opportunities to increase application performance and development agility, while reducing dependencies on their infrastructure. NGINX Plus provides a flexible, scalable, uniformly applicable solution that was purpose built for these modern, distributed application architectures.

Considering the pricing plans ($1,500 per year per instance) and the additional features made available, this platform is indeed clearly aimed at large corporations looking to integrate Nginx into their global architecture seamlessly and effortlessly. Professional support from the Nginx team is included and discounts can be offered for multiple-instance subscriptions. This book covers the open source version of Nginx only and does not detail advanced functionality offered by Nginx Plus. For more information about the paid subscription, take a look at `https://www.nginx.com/`.

Summary

This chapter covered a number of critical steps. We first made sure that your system contained all the required components for compiling Nginx. We then proceeded to select the proper version branch for your usage – will you be using the stable version or a more advanced yet potentially less stable one? After downloading the source and configuring the compilation process by enabling or disabling features and modules such as SSL, GeoIP, and more, we compiled the application and installed it on the system in the directory of your choice. We created an `init` script and modified the system boot sequence to schedule for the service to be started.

From this point on, Nginx is installed on your server and automatically starts with the system. Your web server is functional, though it does not yet answer the most basic functionality – serving a website. The first step towards hosting a website will be to prepare a suitable configuration file. The next chapter will cover the basic configuration of Nginx and will teach you how to optimize performance based on the expected audience and system resources.

2
Basic Nginx Configuration

In this chapter, we will begin to establish an appropriate configuration for your web server. For this purpose, we need to first discover the syntax that is used in the Nginx configuration files. Then we need to understand the various directives that will let you prepare and optimize your web server for different traffic patterns and hardware setups. Finally, we will create some test pages to make sure that everything has been done correctly and that the configuration is valid. We will only approach basic configuration directives here. The following chapters will detail more advanced topics, such as HTTP module configuration and usage, creating virtual hosts, and more.

This chapter covers the following topics:

- Presentation of the configuration syntax
- Basic configuration directives
- Establishing an appropriate configuration for your profile
- Serving a test website
- Testing and maintaining your web server

Configuration file syntax

A configuration file is generally a text file that is edited by the administrator and parsed by a program. By specifying a set of values, you define the behavior of the program. In Linux-based operating systems, the majority of applications rely on vast, complex configuration files which often turn out to be a nightmare to manage. Apache, Qmail, and Bind—all of these names bring up bad memories in the mind of a Linux system administrator.

The fact is that all of these applications use their own configuration files with different syntaxes and styles. PHP works with a Windows-style `.ini` file, Sendmail uses the M4 macro-processor to compile configuration files, Zabbix pulls its configuration from a MySQL database, and so on. There is, unfortunately, no well-established standard, and the same applies to Nginx—you will be required to study a new syntax with its own particularities and its own vocabulary:

Why isn't there a universal standard for configuration file syntax? A possible explanation is provided by Randall Munroe at `https://xkcd.com/` (reproduced with authorization).

On the other hand (and this is one of its advantages), configuring Nginx turns out to be rather simple, at least in comparison to Apache or other mainstream web servers. There are only a few mechanisms that need to be mastered: directives, blocks, and the overall logical structure. Most of the actual configuration process will consist of writing values for directives.

Configuration directives

The Nginx configuration file can be described as a list of directives organized in a logical structure. The entire behavior of the application is defined by the values that you give to those directives.

By default, Nginx makes use of one main configuration file. The path of this file was defined in the steps described in `Chapter 1`, *Downloading and Installing Nginx*, under the *Build configuration issues* section. If you did not edit the configuration file path and prefix options, it should be located at `/usr/local/nginx/conf/nginx.conf`.

However, if you installed Nginx with a package manager, your configuration file will likely be located in `/etc/nginx/folder`, and the contents of the file may be quite different from the version that comes in the original Nginx source code package. Now let's take a quick peek at the first few lines of this initial setup:

```
nginx.conf - Notepad
File  Edit  Format  View  Help
#user    nobody;
worker_processes   1;

#error_log  logs/error.log;
#error_log  logs/error.log   notice;
#error_log  logs/error.log   info;

#pid         logs/nginx.pid;


events {
    worker_connections   1024;
}


http {
    include        mime.types;
```

Default configuration file bundled with the Nginx 1.8.0 source code package.

Let's take a closer look at the first two lines:

```
#user nobody;
worker_processes 1;
```

As you can probably make out from the # character, the first line is a comment. In other words, it is a piece of text that is not interpreted and has no value whatsoever. Its sole purpose is to be read by whoever opens the file, or to temporarily disable parts of an existing configuration section. You may use the # character at the beginning of a line or following a directive.

The second line is an actual statement: a directive. The first bit (`worker_processes`) represents a setting key, to which you append one or more values. In this case, the value is 1, indicating that Nginx should function with a single worker process (more information about this particular directive is given in further sections).

Directives always end with a semicolon (;).

Each directive has a unique meaning and defines a particular feature of the application. It may also have a particular syntax. For example, the `worker_process` directive only accepts one numeric value, whereas the `user` directive lets you specify up to two character strings, one for the user account (that the Nginx worker processes should run as) and a second for the `user` group.

Nginx works in a modular way, and as such, each module comes with a specific set of directives. The most fundamental directives are part of the Nginx core module and will be detailed in this chapter. As for other directives brought in by other modules, they will be explored in the later chapters.

Organization and inclusions

In the preceding screenshot, you may have noticed a particular directive—`include`:

```
include mime.types;
```

As the name suggests, this directive will perform an inclusion of the specified file. In other words, the contents of the file will be inserted at this exact location. Here is a practical example that will help you understand:

`nginx.conf`:

```
user nginx nginx;
worker_processes 4;
include other_settings.conf;
```

`other_settings.conf`:

```
error_log logs/error.log;
pid logs/nginx.pid;
```

The final result, as interpreted by Nginx, is as follows:

```
user nginx nginx;
worker_processes 4;
error_log logs/error.log;
pid logs/nginx.pid;
```

Inclusions are processed recursively. In this case, you have the possibility to use the `include` directive again in the `other_settings.conf` file, in order to include yet another file.

In the initial configuration setup, there are two files at use: `nginx.conf` and `mime.types`. However, in the case of a more advanced configuration, there may be five or more files, as described in the following table:

Standard name	Description
nginx.conf	Base configuration of the application.
mime.types	A list of file extensions and their associated MIME types.
fastcgi.conf	FastCGI-related configuration.
proxy.conf	Proxy-related configuration.
sites.conf	Configuration of the websites served by Nginx, also known as **virtual hosts**. It's recommended to create separate files for each domain.

These filenames were defined conventionally; nothing actually prevents you from regrouping your FastCGI and proxy settings into a common file named `proxy_and_fastcgi_config.conf`.

The `include` directive supports filename globbing, in other words, filenames referenced with the * wildcard, where * may match zero, one, or more consecutive characters:

```
include sites/*.conf;
```

This will include all files with a name that ends with `.conf` in the `sites` folder. This mechanism allows you to create a separate file for each of your websites and include them all at once.

Be careful when including a file. If the specified file does not exist, the configuration checks will fail and Nginx will not start:

```
[alex@example sbin]# ./nginx -t
[emerg]: open() "/usr/local/nginx/conf/dummyfile.conf" failed (2: No such
file or directory) in /usr/local/nginx/conf/nginx.conf:48
```

The previous statement is not true for inclusions with wildcards. Moreover, if you insert `include dummy*.conf` in your configuration and test it (whether there is any file matching this pattern on your system or not), here is what should happen:

```
[alex@example sbin]# ./nginx -t
the configuration file /usr/local/nginx/conf/nginx.conf syntax is ok
configuration file /usr/local/nginx/conf/nginx.conf test is successful
```

Directive blocks

Directives are brought in by modules; if you activate a new module, a specific set of directives become available. Modules may also enable **directive blocks**, which allow for a logical construction of the configuration:

```
events {
    worker_connections 1024;
}
```

The `events` block that you can find in the default configuration file is brought in by the `events` module. The directives that the module enables can only be used within that block. In the preceding example, `worker_connections` will only make sense in the context of the `events` block. On the other hand, some directives must be placed at the root of the configuration file because they have a global effect on the server. The root of the configuration file is also known as the **main block**.

For the most part, blocks can be nested into each other, following a specific logic. The following sequence demonstrates the structure of a simple website setup, making use of nested blocks:

```
http {
    server {
        listen 80;
        server_name example.com;
        access_log /var/log/nginx/example.com.log;
        location ^~ /admin/ {
            index index.php;
        }
    }
}
```

The topmost directive block is the `http` block, in which you may declare a variety of configuration directives, as well as one or more `server` blocks. A `server` block allows you to configure a virtual host, in other words, a website that is to be hosted on your machine. The `server` block, in this example, contains some configuration that applies to all HTTP requests with a `Host` header exactly matching `example.com`.

Within this `server` block, you may insert one or more `location` blocks. These allow you to enable settings only when the requested URI matches the specified path. More information is provided in the The *Location block* section of `Chapter 3`, *HTTP Configuration*.

Last but not least, configuration is inherited within children blocks. The `access_log` directive (defined at the `server` block level in this example) specifies that all HTTP requests for this server should be logged into a text file. This is still true within the `location` child block, although you have the possibility of disabling it by reusing the `access_log` directive:

```
[...]
    location ^~ /admin/ {
        index index.php;
        access_log off;
    }
[...]
```

In this case, logging will be enabled everywhere on the website, except for the `/admin/` location path. The value set for the `access_log` directive at the `server` block level is overridden by the one at the `location` block level.

Advanced language rules

There are a number of important observations regarding the Nginx configuration file syntax. These will help you understand certain language rules that may seem confusing if you have never worked with Nginx before.

Directives accept specific syntaxes

You may indeed stumble upon complex syntaxes that can be confusing at first sight:

```
rewrite ^/(.*)\.(png|jpg|gif)$ /image.php? file=$1&format=$2 last;
```

Syntaxes are directive-specific. While the `root` directive only accepts a simple character string defining the folder containing files that should be served for a website, the `location` block or the `rewrite` directive support complex expressions in order to match particular patterns. Some other directives, such as `listen`, accept up to *17* different parameters. Syntaxes will be explained along with directives in their respective chapters.

Later on, we will detail a module (the *rewrite* module) which allows for a much more advanced logical structure through the `if`, `set`, `break`, and `return` blocks and directives, and the use of variables. With all of these new elements, configuration files will begin to look like programming scripts. Anyhow, the more modules we discover, the richer the syntax becomes.

Diminutives in directive values

Finally, you may use the following diminutives for specifying a file size in the context of a directive value:

- **k** or **K**: **Kilobytes**
- **m** or **M**: **Megabytes**
- **g** or **G**: **Gigabytes**

As a result, the following three syntaxes are correct and equal:

```
client_max_body_size 2G;
client_max_body_size 2048M;
client_max_body_size 2097152k;
```

Nginx does not allow you to insert the same directive more than once within the same block (although there are a few exceptions, such as `allow` or `deny`); should you do so, the configuration will be considered invalid and Nginx will refuse to start up or reload.

Additionally, when specifying a time value, you may use the following shortcuts:

- **ms**: **Milliseconds**
- **s**: **Seconds**
- **m**: **Minutes**
- **h**: **Hours**
- **d**: **Days**
- **w**: **Weeks**

- **M**: **Months** (30 days)
- **y**: **Years** (365 days)

This becomes especially useful in the case of directives accepting a period of time as a value:

```
client_body_timeout  3m;
client_body_timeout  180s;
client_body_timeout  180;
```

The default time unit is seconds; the last two lines above thus result in identical behavior. It is also possible to combine two values with different units:

```
client_body_timeout  1m30s;
client_body_timeout  '1m 30s 500ms';
```

The latter variant is enclosed in quotes since values are separated by spaces.

Variables

Modules also provide variables that can be used in the definition of directive values. For example, the Nginx HTTP core module defines the `$nginx_version` variable. Variables in Nginx always start with `$`—the dollar sign. When setting the `log_format` directive, you may include all kinds of variables in the format string:

```
[...]
location ^~ /admin/ {
    access_log logs/main.log;
    log_format main '$pid - $nginx_version - $remote_addr';
}
[...]
```

Some directives do not allow you to use variables:

```
error_log logs/error-$nginx_version.log;
```

The preceding directive is valid, syntax-wise. However, it simply generates a file named `error-$nginx_version.log`, without parsing the variable.

String values

Character strings that you use as directive values can be written in three forms. First, you may enter the value without quotes:

```
root /home/example.com/www;
```

However, if you want to use a particular character, such as a blank space ( ), a semicolon (;), or a pair of curly braces ({ }), you will need to either prefix said character with a backslash (\), or enclose the entire value in single or double quotes:

```
root '/home/example.com/my web pages';
```

Nginx makes no difference whether you use single or double quotes. Note that variables inserted in strings within quotes will be expanded normally, unless you prefix the $ character with a backslash (\).

Base module directives

In this section, we will take a closer look at the base modules. We are particularly interested in answering two questions: what are base modules? And what directives are made available?

What are base modules?

The base modules offer directives that allow you to define parameters of the basic functionality of Nginx. They cannot be disabled at compile time, and as a result, the directives and blocks they offer are always available. Three base modules are distinguished:

- **Core module**: Essential features and directives, such as process management and security
- **Events module**: Lets you configure the inner mechanisms of the networking capabilities
- **Configuration module**: Enables the inclusion mechanism

These modules offer a large range of directives; we will be detailing them individually, with their syntaxes and default values.

Nginx process architecture

Before we start detailing the basic configuration directives, it is necessary to understand the overall process architecture, that is, how the Nginx daemon works behind the scenes. Although the application comes as a simple binary file (and a somewhat lightweight background process), the way it functions at runtime can be relatively complex.

At the very moment of starting Nginx, one unique process exists in memory: the `master process`. It is launched with the current user and group permissions, usually root/root if the service is launched at boot time by an `init` script. The master process itself does not process any client requests; instead, it spawns processes that do: the `worker processes`, which are affected to a customizable user and group.

From the configuration file, you are able to define the amount of worker processes, the maximum connections per worker process, the user and group the worker processes are running under, and more. The following screenshot shows an example of a running instance of Nginx with eight worker processes running under the `www-data` user account:

```
                                           PuTTY                                    _ □ x
root@example:~# ps fuax | grep nginx
root     17485  0.0  0.0   7772   852 pts/0    S+   03:15   0:00           \_ grep nginx
root     20286  0.0  0.0  35752  3840 ?        Ss   Apr10   0:00 nginx: master process /usr/local/nginx/sbin/nginx
www-data  8910  0.0  0.0  37052  5460 ?        S    Apr24   1:26  \_ nginx: worker process
www-data  8911  0.0  0.0  37316  5756 ?        S    Apr24   1:28  \_ nginx: worker process
www-data  8912  0.0  0.0  36960  5668 ?        S    Apr24   1:29  \_ nginx: worker process
www-data  8913  0.0  0.0  37052  5492 ?        S    Apr24   1:27  \_ nginx: worker process
www-data  8914  0.0  0.0  37316  5756 ?        S    Apr24   1:35  \_ nginx: worker process
www-data  8915  0.0  0.0  36788  5232 ?        S    Apr24   1:30  \_ nginx: worker process
www-data  8916  0.0  0.0  37052  5492 ?        S    Apr24   1:30  \_ nginx: worker process
www-data  8917  0.0  0.0  37316  5748 ?        S    Apr24   1:26  \_ nginx: worker process
root@example:~#
```

Core module directives

The following is the list of directives made available by the core module. Most of these directives must be placed at the `root` of the configuration file and can only be used once. However, some of them are valid in multiple contexts.

If that is the case, the following is the list of valid contexts under the directive name:

Name and context	Syntax and description
daemon	• Accepted values: `on` or `off`. • Syntax: `daemon on;`. • Default value: `on`. • Enables or disables daemon mode. If you disable it, the program will not be started in the background; it will stay in the foreground when launched from the shell. This may come in handy for debugging, in situations where you need to know what causes Nginx to crash, and when.
debug_points	• Accepted values: `stop` or `abort`. • Syntax: `debug_points stop;`. • Default value: None. • Activates debug points in Nginx. Use `stop` to interrupt the application when a debug point comes about in order to attach a debugger. Use `abort` to abort the debug point and create a core dump file. • To disable this feature, simply do not use the directive.
env	• Syntax: `env MY_VARIABLE;` `env MY_VARIABLE=my_value;` • Allows you to define or redefine environment variables

Name and context	Syntax and description
`error_log` **Context**: `main`, `http`, `server`, and `location`	• Syntax: `error_log /file/path level;`. • Default value: `logs/error.log error`. • Where level is one of these values: `debug`, `info`, `notice`, `warn`, `error`, `crit`, `alert`, `emerg` (from most to least detailed: debug provides frequent log entries, emerg only reports the most critical errors). • Enables error logging at different levels: Application, HTTP server, virtual host, and virtual host directory. • By redirecting the log output to `/dev/null`, you can disable error logging. Use the following directive at the root of the configuration file: `error_log /dev/null crit;` • Instead of specifying a file path, you might also select one of the following alternatives: `stderr` will send log entries to the standard error file, and Syslog to the system log. These alternatives are further detailed in Chapter 11, *Troubleshooting*.
`lock_file`	• Syntax (file path): `lock_file logs/nginx.lock;`. • Default value: Defined at compile time. • Use a lock file for mutual exclusion. This is disabled by default, unless you enabled it at compile time. On most operating systems, the locks are implemented using atomic operations, so this directive is ignored anyway.
`load_module` **Context**: `main`	• Syntax (file path): `load_module modules/ngx_http_geoip_module.so;` • Default value: None • Load a dynamically compiled module at runtime
`log_not_found` **Context**: `main`, `http`, `server`, and `location`	• Accepted values: `on` or `off`. • Syntax: `log_not_found on;`. • Default value: `on`. • Enables or disables logging of `404` not found HTTP errors. If your logs get filled with `404` errors due to missing `favicon.ico` or `robots.txt` files, you might want to turn this `off`.

Name and context	Syntax and description
master_process	• Accepted values: on or off. • Syntax: master_process on;. • Default value: on. • If enabled, Nginx will start multiple processes: Main process (the master process) and worker processes. If disabled, Nginx works with a unique process. This directive should be used for testing purposes only, as it disables the master process; clients thus cannot connect to your server.
pcre_jit	• Accepted values: on or off. • Syntax: pcre_jit on;. • Enables or disables **Just-In-Time** (**JIT**) compilation for regular expressions (PCRE from version 8.20 and above), which may speed up their processing significantly. For this to work, the PCRE libraries on your system must be specifically built with the --enable-jit configuration argument. When configuring your Nginx build, you must also add the --with-pcre-jit argument.
pid	• Syntax (file path): pid logs/nginx.pid;. • Default value: Defined at compile time. • Path of the pid file for the Nginx daemon. The default value can be configured at compile time. Make sure to enable this directive and set its value properly, since the pid file may be used by the Nginx init script, depending on your operating system.
ssl_engine	• Syntax (character string): ssl_engine enginename;. • Default value: None. • Where enginename is the name of an available hardware SSL accelerator on your system. To check for available hardware SSL accelerators, run this command from the shell: openssl engine -t

Name and context	Syntax and description

thread_pool	• Syntax:
	`thread_pool name threads=number`
	`[max_queue=number];`
	• Default value: `thread_pool default threads=32`
	`max_queue=65536;`
	• Defines a thread pool reference that can be used with the `aio` directive, in order to serve larger files asynchronously. Further details are provided in `Chapter 9`, *Introduction to Load Balancing and Optimization.*

timer_resolution	• Syntax (numeric (time)): `timer_resolution 100ms;`. • Default value: None. • Controls the interval between system calls to `gettimeofday()` to synchronize the internal clock. If this value is not specified, the clock is refreshed after each kernel event notification.

user	• Syntax:
	`user username groupname;`
	`user username;`
	• Default value: Defined at compile time. If still undefined, the user and group of the Nginx master process are used.
	• Allows you to define the user account, and optionally, the user group used for starting the Nginx worker processes. For security reasons, you should make sure to specify a user and group with limited privileges. For example, create a new user and group dedicated to Nginx, and remember to apply proper permissions on the files that will be served.

Name and context	Syntax and description

`worker_cpu_affinity`	• Syntax:
	`worker_cpu_affinity 1000 0100 0010 0001;`
	`worker_cpu_affinity 10 10 01 01;`
	`worker_cpu_affinity auto;`
	• Default value: None.
	• This directive works in conjunction with `worker_processes`. It lets you affect worker processes to CPU cores.
	• There are as many series of digit blocks as worker processes; there are as many digits in a block as your CPU has cores.
	• If you configure Nginx to use three worker processes, there are three blocks of digits. For a dual-core CPU, each block has two digits:
	`worker_cpu_affinity 01 01 10;`
	• The first block (`01`) indicates that the first worker process should be affected to the second core.
	• The second block (`01`) indicates that the second worker process should be affected to the second core.
	• The third block (`10`) indicates that the third worker process should be affected to the first core.
	• The auto value allows Nginx to automatically manage the process binding. This differs from the default of not being specified, which means the OS will manage it.
	• Note that affinity is only recommended for multi-core CPUs, not for processors with hyperthreading or similar technologies.

`worker_priority`	• Syntax (numeric): `worker_priority 0;`. • Default value: `0`. • Defines the priority of the worker processes, from -20 (highest) to `19` (lowest). The default value is `0`. Note that kernel processes run at priority level -5, so it's not recommended that you set the priority to -5 or less.

Name and context	Syntax and description
`worker_processes`	• Syntax (numeric or auto): `worker_processes 4;`. • Default value: `1`. • Defines the amount of worker processes. Nginx offers to separate the treatment of requests into multiple processes. The default value is `1`, but it's recommended to increase this value if your CPU has more than one core. Besides, if a process gets blocked due to slow I/O operations, incoming requests can be delegated to the other worker processes. • Alternatively, you may use the `auto` value, which will let Nginx select an appropriate value for this directive. By default, it is the amount of CPU cores detected on the system.
`worker_rlimit_core`	• Syntax (numeric (size)): `worker_rlimit_core 100m;` • Default value: None • Defines the size of core files per worker process
`worker_rlimit_nofile`	• Syntax (numeric): `worker_rlimit_nofile 10000;` • Default value: None • Defines the number of files a worker process may use simultaneously
`working_directory`	• Syntax (directory path): `working_directory /usr/local/nginx/;`. • Default value: The prefix switch defined at compile time. • Working directory used for worker processes; it is only used to define the location of core files. The worker process user account (`user` directive) must have write permissions on this folder in order to be able to write core files.
`worker_aio_requests`	• Syntax (numeric): `worker_aio_requests 10000;`. • If you are using `aio` with the `epoll` connection processing method, this directive sets the maximum number of outstanding asynchronous I/O operations for a single worker process.

Name and context	Syntax and description
`worker_shutdown_timeout`	• Syntax (time): `worker_shutdown_timeout 5s;`. • Configures the time limit for graceful shutdown of worker processes. If exceeded, Nginx will try to forcefully close workers to complete the shutdown.

Events module

The `events` module comes with directives that allow you to configure network mechanisms. Some of the parameters have an important impact on the application's performance.

All of the directives listed in the following table must be placed in the events block, which is located at the root of the configuration file:

```
user nginx nginx;
master_process on;
worker_processes 4;
events {
  worker_connections 1024;
  use epoll;
}
[...]
```

These directives cannot be placed elsewhere (if you do so, the configuration test will fail):

Directive name	Syntax and description
`accept_mutex`	• Accepted values: `on` or `off` • Syntax: `accept_mutex on;` • Default value: As of version 1.11.3 `off`; prior to version 1.11.3, was `on` • Enables or disables the use of an accept mutex (mutual exclusion) to open listening sockets
`accept_mutex_delay`	• Syntax (numeric (time)): `accept_mutex_delay 500ms;`. • Default value: 500 milliseconds. • Defines the amount of time a worker process should wait before trying to acquire the resource again. This value is not used if the `accept_mutex` directive is set to `off`.

`debug_connection`	• Syntax (IP address or CIDR block):
	`debug_connection    172.63.155.21;`
	`debug_connection    172.63.155.0/24;`
	• Default value: None.
	• Writes detailed logs for clients matching this IP address or address block. The debug information is stored in the file specified with the `error_log` directive, enabled with the debug level.
	• Nginx must be compiled with the `--debug` switch in order to enable this feature.

`multi_accept`	• Syntax (`on` or `off`): `multi_accept off;` • Default value: `off` • Defines whether or not Nginx should accept all incoming connections at once from the listening queue

Directive name	Syntax and description
use	• Accepted values: `/dev/poll`, `epoll`, `eventport`, `kqueue`, `rtsig`, or `select`. • Syntax: `use kqueue;`. • Default value: Defined at compile time. • Selects the `event` model among the available ones (the ones that you enabled at compile time). Nginx automatically selects the most appropriate one, so you should not have to modify this value. The supported models are: • `select`: The default and standard module, it is used if the OS does not support a more efficient one (it's the only available method under Windows). This method is not recommended for servers that expect to be under high load. • `poll`: It is automatically preferred over `select`, but is not available on all systems. • `kqueue`: An efficient method for FreeBSD 4.1+, OpenBSD 2.9+, NetBSD 2.0, and macOS operating systems. • `epoll`: An efficient method for Linux 2.6+ based operating systems. • `rtsig`: Real-time signals, available as of Linux 2.2.19, but unsuited for high-traffic profiles, as default system settings only allow 1,024 queued signals. • `/dev/poll`: An efficient method for Solaris 7 11/99+, HP/UX 11.22+, IRIX 6.5.15+, and Tru64 UNIX 5.1A+ operating systems. • `eventport`: An efficient method for Solaris 10, though a security patch is required.
worker_connections	• Syntax (numeric): `worker_connections 1024;` • Default value: None • Defines the amount of connections that a worker process may treat simultaneously

Configuration module

The Nginx `configuration` module is a simple module enabling file inclusions with the `include` directive, as previously described in the *Organization and inclusions* section. The directive can be inserted anywhere in the configuration file and accepts a single parameter—a file path:

```
include /file/path.conf;
include sites/*.conf;
```

 If you do not specify an absolute path, the file path is relative to the configuration directory. By default, `include sites/example.conf` will include the following file: `/usr/local/nginx/conf/sites/example.conf`

Necessary adjustments

Several core directives deserve to be adjusted carefully upon preparing the initial setup of Nginx on your server. We will review several of these directives and the possible values you may set:

- `user root;`: This directive specifies that the worker processes will be started as `root`. It is dangerous for security, as it grants Nginx full permissions over your file system. You need to create a new user account on your system and make use of it here. Recommended value (granted that a `www-data` user account and group exist on the system) `user www-data www-data;`.

- `worker_processes 1;`: With this setting, only one worker process will be started, which implies that all requests will be processed by a unique execution flow. This also implies that the execution is delegated to only one core of your CPU. It is highly recommended to increase this value; you should have at least one process per CPU core. Alternatively, just set this to auto to leave it up to Nginx to determine the optimal value. Recommended value: `worker_processes auto;`.

- `worker_priority 0;`: By default, the worker processes are started with a regular priority. If your system performs other tasks simultaneously, you might want to grant a higher priority to the Nginx worker processes. In this case, you should decrease the value; the *smaller the value, the higher the priority*. Values range from `-20` (highest priority) to `19` (lowest priority). There is no recommended value here, as it completely depends on your situation. However, you should not set it under `-5`, as it is the default priority for kernel processes.

- `log_not_found on;`: This directive specifies whether Nginx should log `404 errors` or not. While these errors may of course provide useful information about missing resources, a lot of them may be generated by web browsers trying to reach the *favicon* (the conventional `/favicon.ico` of a website) or robots trying to access the indexing instructions (`robots.txt`). Set this to `off` if you want to ensure your log files don't get cluttered by **Error 404** entries, but keep in mind that this could deprive you from potentially important information about other pages that visitors failed to reach. Note that this directive is part of the HTTP core module. Refer to the next chapter for more information.

- `worker_connections 1024;`: This setting, combined with the amount of worker processes, allows you to define the total amount of connections accepted by the server simultaneously. If you enable four worker processes, each accepting 1,024 connections, your server will treat a total of 4,096 simultaneous connections. You need to adjust this setting to match your hardware: the more RAM and CPU power your server relies on, the more connections you can accept concurrently. If your server is a huge monster meant to host high traffic sites, you will want to increase this value.

Testing your server

At this point, you have configured several basic directives that affect the core functioning of Nginx. We will perform a simple test to ensure that all is working as expected, and that you are ready to further configure and deploy your websites.

Creating a test server

In order to perform simple tests, such as connecting to the server with a web browser, we need to set up a website for Nginx to serve. A test page comes with the default package in the `html` folder (`/usr/local/nginx/html/index.html`) and the original `nginx.conf` is configured to serve this page. Here is the section that we are interested in for now:

```
http {
    include       mime.types;
    default_type  application/octet-stream;
    sendfile        on;
    keepalive_timeout  65;
    server {
        listen        80;
        server_name  localhost;
        location / {
            root    html;
            index   index.html index.htm;
        }
        error_page   500 502 503 504   /50x.html;
        location = /50x.html {
            root    html;
        }
    }
}
```

As you can perhaps already tell, this segment configures Nginx to serve a website:

- By opening a listening socket on port: `80`
- Accessible at the address: `http://localhost/`
- With the index page: `index.html`

For more details about these directives, please refer to `Chapter 3`, *HTTP Configuration*, and go to the HTTP module configuration section. Anyhow, fire up your favorite web browser and visit `http://localhost/`:

You should be greeted with a welcome message; if you aren't, then check the configuration again and make sure you reloaded Nginx in order to apply the changes.

Performance tests

Having configured the basic functioning and the architecture of your Nginx setup, you may already want to proceed with running some tests. The methodology here is experimental: run the tests, edit the configuration, reload the server, run the tests again, edit the configuration again, and so on. Ideally, you should avoid running the testing tool on the same computer that is used to run Nginx, as it may cause the results to be biased.

One could question the pertinence of running performance tests at this stage. On one hand, virtual hosts and modules are not fully configured yet, and your website might use FastCGI applications (PHP, Python, and so on). On the other hand, we are testing the raw performance of the server without additional components (for example, to make sure that it fully makes use of all CPU cores). Besides, it's always better to come up with a polished configuration before the server is put into production.

We have retained three tools to evaluate the server performance here. All three applications were specifically designed for load tests on web servers and have different approaches due to their origins:

- `httperf`: A relatively well-known open source utility developed by HP, for Linux operating systems only
- `Autobench`: Perl wrapper for `httperf`, improving the testing mechanisms and generating detailed reports
- `OpenWebLoad`: Smaller scale open source load testing application that supports both Windows and Linux platforms

The principle behind each of these tools is to generate a massive amount of HTTP requests in order to clutter the server and study the results.

Httperf

The `httperf` is a simple command-line tool that can be downloaded from its official website at `http://www.hpl.hp.com/research/linux/httperf/` (it might also be available in the default repositories of your operating system). The source comes as a `tar.gz` archive and needs to be compiled using the standard method: `./configure`, `make`, and `make install`.

Once installed, you may execute the following command:

```
[alex@example ~]$ httperf --server 192.168.1.10 --port 80 --uri /index.html
--rate 300 --num-conn 30000 --num-call 1 --timeout 5
```

Replace the values in the preceding command with your own:

- `--server`: The website hostname you wish to test
- `--uri`: The path of the file that will be downloaded
- `--rate`: How many requests should be sent every second
- `--num-conn`: The total amount of connections
- `--num-call`: How many requests should be sent per connection
- `--timeout`: Quantity of seconds elapsed before a request is considered lost

In this example, `httperf` will download `http://192.168.1.10/index.html` repeatedly, 300 times per second, resulting in a total of 30,000 requests:

```
alex@example: /home/alex                                                    _ □ x
Maximum connect burst length: 6298

Total: connections 21767 requests 21710 replies 21710 test-duration 14.692 s

Connection rate: 1481.6 conn/s (0.7 ms/conn, <=1022 concurrent connections)
Connection time [ms]: min 1.4 avg 563.4 max 3922.6 median 197.5 stddev 988.4
Connection time [ms]: connect 397.6
Connection length [replies/conn]: 1.000

Request rate: 1477.7 req/s (0.7 ms/req)
Request size [B]: 72.0

Reply rate [replies/s]: min 1942.8 avg 2077.3 max 2211.8 stddev 190.2 (2 samples)
Reply time [ms]: response 165.7 transfer 0.0
Reply size [B]: header 215.0 content 151.0 footer 0.0 (total 366.0)
Reply status: 1xx=0 2xx=21702 3xx=0 4xx=0 5xx=8

CPU time [s]: user 0.22 system 8.88 (user 1.5% system 60.5% total 62.0%)
Net I/O: 633.5 KB/s (5.2*10^6 bps)

Errors: total 78290 client-timo 57 socket-timo 0 connrefused 0 connreset 0
Errors: fd-unavail 78233 addrunavail 0 ftab-full 0 other 0
```

The results indicate the response times and the number of successful requests. If the success ratio is 100 percent or the response time near 0 ms, increase the request rate and run the test again until the server shows signs of weakness. Once the results begin to look a little less perfect, tweak the appropriate configuration directives and run the test again.

Autobench

Autobench is a Perl script that makes use of `httperf` more efficiently. It runs continuous tests and automatically increases request rates until your server gets saturated. One of the interesting features of Autobench is that it generates a `.tsv` report that you can open with various applications to generate graphs. You may download the source code from the author's personal website at `http://www.xenoclast.org/autobench/`. Once again, extract the files from the archive, run `make`, then `make install`.

Although it supports testing of multiple hosts at once, we will only be using the single host test for more simplicity. The command we will execute resembles the `httperf` one:

```
[alex@example ~]$ autobench --single_host --host1 192.168.1.10 --uri1
/index.html --quiet --low_rate 20 --high_rate 200 --rate_step 20 --num_call
10 --num_conn 5000 --timeout 5 --file results.tsv
```

The switches can be configured as follows:

- `--host1`: The website hostname you wish to test
- `--uri1`: The path of the file that will be downloaded
- `--quiet`: Does not display `httperf` information on the screen
- `--low_rate`: Connections per second at the beginning of the test
- `--high_rate`: Connections per second at the end of the test
- `--rate_step`: The number of connections to increase the rate by after each test
- `--num_call`: How many requests should be sent per connection
- `--num_conn`: Total amount of connections
- `--timeout`: The number of seconds elapsed before a request is considered lost
- `--file`: Export results as specified (`.tsv` file)

Once the test terminates, you end up with a `.tsv` file that you can import in applications such as Microsoft Excel. Here is a graph generated from results on a test server (note that the report file contains up to 10 series of statistics):

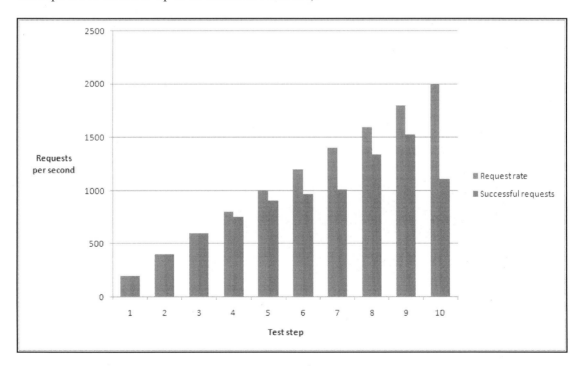

As you can tell from the graph, this test server supports up to 600 requests per second without a loss. Past this limit, some connections get dropped, as Nginx cannot handle the load. It stills gets up to over 1,500 successful requests per second at step 9.

OpenWebLoad

OpenWebLoad is a free open source application. It is available for both Linux and Windows platforms and was developed in the early 2000s, back in the days of Web 1.0. A different approach is offered here. Instead of throwing loads of requests at the server and seeing how many are handled correctly, it will simply send as many requests as possible using a variable amount of connections and report to you every second.

You may download it from its official website at `http://openwebload.sourceforge.net`. Extract the source from the `.tar.gz` archive, then run `./configure`, `make`, and `make install`.

Its usage is simpler than the previous two utilities:

```
[alex@example ~]$ openload example.com/index.html 10
```

The first argument is the URL of the website you want to test. The second one is the number of connections that should be opened:

```
C:\WINDOWS\system32\cmd.exe

C:\>openload.exe example.com/index.html 10
URL: http://example.com:80/index.html
Clients: 10
MaTps 210.37, Tps 210.37, Resp Time 0.046, Err  0%, Count   211
MaTps 211.51, Tps 221.78, Resp Time 0.045, Err  0%, Count   433
MaTps 212.69, Tps 223.33, Resp Time 0.045, Err  0%, Count   657
MaTps 213.38, Tps 219.56, Resp Time 0.046, Err  0%, Count   877
MaTps 214.63, Tps 225.87, Resp Time 0.044, Err  0%, Count  1104
MaTps 215.20, Tps 220.34, Resp Time 0.045, Err  0%, Count  1325
Total TPS: 216.40
Avg. Response time:  0.045 sec.
Max Response time:   0.097 sec
Total Requests:     1325
Total Errors:          0

C:\>
```

A new result line is produced every second. Requests are sent continuously until you press the *Enter* key; following that, a result summary is displayed. Here is how to decipher the output:

- `Tps` (**transactions per second**): A transaction corresponds to a completed request (back and forth)
- `MaTps`: Average `Tps` over the last 20 seconds
- `Resp Time`: Average response time for the elapsed second
- `Err` (**error rate**): Errors occur when the server returns a response that is not the expected, `HTTP 200 OK`
- `Count`: Total transaction count

You can fiddle with the amount of simultaneous connections and see how your server performs in order to establish a balanced configuration for your setup. Three tests were run here, with a different number of connections. The results speak for themselves:

	Test 1	Test 2	Test 3
Simultaneous connections	1	20	1000
Transactions per second (TPS)	67.54	205.87	185.07
Average response time	14 ms	91 ms	596 ms

Too few connections result in a low TPS rate, however, the response times are optimal. Too many connections produce a relatively high TPS, but the response times are critically high. You thus need to find a happy medium.

Upgrading Nginx gracefully

There are many situations where you will need to replace the Nginx binary, for example, when you compile a new version and wish to put it in production, or simply after having enabled new modules and rebuilt the application. What most administrators would do in this situation is stop the server, copy the new binary over the old one, and start Nginx again. While this is not considered to be a problem for most websites, there may be some cases where uptime is critical and connection losses should be avoided at all costs.

Fortunately, Nginx embeds a mechanism allowing you to switch binaries with uninterrupted uptime; zero percent request loss is guaranteed if you follow these steps carefully:

1. Replace the old Nginx binary (by default, `/usr/local/nginx/sbin/nginx`) with the new one.
2. Find the `pid` of the Nginx master process, for example, with `ps x | grep nginx | grep master` or by looking at the value found in the `.pid` file.
3. Send a `USR2` (12) signal to the master process: `kill -USR2 1234`, replacing `1234` with the `pid` found in step 2. This will initiate the upgrade by renaming the old `.pid` file and running the new binary.
4. Send a `WINCH` (28) signal to the old master process: `kill -WINCH 1234`, replacing `1234` with the `pid` found in step 2. This will engage a graceful shutdown of the old worker processes.
5. Make sure that all of the old worker processes are terminated, and then send a `QUIT` signal to the old master process: `kill -QUIT 1234`, replacing `1234` with the `pid` found in step 2.

Congratulations! You have successfully upgraded Nginx and have not lost a single connection.

Summary

This chapter provided a first approach to the configuration architecture by studying the syntax and the core module directives that have an impact on the overall server performance. We then went through a series of adjustments in order to fit your own profile, followed by performance tests that have probably led you to fine-tune some more.

This is just the beginning, though. Practically everything that we will be doing from now on is to prepare configuration sections. The next chapter will detail more advanced directives by further exploring the module system and the exciting possibilities that are offered to you.

3
HTTP Configuration

At this stage, we have a working Nginx setup—not only is it installed on the system and launched automatically on startup, but it's also organized and optimized with the help of basic directives. It's now time to go one step further into the configuration by discovering the HTTP core module. This module is an essential component of the HTTP configuration—it allows you to set up websites to be served, also referred to as virtual hosts.

This chapter will cover:

- An introduction to the HTTP Core module
- The HTTP/server/location structure
- HTTP core module directives, thematically
- HTTP core module variables
- An in-depth look at the location block

HTTP core module

The HTTP core module is the component that contains all of the fundamental blocks, directives, and variables of the HTTP server. It's enabled by default when you configure the build (as described in Chapter 1, *Downloading and Installing Nginx*), but it's actually optional—you can decide not to include it in your custom build. Doing so will completely disable all HTTP functionalities, and all of the other HTTP modules will not be compiled. Obviously, if you purchased this book, it's highly likely that you are interested in the web-serving capacities of Nginx, so you will have this enabled.

This module is the largest of all standard Nginx modules—it provides an impressive number of directives and variables. In order to understand all of these new elements and how they come into play, we first need to understand the logical organization introduced by the three main blocks – http, server, and location.

Structure blocks

In the previous chapter, we discovered the core module by studying the default Nginx configuration file which includes a sequence of directives and values, with no apparent organization. Then came the events module, which introduced the first block, (events). This block is the only placeholder for all of the directives brought in by the events module.

As it turns out, the HTTP module introduces three new logical blocks:

- http: This block is inserted at the root of the configuration file. It allows you to start defining directives and blocks from all modules related to the HTTP facet of Nginx. Although there is no real purpose in doing so, the block can be inserted multiple times, in which case the directive values inserted in the last block will override the previous ones.
- server: This block allows you to declare a website. In other words, a specific website (identified by one or more hostnames, for example, www.mywebsite.com) becomes acknowledged by Nginx and receives its own configuration. This block can only be used within the http block.
- location: Lets you define a group of settings to be applied to a particular location on a website. This block can be used within a server block or nested within another location block.

The following diagram summarizes the final structure by providing a couple of basic examples corresponding to actual situations:

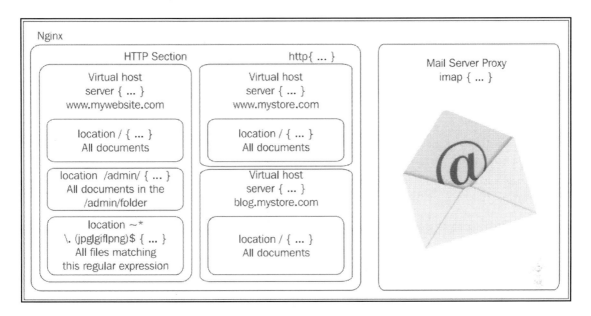

The HTTP section, defined by the `http{...}` block, encompasses the entire web-related configuration. It may contain one or more `server{...}` blocks, defining the domains and subdomains that you are hosting. For each of these websites, you have the possibility of defining location blocks that let you apply additional settings to a particular request URI, or request URIs matching a pattern.

Remember that the principle of setting inheritance applies here. If you define a setting at the `http{...}` block level (for example, `gzip on` to enable gzip compression), the setting will preserve its value in the potentially incorporated `server` and `location` blocks:

```
http {
    # Enable gzip compression at the http block level
    gzip on;
    server {
        server_name localhost;
        listen 80;
        # At this stage, gzip still set to on

        location /downloads/ {
            gzip off;
    #       This directive only applies to documents found
    #       in /downloads/
        }
    }
}
```

Module directives

At each of the three levels, directives can be inserted in order to affect the behavior of the web server. The following is a list of all directives that are introduced by the main HTTP module, grouped thematically. For each directive, an indication regarding the context is given. Some cannot be used at certain levels. For instance, it would make no sense to insert a `server_name` directive at the `http` block level, since `server_name` is a directive directly affecting a virtual host—it should only be inserted in the `server` block. To that extent, the table indicates the possible levels where each directive is allowed—the `http` block, the `server` block, the `location` block, and additionally the `if` block, later introduced in the *Rewrite module* section.

> This documentation is valid as of Stable version 1.8.0. Future updates may alter the *syntax of some directives* or provide new features that are not discussed here.

Socket and host configuration

This set of directives will allow you to configure your virtual hosts, in practice, by creating `server` blocks that you identify either by a hostname, or by an IP address and port combination. In addition, some directives will let you fine-tune your network settings by configuring TCP socket options.

listen

Context: `server`

Specifies the IP address and/or the port to be used by the listening socket that will serve the website. Sites are generally served on port 80 (the default value) via HTTP, or 443 via HTTPS.

Syntax: `listen [address][:port] [additional options];`

Additional options:

- `default_server`: Specifies that this `server` block is to be used as the default website for any request received at the specified IP address and port
- `ssl`: Specifies that the website should be served using SSL
- `http2`: Enables support for the HTTP2 protocol, if the `http2` module is present
- `proxy_protocol`: Enables the proxy protocol for all connections accepted on this port
- Other options are related to the bind and listen system calls:

    ```
    backlog=num, rcvbuf=size, sndbuf=size, accept_filter=filter,
    deferred, setfib=number, fastopen=number, ipv6only=on|off,
    reuseport, so_keepalive=on|off|[keepidle]:[keepintvl]:[keepcnt],
    bind
    ```

- Examples:

    ```
    listen 192.168.1.1:80; listen 127.0.0.1;
    listen 80 default;
    listen [:::a8c9:1234]:80; # IPv6 addresses must be put between
    square brackets
    listen 443 ssl;
    ```

This directive also allows Unix sockets:

```
listen unix:/tmp/nginx.sock;
```

server_name

Context: `server`

Assigns one or more hostnames to the `server` block. When Nginx receives an HTTP request, it matches the `Host` header of the request against all of the `server` blocks. The first `server` block to match this hostname is selected.

If no `server` block matches the desired host, Nginx selects the first `server` block that matches the parameters of the `listen` directive (for example, `listen *:80` would be a catch-all for all requests received on port `80`), giving priority to the first block that has the `default_server` option enabled on the `listen` directive.

This directive accepts wildcards as well as regular expressions. In this case, the hostname should start with the ~ character.

Syntax: `server_name hostname1 [hostname2...];`

Examples:

```
server_name www.website.com;
server_name www.website.com website.com;
server_name *.website.com;
server_name .website.com; # combines both *.website.com and website.com
server_name *.website.*;
server_name ~^(www)\.example\.com$; # $1 = www
```

You may use an empty string as the directive value in order to catch all of the requests that do not come with a `Host` header, but only after at least one regular name (or _ for a dummy hostname):

```
server_name website.com "";
server_name _  "";
```

server_name_in_redirect

Context: `http`, `server`, and `location`

This directive applies to internal redirects (for more information about internal redirects, check the *Rewrite module* section). If set to `on`, Nginx will use the first hostname specified in the `server_name` directive. If set to `off`, Nginx will use the value of the `Host` header from the HTTP request.

Syntax: `on` or `off`

Default value: `off`

server_names_hash_max_size

Context: `http`

Nginx uses hash tables for various data collections in order to speed up the processing of requests. This directive defines the maximum size of the server names hash table. The default value should fit with most configurations. If this needs to be changed, Nginx will automatically tell you on startup, or when you reload its configuration.

Syntax: Numeric value

Default value: `512`

server_names_hash_bucket_size

Context: `http`

Sets the bucket size for the server names hash table. Similarly, you should only change this value if Nginx tells you to.

Syntax: Numeric value

Default value: `32` (or `64`, or `128`, depending on your processor cache specifications).

port_in_redirect

Context: `http`, `server`, and `location`

If disabled, redirects issued by Nginx will be relative.

Syntax: `on` or `off`

Default value: `on`

absolute_redirect

Context: `http`, `server`, `location`

In the case of a redirect, this directive defines whether or not Nginx should append the port number to the redirection URL.

Syntax: on or off

Default value: on

tcp_nodelay

Context: http, server, and location

Enables or disables the TCP_NODELAY socket option for keep-alive connections only. To quote the Linux documentation on sockets programming:

> *"TCP_NODELAY is for a specific purpose; to disable the Nagle buffering algorithm. It should only be set for applications that send frequent small bursts of information without getting an immediate response, where timely delivery of data is required (the canonical example is mouse movements)."*

Syntax: on or off

Default value: on

tcp_nopush

Context: http, server, location

Enables or disables the TCP_NOPUSH (FreeBSD) or TCP_CORK (Linux) socket option. Note that this option only applies if the sendfile directive is enabled. If tcp_nopush is set to on, Nginx will attempt to transmit the entire HTTP response headers in a single TCP packet.

Syntax: on or off

Default value: off

sendfile

Context: http, server, location

If this directive is enabled, Nginx will use the sendfile kernel call to handle file transmission. If disabled, Nginx will handle the file transfer by itself. Depending on the physical location of the file being transmitted (such as NFS), this option may affect the server performance.

On Linux, using `sendfile` automatically disables asynchronous IO. If using FreeBSD, it is possible to combine the use of `aio` and `sendfile`; more on this in `Chapter 8`, *From Apache to Nginx*.

Syntax: `on` or `off`

Default value: `off`

sendfile_max_chunk

Context: `http`, `server`

This directive defines a maximum data size to be used for each call to `sendfile` (read the previous entry).

Syntax: Numeric value (size)

Default value: `0`

send_lowat

Context: `http`, `server`

An option allowing you to make use of the `SO_SNDLOWAT` flag for TCP sockets under FreeBSD only. This value defines the minimum number of bytes in the buffer for output operations.

Syntax: Numeric value (size)

Default value: `0`

reset_timedout_connection

Context: `http`, `server`, and `location`

When a client connection times out, its associated information may remain in memory depending on the state it was on. Enabling this directive will erase all memory associated with the connection after it times out.

Syntax: `on` or `off`

Default value: `off`

Paths and documents

This section describes directives that configure the documents that should be served for each website, such as the document root, the site index, error pages, and so on.

root

Context: `http`, `server`, `location`, and `if`. Variables are accepted.

Defines the document root, containing the files you wish to serve to your visitors.

Syntax: Directory path

Default value: `html`

```
root /home/website.com/public_html;
```

alias

Context: `location`. Variables are accepted.

`alias` is a directive that you place in a `location` block only. It assigns a different path for Nginx to retrieve documents for a specific request. As an example, consider the following configuration:

```
http {
    server {
        server_name localhost;
        root /var/www/website.com/html;
         location /admin/ {
         alias /var/www/locked/;
        }
    }
}
```

When a request for `http://localhost/` is received, files are served from the `/var/www/website.com/html/` folder. However, if Nginx receives a request for `http://localhost/admin/`, the path used to retrieve the files is `/home/website.com/locked/`. Moreover, the value of the document root directive (`root`) is not altered. This procedure is invisible in the eyes of dynamic scripts.

Syntax: Directory (do not forget the trailing `/`) or file path

error_page

Context: `http`, `server`, `location`, and `if`. Variables are accepted.

Allows you to affect URIs to HTTP response code and optionally to replace the code with another.

Syntax: `error_page code1 [code2...] [=replacement code] [=@block | URI]`

Where the replacement code (denoted by =code) is one of 301, 302, 303, 307, or 308

Examples :

```
error_page 404 /not_found.html;
error_page 500 501 502 503 504 /server_error.html;
error_page 403 http://website.com/;
error_page 404 @notfound; # jump to a named location block
error_page 404 =200 /index.html; # in case of 404 error, redirect to
index.html with a 200 OK response code
```

if_modified_since

Context: `http`, `server`, and `location`

Defines how Nginx handles the `If-Modified-Since` HTTP header. This header is mostly used by search engine spiders (such as Google web crawling bots). The robot indicates the date and time of the last pass. If the requested file has not been modified since then, the server simply returns a `304 Not Modified` response code with no body.

This directive accepts the following three values:

- `off`: Ignores the `If-Modified-Since` header.
- `exact`: Returns `304 Not Modified` if the date and time specified in the HTTP header are an exact match with the actual requested file modification date. If the file modification date is earlier or later, the file is served normally (`200 OK` response).
- `before`: Returns `304 Not Modified` if the date and time specified in the HTTP header is earlier than, or equal to, the requested file modification date.

Syntax: `if_modified_since off | exact | before`

Default value: `exact`

index

Context: `http`, `server`, `location`. Variables are accepted.

Defines the default page that Nginx will serve if no filename is specified in the request (in other words, the index page). You may specify multiple filenames and the first file to be found will be served. If none of the specified files are found, Nginx will either attempt to generate an automatic index of the files, if the `autoindex` directive is `enabled` (check the HTTP Autoindex module) or returns a `403 Forbidden` error page. Optionally, you may insert an absolute filename (such as `/page.html`, based on the document root directory) but only as the last argument of the directive.

Syntax: `index file1 [file2...] [absolute_file];`

Default value: `index.html`

```
index index.php index.html index.htm;
index index.php index2.php /catchall.php;
```

recursive_error_pages

Context: `http`, `server`, `location`

Sometimes an error page, itself served by the `error_page` directive, may trigger an error; in this case the `error_page` directive is used again (recursively). This directive enables or disables recursive error pages.

Syntax: `on` or `off`

Default value: `off`

try_files

Context: `server`, `location`. Variables are accepted.

Attempts to serve the specified files (arguments *1* to *N-1*); if none of these files exist, it jumps to the respective named `location` block (last argument) or serves the specified URI.

Syntax: Multiple file paths, followed by a named `location` block or a URI

Example:

```
location / {
    try_files $uri $uri.html $uri.xml @proxy;
}
# the following is a "named location block"
location @proxy {
    proxy_pass 127.0.0.1:8080;
}
```

In this example, Nginx tries to serve files normally. If the request URI does not correspond to any existing file, Nginx appends `.html` to the URI and tries to serve the file again. If it still fails, it tries with `.xml`. Eventually, if all of these possibilities fail, another `location` block (`@proxy`) handles the request.

It is important to note that, except for the final argument, `try_files` will serve the literal file with no internal redirect. That means you *cannot* do a `try_files` directive as follows, as this would result in any file matching `$uri.php` being served with the PHP source code. This would leave a security vulnerability where a user could request a URI `/config` and get the contents of `/config.php`:

```
location / {
    try_files $uri $uri.php @proxy;
}
# the following is a "named location block"
location @proxy {
    proxy_pass 127.0.0.1:8080;
}
```

You may also specify `$uri/` in the list of values in order to test for the existence of a directory with that name.

Client requests

This section documents the way that Nginx handles client requests. Among other things, you are allowed to configure the keep-alive mechanism behavior, and possibly log client requests into files.

keepalive_requests

Context: `http`, `server`, and `location`

Maximum number of requests served over a single keep-alive connection.

Syntax: Numeric value

Default value: `100`

keepalive_timeout

Context: `http`, `server`, and `location`

This directive defines the number of seconds the server will wait before closing a keep-alive connection. The second (optional) parameter is transmitted as the value of the `Keep-Alive: timeout= <HTTP response header>`. The intended effect is to let the client browser close the connection itself after this period has elapsed. Note that some browsers ignore this setting. Internet Explorer, for instance, automatically closes the connection after around 60 seconds.

Syntax: `keepalive_timeout time1 [time2];`

Default value: `75`

```
keepalive_timeout 75;
keepalive_timeout 75 60;
```

keepalive_disable

Context: `http`, `server`, and `location`

This option allows you to disable the `keepalive` functionality for browser families of your choice.

Syntax: `keepalive_disable browser1 browser2;`

Default value: `msie6`

send_timeout

Context: `http`, `server`, `location`

The number of time after which Nginx closes an inactive connection. A connection becomes inactive the moment a client stops transmitting data.

Syntax: Time value (in seconds)

Default value: `60`

client_body_in_file_only

Context: `http`, `server`, and `location`

If this directive is enabled, the body of incoming HTTP requests will be stored into actual files on the disk. The client body corresponds to the client HTTP request raw data, minus the headers (in other words, the content transmitted in `POST` requests). Files are stored as plain-text documents.

This directive accepts three values:

- `off`: Do not store the request body in a file
- `clean`: Store the request body in a file and remove the file after a request is processed
- `on`: Store the request body in a file, but do not remove the file after the request is processed (not recommended unless for debugging purposes)

Syntax: `client_body_in_file_only on | clean | off`

Default value: `off`

client_body_in_single_buffer

Context: `http`, `server`, and `location`

Defines whether or not Nginx should store the request body in a single buffer in memory.

Syntax: `on` or `off`

Default value: `off`

client_body_buffer_size

Context: `http`, `server`, and `location`

Specifies the size of the buffer holding the body of client requests. If this size is exceeded, the body (or at least part of it) will be written to the disk. Note that, if the `client_body_in_file_only` directive is enabled, request bodies are always stored to a file on the disk, regardless of their size (whether they fit in the buffer or not).

Syntax: Size value

Default value: `8k` or `16k` (2 memory pages) depending on your computer architecture

client_body_temp_path

Context: `http`, `server`, and `location`

Allows you to define the path of the directory that will store the client request body files. An additional option lets you separate those files into a folder hierarchy over as many as three levels.

Syntax: `client_body_temp_path path [level1] [level2] [level3]`

Default value: `client_body_temp`

```
client_body_temp_path /tmp/nginx_rbf;
client_body_temp_path temp 2; # Nginx will create 2-digit folders to hold
request body files
client_body_temp_path temp 1 2 4; # Nginx will create 3 levels of folders
(first level: 1 digit, second level: 2 digits, third level: 4 digits)
```

client_body_timeout

Context: `http`, `server`, and `location`

Defines the inactivity timeout while reading a client request body. A connection becomes inactive the moment the client stops transmitting data. If the delay is reached, Nginx returns a `408 Request timeout` HTTP error.

Syntax: Time value (in seconds)

Default value: `60`

client_header_buffer_size

Context: `http`, `server`, and `location`

This directive allows you to define the size of the buffer that Nginx allocates to request headers. Usually, `1k` is enough. However, in some cases, the headers contain large chunks of cookie data or the request URI is lengthy. If that is the case, then Nginx allocates one or more larger buffers (the size of larger buffers is defined by the `large_client_header_buffers` directive).

Syntax: Size value

Default value: `1k`

client_header_timeout

Context: `http`, `server`, and `location`

Defines the inactivity timeout while reading a client request header. A connection becomes inactive the moment the client stops transmitting data. If the delay is reached, Nginx returns a `408 Request timeout` HTTP error.

Syntax: Time value (in seconds)

Default value: `60`

client_max_body_size

Context: `http`, `server`, and `location`

This is the maximum size of a client request body. If this size is exceeded, Nginx returns a `413 Request entity too large` HTTP error. This setting is particularly important if you are going to allow users to upload files to your server over HTTP.

Syntax: Size value

Default value: `1m`

large_client_header_buffers

Context: `http`, `server`, and `location`

Defines the number and size of larger buffers to be used for storing client requests, in the event the default buffer (`client_header_buffer_size`) was insufficient. Each line of the header must fit in the size of a single buffer. If the request URI line is greater than the size of a single buffer, Nginx returns the `414 Request URI too large` error. If another header line exceeds the size of a single buffer, Nginx returns a `400 Bad request` error.

Syntax: `large_client_header_buffers amount size`

Default value: *4*8* kilobytes

lingering_time

Context: `http`, `server`, and `location`

This directive applies to client requests with a request body. As soon as the number of uploaded data exceeds `max_client_body_size`, Nginx immediately sends a `413 Request entity too large` HTTP error response. However, most browsers continue uploading data regardless of that notification. This directive defines the number of time Nginx should wait after sending this error response before closing the connection.

Syntax: Numeric value (time)

Default value: 30 seconds

lingering_timeout

Context: http, server, and location

This directive defines the number of time that Nginx should wait between two read operations before closing the client connection.

Syntax: Numeric value (time)

Default value: 5 seconds

lingering_close

Context: http, server, and location

Controls the way Nginx closes client connections. Set this to off to immediately close connections after all of the request data has been received. The default value (on) allows waiting time to process additional data if necessary. If set to always, Nginx will always wait to close the connection. The number of waiting time is defined by the lingering_timeout directive.

Syntax: on, off, or always

Default value: on

ignore_invalid_headers

Context: http, and server

If this directive is disabled, Nginx returns a 400 Bad Request HTTP error if request headers are malformed.

Syntax: on or off

Default value: on

chunked_transfer_encoding

Context: `http`, `server`, and `location`

Enables or disables chunked transfer encoding for HTTP 1.1 requests.

Syntax: `on` or `off`

Default value: `on`

max_ranges

Context: `http`, `server`, and `location`

Defines how many byte ranges Nginx will serve when a client requests partial content from a file. If you do not specify a value, there is no limit. If you set this to `0`, the byte range functionality is disabled.

Syntax: Size value

MIME types

Nginx offers two particular directives that will help you configure MIME types: `types` and `default_type`, which defines the default MIME types for documents. This will affect the `Content-Type` HTTP header sent within responses. Read on.

types

Context: `http`, `server`, and `location`

This directive allows you to establish correlations between MIME types and file extensions. It's actually a block accepting a particular syntax:

```
types {
  mimetype1  extension1;
  mimetype2  extension2 [extension3...];
  [...]
}
```

When Nginx serves a file, it checks the file extension in order to determine the MIME type. The MIME type is then sent as the value of the `Content-Type` HTTP header in the response. This header may affect the way browsers handle files. For example, if the MIME type of the file you are requesting is `application/pdf`, your browser may, for instance, attempt to render the file using a plugin associated with that MIME type instead of merely downloading it.

Nginx includes a basic set of MIME types as a standalone file (`mime.types`) to be included with the `include` directive:

```
include mime.types;
```

This file already covers the most important file extensions so you will probably not need to edit it. If the extension of the served file is not found within the listed types, the default type is used, as defined by the `default_type` directive (see the next entry).

Note that you may override the list of types by re-declaring the `types` block. A useful example would be to force all files in a folder to be downloaded instead of being displayed:

```
http {
    include mime.types;
    [...]
    location /downloads/ {
        # removes all MIME types
        types { }
        default_type application/octet-stream;
    }
    [...]
}
```

Some browsers ignore MIME types and may still display files if their filename ends with a known extension, such as `.html` or `.txt`.

To control the way files are handled by your visitors' browsers in a more certain and definitive manner, you should make use of the `Content-Disposition` HTTP header via the `add_header` directive, detailed in the *HTTP headers* module (`Chapter 4`, *Module Configuration*).

The default values, if the `mime.types` file is not included, are as follows:

```
types {
  text/html html;
  image/gif gif;
  image/jpeg jpg;
}
```

default_type

Context: http, server, and location

Defines the default MIME type. When Nginx serves a file, the file extension is matched against the known types declared within the types block in order to return the proper MIME type as a value of the Content-Type HTTP response header. If the extension doesn't match any of the known MIME types, the value of the default_type directive is used.

Syntax: MIME type

Default value: text/plain

types_hash_max_size

Context: http, server, and location

Defines the maximum size of an entry in the MIME types hash tables.

Syntax: Numeric value

Default value: 4k or 8k (1 line of CPU cache)

types_hash_bucket_size

Context: http, server, and location

Sets the bucket size for the MIME types hash tables. You should only change this value if Nginx tells you to.

Syntax: Numeric value

Default value: 64

Limits and restrictions

This set of directives will allow you to add restrictions that apply when a client attempts to access a particular location or document on your server. Note that you will find additional directives for restricting access in the next chapter.

limit_except

Context: `location`

This directive allows you to prevent the use of all HTTP methods, except the ones that you explicitly allow. Within a `location` block, you may want to restrict the use of some HTTP methods, such as forbidding clients from sending `POST` requests. You need to define two elements: first, the methods that are not forbidden (the allowed methods; all others will be forbidden); and second, the audience that is affected by the restriction:

```
location /admin/ {
    limit_except GET {
      allow 192.168.1.0/24;
      deny all;
    }
}
```

This example applies a restriction to the `/admin/` location—all visitors are only allowed to use the `GET` method. Visitors that have a local IP address, as specified with the `allow` directive (detailed in the HTTP access module), are not affected by this restriction. If a visitor uses a forbidden method, Nginx will return in a `403 Forbidden` HTTP error. Note that the `GET` method implies the `HEAD` method (if you allow `GET`, both `GET` and `HEAD` are allowed).

The syntax is specific:

```
limit_except METHOD1 [METHOD2...] {
  allow | deny | auth_basic | auth_basic_user_file | proxy_pass | perl;
}
```

The directives that you are allowed to insert within the block are documented in their respective module section in `Chapter 4`, *Module Configuration*.

limit_rate

Context: `http`, `server`, `location`, and `if`

Allows you to limit the transfer rate of individual client connections. The rate is expressed in bytes per second:

```
limit_rate 500k;
```

This will limit connection transfer rates to *500* kilobytes per second. If a client opens two connections, the client will be allowed *2*500* kilobytes.

Syntax: Size value

Default value: No limit

limit_rate_after

Context: `http`, `server`, `location`, and `if`

Defines the number of data transferred before the `limit_rate` directive takes effect.

```
limit_rate 10m;
```

Nginx will send the first 10 megabytes at maximum speed. Past this size, the transfer rate is limited by the value specified with the `limit_rate` directive (see previous entry). Similar to the `limit_rate` directive, this setting only applies to a single connection.

Syntax: Size value

Default: None

satisfy

Context: `location`

The `satisfy` directive defines whether clients require all access conditions to be valid (satisfy all), or at least one (satisfy any):

```
location /admin/ {
    allow 192.168.1.0/24;
    deny all;
    auth_basic "Authentication required";
    auth_basic_user_file conf/htpasswd;
}
```

In the previous example, there are two conditions for clients to be able to access the resource:

- Through the `allow` and `deny` directives (HTTP access module), we only allow clients that have a local IP address; all other clients are denied access
- Through the `auth_basic` and `auth_basic_user_file` directives (the HTTP auth basic module), we only allow clients that provide a valid username and password

With `satisfy all`, the client must satisfy both conditions in order to gain access to the resource. With `satisfy any`, if the client satisfies either condition, they are granted access.

Syntax: `satisfy any | all`

Default value: `all`

internal

Context: `location`

This directive specifies that the `location` block is internal. In other words, the specified resource cannot be accessed by external requests:

```
server {
    [...]
    server_name .website.com;
    location /admin/ {
        internal;
    }
}
```

With the previous configuration, clients will not be able to browse `http://website.com/admin/`. Such requests will be met with 404 Not Found errors. The only way to access the resource is via internal redirects (check the *Rewrite module* section for more information on internal redirects).

File processing and caching

It's important for your websites to be built upon solid foundations. File access and caching are critical aspects of web serving. In this regard, Nginx lets you perform precise tweaking with the use of the following directives.

disable_symlinks

This directive allows you to control the way Nginx handles symbolic links when they are to be served. By default (the directive value is `off`), symbolic links are allowed and Nginx follows them. You may decide to disable the following symbolic links under different conditions by specifying one of these values:

- `on`: If any part of the requested URI is a symbolic link, access to it is denied and Nginx returns a `403 HTTP` error page.
- `if_not_owner`: Similar to the previous, but access is denied only if the link and the object it points to have different owners.
- The optional parameter `from=` allows you to specify a part of the URL that will not be checked for symbolic links. For example, `disable_symlinks on from=$document_root` will tell Nginx to normally follow symbolic links in the URI up to the `$document_root` folder. If a symbolic link is found in the URI parts after that, access to the requested file will be denied.

directio

Context: `http`, `server`, and `location`

If this directive is enabled, files with a size greater than the specified value will be read with the Direct I/O system mechanism. This allows Nginx to read data from the storage device and place it directly in memory with no intermediary caching process involved.

Syntax: Size value, or `off`

Default value: `off`

directio_alignment

Context: `http`, `server`, and `location`

Sets byte alignment when using `directio`. Set this value to `4k` if you use XFS under Linux.

Syntax: Size value

Default value: `512`

open_file_cache

Context: http, server, and location

This directive allows you to enable the cache that stores information about open files. It does not actually store file contents but only information such as:

- File descriptors (file size, modification time, and so on).
- The existence of files and directories.
- File errors, such as permission denied, file not found, and so on. Note that this can be disabled with the open_file_cache_errors directive.

This directive accepts two arguments:

- max=X, where X is the number of entries that the cache can store. If this number is reached, older entries will be deleted in order to leave room for newer entries.
- Optionally inactive=Y, where Y is the of seconds that a cache entry should be stored. By default, Nginx will wait *60* seconds before clearing a cache entry. If the cache entry is accessed, the timer is reset. If the cache entry is accessed more than the value defined by open_file_cache_min_uses, the cache entry will not be cleared (until Nginx runs out of space and decides to clear out older entries).

Syntax: open_file_cache max=X [inactive=Y] | off

Default value: off

Example:

```
open_file_cache max=5000 inactive=180;
```

open_file_cache_errors

Context: http, server, and location

Enables or disables the caching of file errors with the open_file_cache directive (read the previous entry).

Syntax: on or off

Default value: off

open_file_cache_min_uses

Context: `http`, `server`, and `location`

By default, entries in the `open_file_cache` are cleared after a period of inactivity (60 seconds, by default). If there is activity though, you can prevent Nginx from removing the cache entry. This directive defines the number of times an entry must be accessed in order to be eligible for protection:

```
open_file_cache_min_uses 3;
```

If the cache entry is accessed more than three times, it becomes permanently active and is not removed until Nginx decides to clear out older entries to free up some space.

Syntax: Numeric value

Default value: `1`

open_file_cache_valid

Context: `http`, `server`, and `location`

The open file cache mechanism is important, but cached information quickly becomes obsolete, especially in the case of a fast-moving filesystem. In that regard, information needs to be re-verified after a short period of time. This directive specifies the of seconds that Nginx will wait before revalidating a cache entry.

Syntax: Time value (in seconds)

Default value: `60`

read_ahead

Context: `http`, `server`, and `location`

Defines the of bytes to pre-read from files. Under Linux-based operating systems, setting this directive to a value above `0` will enable reading ahead, but the actual value you specify has no effect. Set this to `0` to disable pre-reading.

Syntax: Size value

Default value: `0`

Other directives

The following directives relate to various aspects of web server-logging, URI composition, DNS, and so on.

log_not_found

Context: `http`, `server`, and `location`

Enables or disables logging of 404 Not Found HTTP errors. If your logs get filled with 404 errors due to missing `favicon.ico` or `robots.txt` files, you might want to turn this `off`.

Syntax: `on` or `off`

Default value: `on`

log_subrequest

Context: `http`, `server`, and `location`

Enables or disables logging of sub-requests triggered by internal redirects (see the *Rewrite module* section) or SSI requests (see the *Server Side Includes* module section).

Syntax: `on` or `off`

Default value: `off`

merge_slashes

Context: `http`, `server`, and `location`

Enabling this directive will have the effect of merging multiple consecutive slashes in a URI. It turns out to be particularly useful in situations resembling the following:

```
server {
    [...]
    server_name website.com;
    location /documents/ {
        type { }
        default_type text/plain;
    }
}
```

By default, if the client attempts to access `http://website.com//documents/` (note the `//` in the middle of the URI), Nginx will return a 404 Not Found HTTP error. If you enable this directive, the two slashes will be merged into one and the location pattern will be matched.

Syntax: `on` or `off`

Default value: `off`

msie_padding

Context: `http`, `server`, and `location`

This directive functions with the **Microsoft Internet Explorer (MSIE)** and Google Chrome browser families. In the case of error pages (with error code 400 or higher), if the length of the response body is less than 512 bytes, these browsers will display their own error page, sometimes at the expense of a more informative page provided by the server. If you enable this option, the body of responses with a status code of 400 or higher will be padded to 512 bytes.

Syntax: `on` or `off`

Default value: `off`

msie_refresh

Context: `http`, `server`, and `location`

This is another MSIE-specific directive that will take effect in the case of the following HTTP response codes, `301 moved permanently` and `302 moved temporarily`. When enabled, Nginx sends clients running an MSIE browser a response body containing a refresh meta tag (`<meta http-equiv="Refresh"...>`) in order to redirect the browser to the new location of the requested resource.

Syntax: `on` or `off`

Default value: `off`

resolver

Context: `http`, `server`, and `location`

Specifies the name servers that should be employed by Nginx to resolve hostnames to IP addresses and vice-versa. DNS query results are cached for some time, either by respecting the TTL provided by the DNS server, or by specifying a time value to the valid argument.

If more than one DNS server is specified, Nginx will query them using a round-robin algorithm.

Syntax: one or more IPv4 or IPv6 addresses, `valid=Time value`, `ipv6=on|off`

Default value: None (system default)

```
resolver 127.0.0.1; # use local DNS
resolver 8.8.8.8 8.8.4.4 valid=1h; # use Google DNS and cache results for 1
hour
```

resolver_timeout

Context: `http`, `server`, and `location`

Timeout for a hostname resolution query.

Syntax: Time value (in seconds)

Default value: `30`

server_tokens

Context: `http`, `server`, and `location`

This directive allows you to define whether or not Nginx should inform clients of the running version number. There are three situations where Nginx indicates its version number:

- In the server header of HTTP responses (such as `nginx/1.8.0`). If you set `server_tokens` to `off`, the server header will only indicate **Nginx**.

- On error pages, Nginx indicates the version number in the footer. If you set `server_tokens` to `off`, the footer on error pages will only indicate **Nginx**.
- If using the build value, Nginx will output the build value specified during compilation.

If you are running an older version of Nginx and do not plan to update it, it might be a good idea to *hide* your version number for security reasons.

Syntax: `on`, `off` , or `build` Default value: `on`

underscores_in_headers

Context: `http`, and `server`

Allows or disallows underscores in custom HTTP header names. If this directive is set to `on`, the following example header is considered valid by `Nginx: test_header: value`.

Syntax: `on` or `off`

Default value: `off`

variables_hash_max_size

Context: `http`

This directive defines the maximum size of variables hash tables. If your server configuration uses a total of more than 1,024 variables, you will have to increase this value.

Syntax: Numeric value

Default value: `1024`

variables_hash_bucket_size

Context: `http`

This directive allows you to set the bucket size for variable hash tables.

Syntax: Numeric value

Default value: `64` (or `32` or `128`, depending on your processor cache specifications)

post_action

Context: `http`, `server`, `location`, and `if`

Defines a post-completion action, a URI that will be called by Nginx after the request has been completed.

Syntax: URI or named `location` block

Example:

```
location /payment/ {
    post_action /scripts/done.php;
}
```

Using HTTP/2

Nginx added support for HTTP/2 in version 1.9.5 and superseded the SPDY (pronounced **SPeeDY**) module, meaning that, as of 1.9.5, SPDY is no longer available and we now have to use HTTP/2.

If you installed Nginx via a package manager this module is most likely enabled; if you compiled it yourself please make sure you compiled Nginx using the `--with_http_v2_module` configure flag.

Similarly to SPDY, HTTP/2 requires the use of SSL, which is good practice regardless. These days, SSL certificates can be issued for free by services such as *Let's Encrypt* so this is highly recommended.

To enable HTTP/v add the `http2` flag to the listen directive:

```
listen 443 ssl http2;
```

Module directives

Let's explore the different module directives in this section.

http2_chunk_size

Context: http, server, and location

Sets the maximum size of chunks into which the response body is sliced.

Syntax: size

Default value: 8k

http2_body_preread_size

Context: http, and server

Sets the size of the request buffer in which the body may be saved before it is processed.

Syntax: size

Default value: 64k

http2_idle_timeout

Context: http, and server

Sets the time after which the connection is closed due to inactivity.

Syntax: time

Default value: 3m

http2_max_concurrent_streams

Context: http, and server

Sets the maximum number of concurrent HTTP/2 streams in a connection.

Syntax: number

Default value: 128

http2_max_field_size

Context: http, and server

Limits the maximum size of a compressed request header field.

Syntax: size

Default value: 4k

http2_max_header_size

Context: http, and server

Limits the maximum size of the entire request header list after decompression.

Syntax: Size

Default value: 16k

http2_max_requests

Context: http, and server

Sets the maximum number of requests that can be served through one HTTP/2 connection, after which the connection is closed and the client should use a new connection.

Syntax: Number

Default value: 1000

http2_recv_buffer_size

Context: http

Sets the size of the per-worker input buffer.

Syntax: Size

Default value: 256k

http2_recv_timeout

Context: `http, server`

Sets the timeout for expecting more data from the client, after which the connection is closed.

Syntax: Time

Default value: `30`

Module variables

The HTTP/2 module sets only a single variable to determine whether HTTP/2 is used or not:

Variable	Description
`$http2`	h2 if HTTP/2 over TLS, h2c if over cleartext TCP. Empty string ( ) if HTTP/2 is not used.

Module variables

The HTTP core module introduces a large set of variables that you can use within the value of directives. Be careful though, as only a handful of directives accept variables in the definition of their value. If you insert a variable in the value of a directive that does not accept variables, no error is reported; instead the variable name appears as raw text.

There are three different kinds of variable that you will come across. The first set represents the values transmitted in the headers of the client request. The second set corresponds to the headers of the response sent to the client. Finally, the third set comprises variables that are completely generated by Nginx.

Request headers

Nginx lets you access client request headers in the form of variables that you will be able to employ later on in the configuration:

Variable	Description
$http_host	Value of the **Host** HTTP header, a string indicating the hostname that the client is trying to reach.
$http_user_agent	Value of the **User-Agent** HTTP header, a string indicating the web browser of the client.
$http_referer	Value of the **Referer** HTTP header, a string indicating the URL of the previous page from which the client comes.
$http_via	Value of the **Via** HTTP header, which informs us about possible proxies used by the client.
$http_x_forwarded_for	Value of the **X-Forwarded-For** HTTP header, which shows the actual IP address of the client if the client is behind a proxy.
$http_cookie	Value of the **Cookie** HTTP header, which contains the cookie data sent by the client.
$http_...	Additional headers sent by the client can be retrieved using $http_ followed by the header name in lowercase and with dashes (–) replaced by underscores (_).

Response headers

In a similar fashion, you are allowed to access the HTTP headers of the response that was sent to the client. These variables are not available at all times—they will only carry a value after the response is sent, for instance, at the time of writing messages in the logs:

Variable	Description
$sent_http_content_type	Value of the Content-Type HTTP header, indicating the MIME type of the resource being transmitted.
$sent_http_content_length	Value of the Content-Length HTTP header informing the client of the response body length.
$sent_http_location	Value of the Location HTTP header, which indicates that the location of the desired resource is different from the one specified in the original request.

Variable	Description
`$sent_http_last_modified`	Value of the `Last-Modified` HTTP header corresponding to the modification date of the requested resource.
`$sent_http_connection`	Value of the `Connection` HTTP header, defining whether the connection will be kept alive or closed.
`$sent_http_keep_alive`	Value of the `Keep-Alive` HTTP header that defines the amount of time a connection will be kept alive.
`$sent_http_transfer_encoding`	Value of the `Transfer-Encoding` HTTP header, giving information about the response body encoding method (such as compress, gzip).
`$sent_http_cache_control`	Value of the `Cache-Control` HTTP header, telling us whether the client browser should cache the resource or not.
`$sent_http_...`	Additional headers sent to the client can be retrieved using `$sent_http_` followed by the header name, in lowercase and with dashes (–) replaced by underscores (_).

Nginx generated

Apart from HTTP headers, Nginx provides a large of variables concerning the request, the way it was and will be handled, as well as settings in use with the current configuration:

Variable	Description
`$arg_XXX`	Allows you to access the query string (GET parameters), where XXX is the name of the parameter you want to utilize.
`$args`	All of the arguments of the query string combined together.
`$binary_remote_addr`	IP address of the client as binary data (4 bytes).
`$body_bytes_sent`	Amount of bytes sent in the body of the response (does not include response headers).

Variable	Description
$bytes_sent	Amount of bytes sent to the client.
$connection	Serial number identifying a connection.
$connection_requests	Amount of requests already served by the current connection.
$content_length	Equates to the Content-Length HTTP header.
$content_type	Equates to the Content-Type HTTP header.
$cookie_XXX	Allows you to access cookie data where XXX is the name of the parameter you want to utilize.
$document_root	Returns the value of the root directive for the current request.
$document_uri	Returns the current URI of the request. It may differ from the original request URI if internal redirects were performed. It is identical to the $uri variable.
$host	This variable equates to the host HTTP header of the request. Nginx itself gives this variable a value for cases where the host header is not provided in the original request.
$hostname	Returns the system hostname of the server computer.
$https	Set to on for HTTPS connections, empty otherwise.
$is_args	If the $args variable is defined, $is_args equates to ?. If $args is empty, $is_args is empty as well. You may use this variable for constructing an URI that optionally comes with a query string, such as index.phpis_argsargs. If there is any query string argument in the request, $is_args is set to ?, making this a valid URI.
$limit_rate	Returns the per-connection transfer rate limit, as defined by the limit_rate directive. You are allowed to edit this variable by using set (directive from the *Rewrite module*): set $limit_rate 128k;.
$msec	Returns the current time (in seconds + milliseconds).

Variable	Description
`$nginx_version`	Returns the version of Nginx you are running.
`$pid`	Returns the Nginx process identifier.
`$pipe`	If the current request is pipelined, this variable is set to `p`; otherwise the value is [.]".
`$proxy_protocol_addr`	If the `proxy_protocol` parameter is enabled on the listen directive, this variable will contain the client address.
`$query_string`	Identical to `$args`.
`$remote_addr`	Returns the IP address of the client.
`$remote_port`	Returns the port of the client socket.
`$remote_user`	Returns the client username if they used authentication.
`$realpath_root`	Returns the document root in the client request, with symbolic links resolved into the actual path.
`$request_body`	Returns the body of the client request, or – if the body is empty.
`$request_body_file`	If the request body was saved (see the `client_body_in_file_only` directive), this variable indicates the path of the temporary file.
`$request_completion`	Returns OK if the request is completed, an *empty string* otherwise.
`$request_filename`	Returns the *full filename* served in the current request.
`$request_length`	Returns the *total length* of the client request.
`$request_method`	Indicates the HTTP method used in the request, such as GET or POST.
`$request_time`	Returns the amount of time elapsed since the first byte was read from the client (seconds + milliseconds value).
`$request_id`	Unique request identifier generated from 16 random bytes, in hexadecimal.

Variable	Description
$request_uri	Corresponds to the original URI of the request; remains unmodified all through the process (unlike $document_uri/$uri).
$scheme	Returns either http or https, depending on the request.
$server_addr	Returns the IP address of the server. Be careful, as each use of the variable requires a system call, which could potentially affect overall performance in the case of high-traffic setups.
$server_name	Indicates the value of the server_name directive that was used while processing the request.
$server_port	Indicates the port of the server socket that received the request data.
$server_protocol	Returns the protocol and version, usually HTTP/1.0 or HTTP/1.1.
$status	Returns the response status code.
$tcpinfo_rtt, $tcpinfo_rttvar, $tcpinfo_snd_cwnd, $tcpinfo_rcv_space	If your operating system supports the TCP_INFO socket option, these variables will be populated with information on the current client TCP connection.
$time_iso8601, $time_local	Provides the current time respectively in *ISO 8601* and local formats for use with the access_log directive.
$uri	Identical to $document_uri.

The location block

We have established that Nginx lets you fine-tune your configuration down to three levels—at the protocol level (http block), the server level (server block), and the requested URI level (location block). Let's now go into more detail about the latter.

Location modifier

Nginx allows you to define `location` blocks by specifying a pattern that will be matched against the requested document URI:

```
server {
    server_name website.com;
    location /admin/ {
    # The configuration you place here only applies to
    # http://website.com/admin/
    }
}
```

Instead of a simple folder name, you can indeed insert complex patterns. The syntax of the `location` block is:

```
location [=|~|~*|^~|@] pattern { ... }
```

The first optional argument is a symbol called `location` that will define the way Nginx matches the specified pattern and also defines the very nature of the pattern (a simple string or regular expression). The following paragraphs detail the different modifiers and their behavior.

The = modifier

The requested document URI must match the specified pattern exactly. The pattern here is limited to a simple literal string; you cannot use a regular expression:

```
server {
    server_name website.com;
    location = /abcd {
    [...]
    }
}
```

The configuration in the `location` block:

- Applies to `http://website.com/abcd` (exact match)
- May apply to `http://website.com/ABCD` (it is case-sensitive if your operating system uses a case-sensitive filesystem)
- Applies to `http://website.com/abcd?param1&param2` (regardless of query string arguments)

- Does not apply to `http://website.com/abcd/` (trailing slash)
- Does not apply to `http://website.com/abcde` (extra characters after the specified pattern)

No modifier

The requested document URI must begin with the specified pattern. You may not use regular expressions:

```
server {
    server_name website.com;
    location /abcd {
    [...]
    }
}
```

The configuration in the `location` block:

- Applies to `http://website.com/abcd` (exact match)
- May apply to `http://website.com/ABCD` (it is case-sensitive if your operating system uses a case-sensitive filesystem)
- Applies to `http://website.com/abcd?param1&param2` (regardless of query string arguments)
- Applies to `http://website.com/abcd/` (trailing slash)
- Applies to `http://website.com/abcde` (extra characters after the specified pattern)

The ~ modifier

The requested URI must be a case-sensitive match for the specified regular expression:

```
server {
    server_name website.com;
    location ~ ^/abcd$ {
    [...]
    }
}
```

The ^/abcd$ regular expression used in this example specifies that the pattern must begin (^) with /, be followed by abc, and finish ($) with d. Consequently, the configuration in the location block:

- Applies to http://website.com/abcd (exact match)
- Does not apply to http://website.com/ABCD (case-sensitive)
- Applies to http://website.com/abcd?param1&param2 (regardless of query string arguments)
- Does not apply to http://website.com/abcd/ (trailing slash) due to the specified regular expression
- Does not apply to http://website.com/abcde (extra characters) due to the specified regular expression

> With operating systems such as Microsoft Windows, ~ and ~* are both case-insensitive, as the OS uses a case-insensitive filesystem.

The ~* modifier

The requested URI must be a case-insensitive match for the specified regular expression:

```
server {
    server_name website.com;
    location ~* ^/abcd$ {
    [...]
    }
}
```

The regular expression used in the example is similar to the previous one. Consequently, the configuration in the location block:

- Applies to http://website.com/abcd (exact match)
- Applies to http://website.com/ABCD (case-insensitive)
- Applies to http://website.com/abcd?param1&param2 (regardless of query string arguments)
- Does not apply to http://website.com/abcd/ (trailing slash) due to the specified regular expression
- Does not apply to http://website.com/abcde (extra characters) due to the specified regular expression

The ^~ modifier

Similar to the no-symbol behavior, the location URI must begin with the specified pattern. The difference is that, if the pattern is matched, Nginx stops searching for other patterns (read the *Search order and priority* section).

The @ modifier

Defines a named `location` block. These blocks cannot be accessed by the client, but only by internal requests generated by other directives, such as `try_files` or `error_page`.

Search order and priority

Since it's possible to define multiple `location` blocks with different patterns, you need to understand that, when Nginx receives a request, it searches for the `location` block that best matches the requested URI:

```
server {
    server_name website.com;
    location /files/ {
    # applies to any request starting with "/files/"
    # for example /files/doc.txt, /files/, /files/temp/
    }
    location = /files/ {
    # applies to the exact request to "/files/"
    # and as such does not apply to /files/doc.txt
    # but only /files/
    }
}
```

When a client visits `http://website.com/files/doc.txt`, the first `location` block applies. However, when they visit `http://website.com/files/`, the second block applies (even though the first one matches) because it has priority over the first one (it is an exact match).

The order you established in the configuration file (placing the `/files/` block before the `=` `/files/` block) is irrelevant. Nginx will search for matching patterns in a specific order:

- `location` blocks with the `=` modifier: If the specified string exactly matches the requested URI, Nginx retains the `location` block

- location blocks with no modifier: If the specified string *exactly* matches the requested URI, Nginx retains the location block
- location blocks with the ^~ modifier: If the specified string matches the beginning of the requested URI, Nginx retains the location block
- location blocks with the ~ or ~* modifier: If the regular expression matches the requested URI, Nginx retains the location block
- location blocks with no modifier: If the specified string matches the *beginning* of the requested URI, Nginx retains the location block

To that extent, the ^~ modifier begins to make sense, and we can envision cases where it becomes useful, as shown here:

Case 1

```
server {
    server_name website.com;
    location /doc {
    [...] # requests beginning with "/doc"
    }
    location ~* ^/document$ {
    [...] # requests exactly matching "/document"
    }
}
```

You might wonder: When a client requests http://website.com/document, which of these two location blocks applies? Indeed, both blocks match this request. Again, the answer does not lie in the order in which the blocks appear in the configuration files. In this case, the second location block will apply as the ~* modifier has priority over the other.

Case 2

```
server {
    server_name website.com;
    location /document {
    [...] # requests beginning with "/document"
    }
    location ~* ^/document$ {
    [...] # requests exactly matching "/document"
    }
}
```

The question remains the same—*What happens when a client sends a request to download* `http://website.com/document`? There is a trick here. The string specified in the first block now exactly matches the requested URI. As a result, Nginx prefers it over the regular expression.

Case 3

```
server {
    server_name website.com;
    location ^~ /doc {
    [...] # requests beginning with "/doc"
    }
    location ~* ^/document$ {
    [...] # requests exactly matching "/document"
    }
}
```

This last case makes use of the `^~` modifier. Which block applies when a client visits `http://website.com/document`? The answer is the first block. The reason is that `^~` has priority over `~*`. As a result, any request with a URI beginning with `/doc` will be affected to the first block, even if the request URI matches the regular expression defined in the second block.

Summary

All through this chapter, we studied the key concepts of the Nginx HTTP configuration. First, we learned about creating virtual hosts by declaring `server` blocks. Then we discovered the directives and variables of the HTTP Core module that can be inserted within those blocks, and eventually understood the mechanisms governing the `location` block.

The job is done—your server now actually serves websites. We are going to take it one step further by discovering the modules that truly form the powerhouse of Nginx. The next chapter will deal with advanced topics, such as the rewrite and SSI modules, as well as additional components of the HTTP server.

4

Module Configuration

The true power of Nginx lies within its modules. The entire application is built on a modular system, and each module can be enabled or disabled at compile time. Some bring up simple functionalities, such as the autoindex module that generates a listing of the files in a directory. Some will transform your perception of a web server (such as the Rewrite module). Developers are also invited to create their own modules. A quick overview of the third-party module system can be found at the end of this chapter.

This chapter covers:

- The Rewrite module, which does more than just rewrite URIs
- The SSI module, a server-side scripting language
- Additional modules enabled in the default Nginx build
- Optional modules that must be enabled at compile time
- A quick note on third-party modules

Rewrite module

This module, in particular, brings much more functionality to Nginx than a simple set of directives. It defines a whole new level of request processing that will be explained throughout this section.

Initially, the purpose of this module (as the name suggests) is to perform URL rewriting. This mechanism allows you to get rid of ugly URLs containing multiple parameters, for instance, `http://example.com/article.php?id=1234&comment=32`—such URLs being particularly uninformative and meaningless for a regular visitor.

Instead, links to your website will contain useful information that indicates the nature of the page you are about to visit. The URL given in the example becomes `http://website.com/article-1234-32-US-economy-strengthens.html`. This solution is not only more interesting for your visitors, but also for search engines. URL rewriting is a key element to **Search Engine Optimization (SEO)**.

The principle behind this mechanism is simple: it consists of rewriting the URI of the client request after it is received, before serving the file. Once rewritten, the URI is matched against `location` blocks in order to find the configuration that should be applied to the request. The technique is further detailed in the coming sections.

Reminder on regular expressions

First and foremost, this module requires a certain understanding of regular expressions, also known as **regexes** or **regexps**. Indeed, URL rewriting is performed by the `rewrite` directive, which accepts a pattern followed by the replacement URI.

It is a vast topic; entire books are dedicated to explaining the ins and outs. However, the simplified approach that we are about to examine should be more than sufficient to make the most of the mechanism.

Purpose

The first question we must answer is: what is the purpose of regular expressions? To put it simply, the main purpose is to verify that a string of characters matches a given pattern. The pattern is written in a particular language that allows for defining extremely complex and accurate rules:

String	Pattern	Does it match?	Explanation
hello	^hello$	Yes	The string begins with character h (^h), followed by e, l, l, and then finishes with o (o$).
hell	^hello$	No	The string begins with character h (^h), followed by e, l, l, but does not finish with o.
Hello	^hello$	Depends	If the engine performing the match is case-sensitive, the string doesn't match the pattern.

This concept becomes a lot more interesting when complex patterns are employed, such as one that validates an email addresses: `^[A-Z0-9._%+-]+@[A-Z0-9.-]+\.[A-Z]{2,4}$`. Validating a well-formed email address programmatically would require a great deal of code, while all of the work can be done with a single regular expression pattern matching.

PCRE syntax

The syntax that Nginx employs originates from the **Perl Compatible Regular Expression** (**PCRE**) library, which (if you remember `Chapter 2`, *Basic Nginx Configuration*) is a prerequisite for making your own build, unless you disable modules that make use of it. It's the most commonly used form of regular expression, and nearly everything you learn here remains valid for other language variations.

In its simplest form, a pattern is composed of one character, for example, `x`. We can match strings against this pattern. Does `example` match the pattern x? Yes, `example` contains the character x. It can be more than one specific character; the pattern `[a-z]` matches any character between `a` and `z`, or even a combination of letters and digits: `[a-z0-9]`. In consequence, the pattern `hell[a-z0-9]` validates the following strings: `hello` and `hell4`, but not `hell` or `hell!`.

You probably noticed that we employed the characters `[` and `]`. These are called **metacharacters** and have a special effect on the pattern. There is a total of *11* metacharacters, and all play a different role. If you want to create a pattern that actually contains one of these characters, you need to escape the character with a \ (backslash):

Metacharacter	Description
^ Beginning	The entity after this character must be found at the beginning: • Example pattern: `^h` • Matching strings: `hello`, `h`, `hh` (anything beginning with *h*) • Non-matching strings: `character`, `ssh`
$ End	The entity before this character must be found at the end: • Example pattern: `e$` • Matching strings: `sample`, `e`, `file` (anything ending with *e*) • Non-matching strings: `extra`, `shell`
. (dot) Any	Matches any character: • Example pattern: `hell.` • Matching strings: `hello`, `hellx`, `hell5`, and `hell!` • Non-matching strings: `hell`, `helo`

Metacharacter	Description
[ ] Set	Matches any character within the specified set: • Syntax: `[a-z]` for a range, `[abcd]` for a set, and `[a-z0-9]` for two ranges. Note that if you want to include the – character in a range, you need to insert it right after the `[` or just before the `]`. • Example pattern: `hell[a-y123-]` • Matching strings: `hello`, `hell1`, `hell2`, `hell3`, and `hell-` • Non-matching strings: `hellz`, `hell4`, `heloo`, and `he-llo`
[^] Negate set	Matches any character that is not within the specified set: • Example pattern: `hell[^a-np-z0-9]` • Matching strings: `hello`, and `hell!` • Non-matching strings: `hella`, `hell5`
| Alternation	Matches the entity placed either before or after the `|`: • Example pattern: `hello|welcome` • Matching strings: `hello`, `welcome`, `helloes`, and `awelcome` • Non-matching strings: `hell`, `ellow`, `owelcom`
( ) Grouping	Groups a set of entities, often to be used in conjunction with `|`. Also **captures** the matched entities; captures are detailed further on: • Example pattern: `^(hello|hi) there$` • Matching strings: `hello there`, and `hi there` • Non-matching strings: `hey there`, and `ahoy there`
\\ Escape	Allows you to escape special characters: Example pattern: `Hello\` Matching strings: `Hello.`, `Hello. How are you?`, and `Hi! Hello...` Non-matching strings: `Hello`, and `Hello!how are you?`

Quantifiers

So far, you are able to express simple patterns with a limited number of characters. Quantifiers allow you to extend the amount of accepted entities:

Quantifier	Description
* 0 or more times	The entity preceding * must be found 0 or more times: • Example pattern: `he*llo` • Matching strings: `hllo, hello, heeeello` • Non-matching strings: `hallo, ello`
+ 1 or more times	The entity preceding + must be found 1 or more times: • Example pattern: `he+llo` • Matching strings: `hello, heeeello` • Non-matching strings: `hllo, helo`
? 0 or 1 time	The entity preceding ? must be found 0 or 1 times: • Example pattern: `he?llo` • Matching strings: `hello, hllo` • Non-matching strings: `heello, heeeello`
{x} x times	The entity preceding {x} must be found x times: • Example pattern: `he{3}llo` • Matching strings: `heeello, oh heeello there!` • Non-matching strings: `hello, heello, heeeello`
{x, } At least x times	The entity preceding {x, } must be found at least x times: • Example pattern: `he{3,}llo` • Matching strings: `heeello, heeeeeeello` • Non-matching strings: `hllo, hello, heello`
{x,y} x to y times	The entity preceding {x,y} must be found between x and y times: • Example pattern: `he{2,4}llo` • Matching strings: `heello, heeello, heeeello` • Non-matching strings: `hello, heeeeello`

As you probably noticed, the { and } characters in the regular expressions conflict with the block delimiter of the Nginx configuration file syntax language. If you want to write a regular expression pattern that includes *curly brackets*, you need to place the pattern between quotes (single or double quotes):

```
rewrite hel{2,}o /hello.php; # invalid
rewrite "hel{2,}o" /hello.php; # valid
rewrite 'hel{2,}o' /hello.php; # valid
```

Captures

One last feature of the regular expression mechanism is the ability to capture sub-expressions. Whatever text is placed between parentheses ( ) is captured and can be used after the matching process. The captured characters become available under the form of variables called $N, where N is a numeric index, in order of capture. Alternatively, you can attribute an arbitrary name to each of your captures (see the following example). The variables generated through the captures can be inserted within directive values.

Here are a couple of examples to illustrate the principle:

Pattern	Example of a matching string	Captured
`^(hello|hi) (sir|mister)$`	`hello sir`	`$1 = hello` `$2 = sir`
`^(hello (sir))$`	`hello sir`	`$1 = hello sir` `$2 = sir`
`^(.*)$`	`nginx rocks`	`$1 = nginx rocks`

`^(.{1,3})([0-9]{1,4})([?!]{1,2})$`	`abc1234!?`	`$1 = abc`
		`$2 = 1234`
		`$3 = !?`

Named captures are also supported through the following syntax: `?<name>` Example: `^/(?<folder>[^/]+)/(?<file>.*)$`	`/admin/doc`	`$folder = admin` `$file = doc`

When you use a regular expression in Nginx, for example, in the context of a location block, the buffers that you capture can be employed in later directives:

```
server {
    server_name website.com;
    location ~* ^/(downloads|files)/(.*)$ {
        add_header Capture1 $1;
        add_header Capture2 $2;
    }
}
```

In the preceding example, the `location` block will match the request URI against a regular expression. A few of URIs that would apply here: `/downloads/file.txt`, `/files/archive.zip`, or even `/files/docs/report.doc`. Two parts are captured: `$1` will contain either `downloads` or `files`, and `$2` will contain whatever comes after `/downloads/` or `/files/`. Note that the `add_header` directive (syntax: `add_header header_name header_value`, see the *HTTP headers module* section) is employed here to append arbitrary headers to the client response, for the sole purpose of demonstration.

Internal requests

Nginx differentiates external and internal requests. External requests originate directly from the client; the URI is then matched against possible `location` blocks:

```
server {
    server_name website.com;
    location = /document.html {
        deny all; # example directive
    }
}
```

A client request to `http://website.com/document.html` would directly fall into the preceding `location` block.

Opposite to this, internal requests are triggered by Nginx via specific directives. Among the directives offered by the default Nginx modules, there are several directives capable of producing internal requests: `error_page`, `index`, `rewrite`, `try_files`, `add_before_body`, and `add_after_body` (from the addition module), the `include` SSI command, and more.

There are two different types of internal requests:

- * **Internal redirects:** Nginx redirects the client requests internally. The URI is changed, and the request may therefore match another `location` block and become eligible for different settings. The most common case of internal redirects is when using the `rewrite` directive, which allows you to rewrite the request URI.

- **Sub-requests**: Additional requests that are triggered internally to generate content that is complementary to the main request. A simple example would be with the addition module. The `add_after_body` directive allows you to specify a URI that will be processed after the original one, the resulting content being appended to the body of the original request. The SSI module also makes use of sub-requests to insert content with the `include` SSI command.

error_page

Detailed in the module directives of the Nginx HTTP Core module, `error_page` allows you to define the server behavior when a specific error code occurs. The simplest form is to affect a URI to an error code:

```
server {
    server_name website.com;
    error_page 403 /errors/forbidden.html;
    error_page 404 /errors/not_found.html;
}
```

When a client attempts to access a URI that triggers one of these errors (such as loading a document or file that does not exist on the server, resulting in a 404 error), Nginx is supposed to serve the page associated to the error code. In fact, it does not just send the client the error page; it actually initiates a completely new request, based on the new URI.

Consequently, you can end up falling back on a different configuration, like in the following example:

```
server {
    server_name website.com;
    root /var/www/vhosts/website.com/httpdocs/;
    error_page 404 /errors/404.html;
    location /errors/ {
        alias /var/www/common/errors/;
        internal;
    }
}
```

When a client attempts to load a document that does not exist, they will initially receive a 404 error. We employed the `error_page` directive to specify that 404 errors should create an internal redirect to `/errors/404.html`. As a result, a new request is generated by Nginx, with the URI `/errors/404.html`. This URI falls under the location `/errors/` block, so the corresponding configuration applies.

Logs can prove to be particularly useful when working with redirects and URL rewrites. Be aware that information on internal redirects will show up in the logs only if you set the error_log directive to debug. You can also get it to show up at the notice level, under the condition that you specify rewrite_log on; wherever you need it.

A raw but trimmed excerpt from the debug log summarizes the mechanism:

```
->http request line: "GET /page.html HTTP/1.1"
->http uri: "/page.html"
->test location: "/errors/"
->using configuration ""
->http filename: "/var/www/vhosts/website.com/httpdocs/page.html"
-> open() "/var/www/vhosts/website.com/httpdocs/page.html" failed (2: No
such file or directory), client: 127.0.0.1, server: website.com, request:
"GET /page.html HTTP/1.1", host:"website.com"
->http finalize request: 404, "/page.html?" 1
->http special response: 404, "/page.html?"
->internal redirect: "/errors/404.html?"
->test location: "/errors/"
->using configuration "/errors/"
->http filename: "/var/www/common/errors/404.html"
->http finalize request: 0, "/errors/404.html?" 1
```

Note that the use of the internal directive in the location block forbids clients from accessing the /errors/ directory. This location can thus only be accessed through an internal redirect.

The mechanism is the same for the index directive (detailed further on in the index module). If no file path is provided in the client request, Nginx will attempt to serve the specified index page by triggering an internal redirect.

Rewrite

While the previous directive error_page is not actually part of the Rewrite module, detailing its functionality provides a solid introduction to the way Nginx handles client requests.

Similar to how the `error_page` directive redirects to another location, rewriting the URI with the `rewrite` directive generates an internal redirect:

```
server {
    server_name website.com;
    root /var/www/vhosts/website.com/httpdocs/;
    location /storage/ {
        internal;
        alias /var/www/storage/;
    }
    location /documents/ {
        rewrite ^/documents/(.*)$ /storage/$1;
    }
}
```

A client query to `http://website.com/documents/file.txt` initially matches the second `location` block (`location /documents/`). However, the block contains a rewrite instruction that transforms the URI from `/documents/file.txt` to `/storage/file.txt`. The URI transformation reinitializes the process; the new URI is matched against the `location` blocks. This time, the first `location` block (`location /storage/`) matches the URI (`/storage/file.txt`).

Again, a quick peek at the debug log details the mechanism:

```
->http request line: "GET /documents/file.txt HTTP/1.1"
->http uri: "/documents/file.txt"
->test location: "/storage/"
->test location: "/documents/"
->using configuration "/documents/"
->http script regex: "^/documents/(.*)$"
->"^/documents/(.*)$" matches "/documents/file.txt", client: 127.0.0.1,
server: website.com, request: "GET /documents/file.txt HTTP/1.1", host:
"website.com"
->rewritten data: "/storage/file.txt", args: "", client: 127.0.0.1, server:
website.com, request: "GET /documents/file.txt HTTP/1.1", host:
"website.com"
->test location: "/storage/"
->using configuration "/storage/"
->http filename: "/var/www/storage/file.txt"
->HTTP/1.1 200 OK
->http output filter "/storage/test.txt?"
```

Infinite loops

With all of the different syntaxes and directives, you could easily get confused. Worse, you might get Nginx confused. This happens, for instance, when your rewrite rules are redundant and cause internal redirects to *loop infinitely*:

```
server {
    server_name website.com;
    location /documents/ {
        rewrite ^(.*)$ /documents/2018/$1;
    }
}
```

You thought you were doing well, but this configuration actually triggers an internal redirect of `/documents/anything` to `/documents/2018//documents/anything`. Moreover, since the location patterns are re-evaluated after an internal redirect, `/documents/2018//documents/anything` becomes `/documents/2018//documents/2018//documents/anything`.

Here is the corresponding excerpt from the debug log:

```
->test location: "/documents/"
->using configuration "/documents/"
->rewritten data: "/documents/2018//documents/file.txt", [...]
->test location: "/documents/"
->using configuration "/documents/"
->rewritten data: "/documents/2018//documents/2018//documents/file.txt"
[...]
->test location: "/documents/"
->using configuration "/documents/"
->rewritten data: -
>"/documents/2018//documents/2018//documents/2018//documents/file.txt"
[...]
->[...]
```

You are probably wondering if this goes on indefinitely; the answer is *no*. The amount of cycles is restricted to *10*. You are only allowed 10 internal redirects. Anything past this limit, and Nginx will produce a `500 Internal Server Error`.

It is possible to prevent infinite loops for cases like this where you might want to update the internal path over time. Simply use the `break` flag on the rewrite as documented later, and Nginx will not do an internal redirect.

Server Side Includes

A potential source of sub-requests is the **Server Side Include** (**SSI**) module. The purpose of SSI is for the server to parse documents before sending the response to the client in a somewhat similar fashion to PHP or other preprocessors.

Within a regular HTML file (for example), you have the possibility to insert tags corresponding to commands interpreted by Nginx:

```
<html>
<head>
  <!--# include file="header.html" -->
</head>
<body>
  <!--# include file="body.html" -->
</body>
</html>
```

Nginx processes these two commands; in this case, it reads the contents of `head.html` and `body.html` and inserts them into the document source, which is then sent to the client.

Several commands are at your disposal; they are detailed in the SSI module section in this chapter. The one we are interested in for now is the `include` command, including a file into another file:

```
<!--# include virtual="/footer.php?id=123" -->
```

The specified file is not just opened and read from a static location. Instead, a whole subrequest is processed by Nginx, and the body of the response is inserted instead of the `include` tag.

Conditional structure

The Rewrite module introduces a new set of directives and blocks, among which is the `if` conditional structure:

```
server {
    if ($request_method = POST) {
      [...]
    }
}
```

This offers the possibility to apply a configuration according to the specified condition. If the condition is true, the configuration is applied; otherwise, it isn't.

The following table describes the various syntaxes accepted when forming a condition:

Operator	Description

None	The condition is true if the specified variable or data is not equal to an empty string or a string starting with the character 0:
	
	``
	if ($string) {
	  [...]
	}
	``

=, !=	The condition is true if the argument preceding the = symbol is equal to the argument following it. The following example can be read as, *"If the request_method is equal to* POST, *then apply the configuration"*:
	
	``
	if ($request_method = POST) {
	  [...]
	}
	``
	The != operator does the opposite: *"If the request method is not equal to* GET, *then apply the configuration"*:
	
	``
	if ($request_method != GET) {
	  [...]
	}
	``

~, ~*, !~, !~*	The condition is true if the argument preceding the ~ symbol matches the regular expression pattern placed after it:
	
	``
	if ($request_filename ~ "\.txt$") {
	  [...]
	}
	``
	~ is case-sensitive, and ~* is case-insensitive. Use the ! symbol to negate the matching:
	
	``
	if ($request_filename !~* "\.php$") {
	  [...]
	}
	``
	You can insert capture buffers in the regular expression:
	
	``
	if ($uri ~ "^/search/(.*)$") {
	  set $query $1;
	  rewrite ^ http://google.com/search?q=$query;
	}
	``

Operator	Description

-f, !-f	Tests the existence of the specified file:
	```if (-f $request_filename) {```
	``` [...] # if the file exists```
	```}```
	Use !-f to test the non-existence of the file:
	```if (!-f $request_filename) {```
	``` [...] # if the file does not exist```
	```}```

-d, !-d	Similar to the -f operator, for testing the existence of a directory.
-e, !-e	Similar to the -f operator, for testing the existence of a file, directory, or symbolic link.
-x, !-x	Similar to the -f operator, for testing whether a file exists and is executable.

As of version 1.13.8, there are no else or else if-like instructions. However, other directives allowing you to control the configuration flow sequencing are available.

You might wonder: *What are the advantages of using a* location *block over an* if *block?* Indeed, in the following example, both seem to have the same effect:

```
if ($uri ~ /search/) {
   [...]
}
location ~ /search/ {
    [...]
}
```

As a matter of fact, the main difference lies within the directives that can be employed within either block. Some can be inserted in an if block, and some can't; on the contrary, almost all directives are authorized within a location block, as you probably noticed in the directive listings so far. In general, it's best to only insert directives from the Rewrite module within an if block, as other directives were not originally intended for such usage.

Directives

The Rewrite module provides you with a set of directives that do more than just rewriting a URI. The following table describes these directives, along with the context in which they can be employed:

Directive	Description

`rewrite`
Context: `server, location, if`
	As discussed previously, the `rewrite` directive allows you to rewrite the URI of the current request, thus resetting the treatment of the said request.
	Syntax: `rewrite regexp replacement [flag];`
	Where `regexp` is the regular expression, the URI should match in order for the replacement to apply.
	Flag may take one of the following values:
	• `last`: The current rewrite rule should be the last to be applied. After its application, the new URI is processed by Nginx and a `location` block is searched for. However, further rewrite instructions will be disregarded.
	• `break`: The current rewrite rule is applied, but Nginx does not initiate a new request for the modified URI (does not restart the search for matching `location` blocks). All further rewrite directives are ignored.
	• `redirect`: Returns a `302 Moved temporarily` HTTP response, with the replacement URI set as the value of the `location` header.
	• `permanent`: Returns a `301 Moved permanently` HTTP response, with the replacement URI set as the value of the `location` header.
	• If you specify a URI beginning with `http://` as the replacement URI, Nginx will automatically use the `redirect` flag.
	• Note that the request URI processed by the directive is a relative URI; it does not contain the hostname and protocol. For a request such as `http://website.com/documents/page.html`, the request URI is `/documents/page.html`.
	• If decoded, this URI corresponding to a request, such as `http://website.com/my%20page.html`, would be `/my page.html` (in the encoded URI, `%20` indicates a white space character).
	• Does not contain arguments, for a request such as `http://website.com/page.php?id=1&p=2`, the URI would be `/page.php`. When rewriting the URI, you don't need to consider including the arguments in the replacement URI; Nginx does it for you. If you want Nginx to not include the arguments after the rewritten URI, you must insert a `?` character at the end of the replacement URI: `rewrite ^/search/(.*)$ /search.php?q=$1?`.
	• Examples:
	`rewrite ^/search/(.*)$ /search.php?q=$1;`
	`rewrite ^/search/(.*)$ /search.php?q=$1?;`
	`rewrite ^ http://website.com;`
	• `rewrite ^ http://website.com permanent;`

Directive	Description

break
Context: server, location, if
	The break directive is used to prevent further rewrite directives. Past this point, the URI is fixed and cannot be altered.
	Example:
	``
	if (-f $uri) {
	    break; # break if the file exists
	}
	if ($uri ~ ^/search/(.*)$) {
	    set $query $1;
	    rewrite ^ /search.php?q=$query?;
	}
	``
	This example rewrites /search/anything-like queries to /search.php?q=anything. However, if the requested file exists (such as /search/index.html), the break instruction prevents Nginx from rewriting the URI.

return
Context: **server, location, if**
	Interrupts the processing of the request and returns the specified HTTP status code or specified text.
	Syntax: return code | text;
	Where the code is one of the following status codes: 204, 308, 400, 402 to 406, 408, 410, 411, 413, 416, and 500 to 504. In addition, you may use the Nginx-specific code 444 in order to return a HTTP 200 OK status code with no further response header or body. Alternatively, you may also specify a raw text value that will be returned to the user as a response body. This comes in handy when testing whether your request URIs fall within particular location blocks.
	Example:
	``
	if ($uri ~ ^/admin/) {
	    return 403;
	    # the instruction below is NOT executed
	    # as Nginx already completed the request
	    rewrite ^ http://website.com;
	}
	``

set
Context: server, location, if
	Initializes or redefines a variable. Note that some variables cannot be redefined; for example, you are not allowed to alter $uri.
	Syntax: set $variable value;
	Examples:
	``
	set $var1 "some text";
	if ($var1 ~ ^(.*) (.*)$) {
	    set $var2 $1$2; #concatenation
	    rewrite ^ http://website.com/$var2;
	}
	``

Directive	Description

`uninitialized_variable_warn`
Context: `http, server, location,`
`if`
	If set to `on`, Nginx will issue log messages when the configuration employs a variable that has not yet been initialized.
	Syntax: `on` or `off`
	`uninitialized_variable_warn    on;`

`rewrite_log`
Context: `http, server, location,`
`if`
	If `rewrite_log` is set to `on`, Nginx will issue log messages for every operation performed by the rewrite engine at the `notice` error level (see the `error_log` directive).
	Syntax: `on` or `off`
	Default value: `off`
	`rewrite_log    off;`

Common rewrite rules

Here is a set of rewrite rules that satisfy basic needs for dynamic websites that wish to beautify their page links, thanks to the URL rewriting mechanism. You will obviously need to adjust these rules according to your particular situation, as every website is different.

Performing a search

This rewrite rule is intended for search queries. Search keywords are included in the URL:

Input URI	`http://website.com/search/some-search-keywords`
Rewritten URI	`http://website.com/search.php?q=some-search-keywords`
Rewrite rule	`rewrite ^/search/(.*)$ /search.php?q=$1?;`

User profile page

Most dynamic websites that allow visitors to register, offer a profile view page. URLs of this form can be employed, containing both the user ID and the username:

Input URI	`http://website.com/user/31/James`
Rewritten URI	`http://website.com/user.php?id=31&name=James`
Rewrite rule	`rewrite ^/user/([0-9]+)/(.+)$ /user.php?id=$1&name=$2?;`

Multiple parameters

Some websites may use different syntaxes for the argument string, for example, by separating non-named arguments with slashes:

Input URI	`http://website.com/index.php/param1/param2/param3`
Rewritten URI	`http://website.com/index.php?p1=param1&p2=param2&p3=param3`
Rewrite rule	`rewrite ^/index.php/(.*)/(.*)/(.*)$` `/index.php?p1=$1&p2=$2&p3=$3?;`

Wikipedia-like

Many websites have now adopted the URL style introduced by Wikipedia, including a prefix folder followed by an article name:

Input URI	`http:// website.com/wiki/Some_keyword`
Rewritten URI	`http://website.com/wiki/index.php?title=Some_keyword`
Rewrite rule	`rewrite ^/wiki/(.*)$ /wiki/index.php?title=$1?;`

News website article

This URL structure is often employed by news websites, as URLs contain indications of the articles' contents. It is formed of an article identifier, followed by a slash, then a list of keywords. The keywords can usually be ignored and not included in the rewritten URI:

Input URI	`http://website.com/33526/us-economy-strengthens`
Rewritten URI	`http://website.com/article.php?id=33526`
Rewrite rule	`rewrite ^/([0-9]+)/.*$ /article.php?id=$1?;`

Discussion board

Modern bulletin boards now use *pretty URLs*, for the most part. This example shows how to create a *topic view* URL with two parameters: the topic identifier and the starting post. Once again, keywords are ignored:

Input URI	`http://website.com/topic-1234-50-some-keywords.html`
Rewritten URI	`http://website.com/viewtopic.php?topic=1234&start=50`
Rewrite rule	`rewrite ^/topic-([0-9]+)-([0-9]+)-(.*)\.html$` `/viewtopic.php?topic=$1&start=$2?;`

SSI module

SSI or Server Side Includes, is actually a sort of server-side programming language interpreted by Nginx. Its name originates from the fact that the most used functionality of the language is the `include` command. Back in the 1990s, such languages were employed in order to render web pages dynamically, from simple static `.html` files with client-side scripts to complex pages with server-processed instructions. Within the HTML source code, webmasters could now insert server-interpreted directives, which would then lead the way to much more advanced pre-processors, such as PHP or ASP.

The most famous illustration of SSI is the *quote of the day* example. In order to insert a new quote every day at the top of each page of their website, webmasters would have to edit out the HTML source of every page of the site, updating the old quote manually. With Server Side Includes, a single command suffices to simplify the task:

```
<html>
<head><title>My web page</title></head>
<body>
  <h1>Quote of the day: <!--# include file="quote.txt" -->
  </h1>
</body>
</html>
```

All you would have to do to update the quote is to edit the contents of the `quote.txt` file. Automatically, all pages would show the updated quote. As of today, most of the major web servers (Apache, IIS, Lighttpd, and so on) support Server Side Includes.

Module directives and variables

Having directives inserted within the actual content of files that Nginx serves raises one major issue: *What files should Nginx parse for SSI commands?* It would be a waste of resources to parse binary files, such as images (`.gif`, `.jpg`, `.png`) or other kinds of media, since they are unlikely to contain any SSI commands. You need to make sure to configure Nginx correctly with the directives introduced by this module:

Directive	Description
`ssi` Context: `http, server, location, if`	Enables parsing files for SSI commands. Nginx only parses files corresponding to MIME types selected with the `ssi_types` directive. Syntax: `on` or `off` Default value: `off` `ssi on;`

`ssi_types`
Context: `http, server, location`
	Defines the MIME file types that should be eligible for SSI parsing. The `text/html` type is always included.
	Syntax:
	`ssi_types type1   [type2] [type3...];`
	`ssi_types *;`
	Default value: `text/html`
	`ssi_types   text/plain;`

`ssi_silent_errors` Context: `http, server, location`	Some SSI commands may generate errors; when that is the case, Nginx outputs a message at the location of the command: An error occurred while processing the directive. Enabling this option silences Nginx, and the message does not appear. Syntax: `on` or `off` Default value: `off` `ssi_silent_errors   off;`
`ssi_value_length` Context: `http, server, location`	SSI commands have arguments that accept a value (for example, `<!--# include file="value" -->`). This parameter defines the maximum length accepted by Nginx. Syntax: Numeric Default: `256` (characters) `ssi_value_length   256;`

Directive	Description
`ssi_ignore_recycled_buffers` Context: `http`, `server`, `location`	When set to `on`, this directive prevents Nginx from making use of recycled buffers. Syntax: `on` or `off` Default: `off`
`ssi_min_file_chunk` Context: `http`, `server`, `location`	If the size of a buffer is greater than `ssi_min_file_chunk`, data is stored in a file and then sent via `sendfile`. In other cases, it is transmitted directly from the memory. Syntax: Numeric value (size) Default: `1,024`
`ssi_last_modified` Context: `http`, `server`, `location`	If set to `off`, Nginx removes the `Last-modified` header from the original response during SSI processing in order to increase caching likeliness. The `Last-modified` date is likely to change often, due to dynamically generated elements contained in the response, rendering it non-cacheable. Syntax: `on` or `off` Default: `off`

A quick note regarding possible concerns about the SSI engine resource usage: by enabling the SSI module at the `location` or `server` block level, you enable parsing of at least all `text/html` files (pretty much any page to be displayed by the client browser). While the Nginx SSI module is efficiently optimized, you might want to disable parsing for files that do not require it.

Firstly, all your pages containing SSI commands should have the `.shtml` (**Server HTML**) extension. Then, in your configuration, at the `location` block level, enable the SSI engine under a specific condition. The name of the served file must end with `.shtml`:

```
server {
    server_name website.com;
    location ~* \.shtml$ {
        ssi on;
    }
}
```

On one hand, all HTTP requests submitted to Nginx will go through an additional regular expression pattern matching. On the other hand, static HTML files or files to be processed by other interpreters (.php, for instance) will not be parsed unnecessarily.

Finally, the SSI module enables two variables:

- $date_local: Returns the current time, according to the current system time zone
- $date_gmt: Returns the current GMT time, regardless of the server time zone

SSI commands

Once you have the SSI engine enabled for your web pages, you are ready to start writing your first dynamic HTML page. Again, the principle is simple: design the pages of your website using regular HTML code, inside which you will insert SSI commands.

These commands respect a particular syntax. At first sight, they look like regular HTML comments, such as `<!-- A comment -->`, and that is the good thing about it: if you accidentally disable SSI parsing of your files, the SSI commands do not appear on the client browser. They are only visible in the source code as actual HTML comments. The full syntax is as follows:

```
<!--# command param1="value1" param2="value2" ... -->
```

File includes

The main command of the SSI module is obviously the `include` command. It comes in two different fashions.

First, you are allowed to make a simple file include:

```
<!--# include file="header.html" -->
```

This command generates an HTTP sub-request to be processed by Nginx. The body of the response that was generated is inserted instead of the command itself.

The second possibility is to use the `include` virtual command:

```
<!--# include virtual="/sources/header.php?id=123" -->
```

This also performs a sub-request to the server; the difference lies within the way that Nginx fetches the specified file (when using `include file`, the `wait` parameter is automatically enabled). Indeed, two parameters can be inserted within the `include` command tag. By default, all SSI requests are issued simultaneously, in parallel. This can cause slowdowns and timeouts in the case of heavy loads. Alternatively, you can use the `wait="yes"` parameter to specify that Nginx should wait for the completion of the request before moving on to other includes:

```
<!--# include virtual="header.php" wait="yes" -->
```

If the result of your `include` command is empty or triggered an error (`404`, `500`, and so on), Nginx inserts the corresponding error page with its HTML: `<html>[...]404 Not Found</body></html>`. The message is displayed at the exact same place where you inserted the `include` command. If you wish to revise this behavior, you have the possibility to create a `named` block. By linking the block to the `include` command, the contents of the block will show at the location of the `include` command tag, in case an error occurs:

```
<html>
<head><title>SSI Example</title></head>
<body>
<center>
  <!--# block name="error_footer" -->Sorry, the footer file was not
found.<!--# endblock -->
  <h1>Welcome to nginx</h1>
  <!--# include virtual="footer.html" stub="error_footer" -->
</center>
</body>
</html>
```

The result, as output in the client browser, is shown as follows:

As you can see, the contents of the `error_footer` block were inserted at the location of the `include` command, after the `<h1>` tag.

Working with variables

The Nginx SSI module also offers the possibility to work with variables. Displaying a variable (in other words, inserting the variable value into the final HTML source code) can be done with the `echo` command:

```
<!--# echo var="variable_name" -->
```

The command accepts the following three parameters:

- `var`: The name of the variable you want to display, for example, REMOTE_ADDR to display the IP address of the client.
- `default`: A string to be displayed in case the variable is empty. If you don't specify this parameter, the output is `(none)`.
- `encoding`: Encoding method for the string. The accepted values are `none` (no particular encoding), `url` (encode text like a URL: a blank space becomes `%20`, and so on) and `entity` (uses HTML entities: `&` becomes `&amp;`).

You may also affect your own variables with the `set` command:

```
<!--# set var="my_variable" value="your value here" -->
```

The `value` parameter is itself parsed by the engine; as a result, you are allowed to make use of existing variables:

```
<!--# echo var="MY_VARIABLE" -->
<!--# set var="MY_VARIABLE" value="hello" -->
<!--# echo var="MY_VARIABLE" -->
<!--# set var="MY_VARIABLE" value="$MY_VARIABLE there" -->
<!--# echo var="MY_VARIABLE" -->
```

Here is the code that Nginx outputs for each of the three `echo` commands from the preceding example:

```
(none)
hello
hello there
```

Conditional structure

The following set of commands will allow you to include text or other directives, depending on a condition. The conditional structure can be established with the following syntax:

```
<!--# if expr="expression1" -->
[...]
<!--# elif expr="expression2" -->
[...]
<!--# else -->
[...]
<!--# endif -->
```

The expression can be formulated in three different ways:

- **Inspecting a variable**: `<!--# if expr="$variable" -->`. Similar to the `if` block in the Rewrite module, the condition is true if the variable is not empty.
- **Comparing two strings**: `<!--# if expr="$variable = hello" -->`. The condition is true if the first string is equal to the second string. Use `!=` instead of `=` to revert the condition (the condition is true if the first string is not equal to the second string).
- **Matching a regular expression pattern**: `<!--# if expr="$variable = /pattern/" -->`. Note that the pattern must be enclosed with `/` characters, otherwise it is considered to be a simple string (for example, `<!--# if expr="$MY_VARIABLE = /^/documents//" -->`). Similar to the comparison, use `!=` to negate the condition. Captures in regular expressions are supported.

The content that you insert within a condition block can contain regular HTML code or additional SSI directives, with one exception: you cannot nest `if` blocks.

Configuration

The last, and probably least (for once), of the SSI commands offered by Nginx is the `config` command. It allows you to configure two simple parameters.

First, the message that appears when the SSI engine faces an error is malformed tags or invalid expressions. By default, Nginx displays `[an error occurred while processing the directive]`. If you want it to display something else, enter the following:

```
<!--# config errmsg="Something terrible happened" -->
```

Additionally, you can configure the format of the dates that are returned by the `$date_local` and `$date_gmt` variables using the `timefmt` parameter:

```
<!--# config timefmt="%A, %d-%b-%Y %H:%M:%S %Z" -->
```

The string you specify here is passed as the format string of the `strftime` C function. For more information about the arguments that can be used in the format string, please refer to the documentation of the `strftime` C language function at `http://www.opengroup.org/onlinepubs/009695399/functions/strftime.html`.

Additional modules

The first half of this chapter covered two of the most important Nginx modules, namely, the Rewrite module and the SSI module. There are a lot more modules that will greatly enrich the functionality of the web server; they are regrouped here by theme.

Among the modules described in this section, some are included in the default Nginx build, but some are not. This implies that unless you specifically configured your Nginx build to include these modules (as described in `Chapter 1`, *Downloading and Installing Nginx*), they will not be available to you. But remember that rebuilding Nginx to include additional modules is a relatively quick and easy process.

Website access and logging

The following set of modules allows you to configure how visitors access your website and the way your server logs requests.

Index

The Index module provides a simple directive named `index`, which lets you define the page that Nginx will serve by default if no filename is specified in the client request (in other words, it defines the website `index` page). You may specify multiple filenames; the first file to be found will be served. If none of the specified files are found, Nginx will either attempt to generate an automatic index of the files, if the `autoindex` directive is enabled (check the HTTP `autoindex` module), or return a `403 Forbidden` error page.

Optionally, you may insert an absolute filename (such as `/page.html`), but only as the last argument of the directive.

Syntax: `index file1 [file2...] [absolute_file];`

Default value: `index.html`

```
index index.php index.html index.htm;
index index.php index2.php /catchall.php;
```

This directive is valid in the following contexts: `http`, `server`, and `location`.

Autoindex

If Nginx cannot provide an index page for the requested directory, the default behavior is to return a `403 Forbidden HTTP` error page. With the following set of directives, you enable an automatic listing of the files that are present in the requested directory:

Three columns of information appear for each file: the filename, the file date and time, and the file size in bytes:

Directive	Description

`autoindex`
Context: `http, server,`
`location`
	Enables or disables automatic directory listing for directories missing an `index` page.
	Syntax: `on` or `off`

`autoindex_exact_size`
Context: `http, server,`
`location`
	If set to `on`, this directive ensures that the listing displays file sizes in bytes. Otherwise, another unit is employed, such as KB, MB, or GB.
	Syntax: `on` or `off`
	Default value: `on`

`autoindex_localtime`
Context: `http, server,`
`location`
	By default, this directive is set to `off`, so the date and time of files in the listing appear as GMT time. Set it to `on` to make use of the local server time.
	Syntax: `on` or `off`
	Default value: `off`

`autoindex_format` Context: `http, server,` `location`	Nginx offers to serve the directory index in different formats: HTML, XML, JSON, or JSONP (by default, HTML is used). Syntax: `autoindex_format html	xml	json |` `jsonp;` If you set the directive value to `jsonp`, Nginx will insert the value of the `callback` query argument as JSONP callback. For example, your script should call this URI: `/folder/?callback=MyCallbackName`.

Random index

This module enables a simple directive, `random_index`, which can be used within a `location` block in order for Nginx to return an `index` page selected randomly among the files of the specified directory.

 This module is not included in the default Nginx build.

Syntax: on or off

Log

This module controls the behavior of Nginx regarding access logs. It is a key module for system administrators, as it allows analyzing the runtime behavior of web applications. It is composed of three essential directives:

Directive	Description
access_log Context: http, server, location, if (in location), limit_except	This parameter defines the access log file path, the format of entries in the access log by selecting a template name, or disables access logging. Syntax: access_log path [format [buffer=size]] | off; Some remarks concerning the directive syntax: • Use access_log off to disable access logging at the current level • The format argument corresponds to a template declared with the log_format directive • If the format argument is not specified, the default format is employed (combined) • You may use variables in the file path
log_format Context: http, server, location	Defines a template to be utilized by the access_log directive, describing the contents that should be included in an entry of the access log. Syntax: log_format template_name [escape=default|json] format_string; The default template is called combined and matches the following example: log_format combined '$remote_addr - $remote_user [$time_local] '"$request" $status $body_bytes_sent '"$http_referer" "$http_user_agent"'; # Other example log_format simple '$remote_addr $request';

Directive	Description

`open_log_file_cache`
Context: `http, server,`
`location`
	Configures the cache for log file descriptors. Please refer to the `open_file_cache` directive of the HTTP Core module for additional information.
	Syntax: `open_log_file_cache max=N`
	`[inactive=time] [min_uses=N] [valid=time]`
	`| off;`
	The arguments are similar to the `open_file_cache` and other related directives; the difference being that this applies to access log files only.

The Log module also enables several new variables, though they are only accessible when writing log entries:

- `$connection`: The connection number
- `$pipe`: The variable is set to `p` if the request was pipelined
- `$time_local`: Local time (at the time of writing the log entry)
- `$msec`: Local time (at the time of writing the log entry) to the microsecond
- `$request_time`: Total length of the request processing, in milliseconds
- `$status`: Response status code
- `$bytes_sent`: Total number of bytes sent to the client
- `$body_bytes_sent`: Number of bytes sent to the client for the response body
- `$apache_bytes_sent`: Similar to `$body_bytes`, which corresponds to the `%B` parameter of Apache's `mod_log_config`
- `$request_length`: Length of the request body

Limits and restrictions

The following modules allow you to regulate access to the documents of your websites, require users to authenticate, match a set of rules, or simply restrict access to certain visitors.

Auth_basic module

The `auth_basic` module enables the basic authentication functionality. With the two directives that it brings forth, you can make it so that a specific location of your website (or your server) is restricted to users that authenticate with a username and password:

```
location /admin/ {
    auth_basic "Admin control panel"; # variables are supported
    auth_basic_user_file access/password_file;
}
```

The first directive, `auth_basic`, can be set to either `off` or a text message, usually referred to as *authentication challenge* or *authentication realm*. This message is displayed by web browsers in a username/password box when a client attempts to access the protected resource.

The second one, `auth_basic_user_file`, defines the path of the password file relative to the directory of the configuration file. A password file is formed of lines respecting the syntax `username:[{SCHEME}]password[:comment]`, where:

- `username`: A plain text username
- `{SCHEME}`: Optionally, the password hashing method. There are currently three supported schemes: `{PLAIN}` for plain text passwords, `{SHA}` for SHA-1 hashing, and `{SSHA}` for salted SHA-1 hashing.
- `password`: The password
- `comment`: A plain text comment for your own use

If you fail to specify a scheme, the password will need to be encrypted with the `crypt(3)` function, for example, with the help of the `htpasswd` command-line utility from Apache packages.

 If you aren't too keen on installing Apache on your system just for the sake of the `htpasswd` tool, you may resort to online tools, as there are plenty of them available. Fire up your favorite search engine and type `online htpasswd`.

Access

Two important directives are brought up by this module: `allow` and `deny`. They let you allow or deny access to a resource for a specific IP address or IP address range.

Both directives have the same syntax: `allow IP | CIDR | unix: | all`, where `IP` is an IP address, `CIDR` is an IP address range (CIDR syntax), `unix:` represents all UNIX domain sockets, and `all` specifies that the directive applies to all clients:

```
location {
allow 127.0.0.1; # allow local IP address
allow unix:; # allow UNIX domain sockets
    deny all; # deny all other IP addresses
}
```

 Note that rules are processed from the top down: if your first instruction is `deny all`, all possible `allow` exceptions that you place afterwards will have no effect. The opposite is also true; if you start with `allow all`, all possible `deny` directives that you place afterwards will have no effect, as you already allowed all IP addresses.

Limit connections

The mechanism induced by this module is a little more complex than regular ones. It allows you to define the maximum amount of simultaneous connections to the server for a specific *zone*.

The first step is to define the zone using the `limit_conn_zone` directive:

- Directive syntax is `limit_conn_zone $variable zone=name:size;`
- `$variable` is the variable that will be used to differentiate one client from another, typically `$binary_remote_addr`, the IP address of the client in binary format (more efficient than ASCII)
- `name` is an arbitrary name given to the zone
- `size` is the maximum size you allocate to the table storing session states

The following example defines zones based on the client IP addresses:

```
limit_conn_zone $binary_remote_addr zone=myzone:10m;
```

Now that you have defined a zone, you may limit connections using `limit_conn`:

```
limit_conn zone_name connection_limit;
```

When applied to the previous example, it becomes:

```
location /downloads/ {
    limit_conn myzone 1;
}
```

As a result, requests that share the same `$binary_remote_addr` are subject to the connection limit (one simultaneous connection). If the limit is reached, all additional concurrent requests will be answered with a `503 Service unavailable` HTTP response. This response code can be overridden if you specify another code via the `limit_conn_status` directive. If you wish to log client requests that are affected by the limits you have set, enable the `limit_conn_log_level` directive and specify the log level (`info` | `notice` | `warn` | `error`).

Limit request

In a similar fashion, the Limit request module allows you to limit the amount of requests for a defined zone.

Defining the zone is done via the `limit_req_zone` directive; its syntax differs from the Limit zone equivalent directive:

```
limit_req_zone $variable zone=name:max_memory_size rate=rate;
```

The directive parameters are identical, except for the trailing `rate`, expressed in requests per second (r/s) or requests per minute (r/m). It defines a request rate that will be applied to clients where the zone is enabled. To apply a zone to a location, use the `limit_req` directive:

```
limit_req zone=name burst=burst [nodelay];
```

The `burst` parameter defines the maximum possible bursts of requests. When the amount of requests received from a client exceeds the limit defined in the zone, the responses are delayed in a manner that respects the rate that you defined. To a certain extent, only a maximum of `burst` requests will be accepted simultaneously. Past this limit, Nginx returns a `503 Service Unavailable` HTTP error response. This response code can be overridden if you specify another code via the `limit_req_status` directive:

```
limit_req_zone $binary_remote_addr zone=myzone:10m rate=2r/s;
[...]
location /downloads/ {
limit_req zone=myzone burst=10;
limit_req_status 404; # returns a 403 error if limit is exceeded
```

```
}
```

If you wish to log client requests that are affected by the limits you have set, enable the `limit_req_log_level` directive and specify the log level (`info` | `notice` | `warn` | `error`).

Auth request

The `auth_request` module was implemented in recent versions of Nginx and allows you to allow or deny access to a resource based on the result of a sub-request. Nginx calls the URI that you specify via the `auth_request` directive: if the sub-request returns a `2xx` response code (such as `HTTP/200 OK`), access is allowed. If the sub-request returns a 401 or 403 status code, access is denied, and Nginx forwards the response code to the client. Should the backend return any other response code, Nginx will consider it to be an error and deny access to the resource:

```
location /downloads/ {
    # if the script below returns a 200 status code,
    # the download is authorized
    auth_request /authorization.php;
}
```

Additionally, the module offers a second directive, called `auth_request_set`, allowing you to set a variable after the sub-request is executed. You can insert variables that originate from the sub-request upstream (`$upstream_http_*`), such as `$upstream_http_server` or other HTTP headers, from the server response:

```
location /downloads/ {
    # requests authorization from PHP script
    auth_request /authorization.php;
    # assuming authorization is granted, get filename from
    # sub-request response header and redirect
    auth_request_set $filename "${upstream_http_x_filename}.zip";
    rewrite ^ /documents/$filename;
}
```

Content and encoding

The following set of modules provides functionalities having an effect on the contents served to the client, either by modifying the way the response is encoded, by affecting the headers, or by generating a response from scratch.

Empty GIF

The purpose of this module is to provide a directive that serves a 1x1 transparent GIF image from the memory. Such files are sometimes used by web designers to tweak the appearance of their website. With this directive, you get an empty GIF straight from the memory, instead of reading and processing an actual GIF file from the storage space.

To utilize this feature, simply insert the `empty_gif` directive in the location of your choice:

```
location = /empty.gif {
    empty_gif;
}
```

FLV and MP4

FLV and MP4 are separate modules, enabling a simple functionality that becomes useful when serving Flash (FLV) or MP4 video files. It parses a special argument of the request, `start`, which indicates the offset of the section the client wishes to download or pseudo-stream. The video file must thus be accessed with the following URI: `video.flv?start=XXX`. This parameter is prepared automatically by mainstream video players, such as JWPlayer.

 This module is not included in the default Nginx build.

To utilize this feature, simply insert the `.flv` or `.mp4` directive in the location of your choice:

```
location ~* \.flv {
    flv;
}
location ~* \.mp4 {
    mp4;
}
```

Be aware that if Nginx fails to seek the requested position within the video file, the request will result in a `500 Internal Server Error` HTTP response. JW Player sometimes misinterprets this error and simply displays a `Video not found` error message.

HTTP headers

Three directives are introduced by this module that will affect the header of the response sent to the client.

First, `add_header name value [always]` lets you add a new line in the response headers, respecting the following syntax: `Name: value`. The line is added only for responses of the following codes: `200`, `201`, `204`, `301`, `302`, or `304`. You may insert variables in the `value` argument. If you specify `always` at the end of the directive value, the header will always be added, regardless of the response code.

Additionally, the `add_trailer name value [always]` directive allows you to add a header to the end of the response if the response code is one of `200`, `201`, `204`, `206`, `301`, `302`, `303`, `307`, or `308`. This directive can be specified multiple times to add multiple headers. The `always` flag works similar to the `add_header` version.

Finally, the `expires` directive allows you to control the value of the **Expires** and **Cache-Control** HTTP header sent to the client, affecting requests of the same code, as listed earlier. It accepts a single value among the following:

- `off`: Does not modify either headers.
- A time value: The expiration date of the file is set to *the current time + the time you specify*. For example, `expires 24h` will return an expiry date set to 24 hours from now.
- `epoch`: The expiration date of the file is set to January 1, 1970. The Cache-Control header is set to `no-cache`.
- `max`: The expiration date of the file is set to December 31, 2037. The Cache-Control header is set to 10 years.

Addition

The Addition module allows you to (through simple directives) add content before or after the body of the HTTP response.

This module is not included in the default Nginx build.

The two main directives are:

```
add_before_body file_uri;
add_after_body file_uri;
```

As stated previously, Nginx triggers a sub-request for fetching the specified URI. Additionally, you can define the types of files to which the content is appended in case your `location` block pattern is not specific enough (default: `text/html`):

```
addition_types mime_type1 [mime_type2...];
addition_types *;
```

Substitution

Along the lines of the previous module, the Substitution module allows you to search and replace text directly from the response body:

```
sub_filter searched_text replacement_text;
```

 This module is not included in the default Nginx build.

Two additional directives provide more flexibility:

- `sub_filter_once` (on or off, default on): Only replaces the text once, and stops after the first occurrence.
- `sub_filter_types` (default `text/html`): Affects additional MIME types that will be eligible for the text replacement. The * wildcard is allowed.

Gzip filter

This module allows you to compress the response body with the Gzip algorithm before sending it to the client. To enable Gzip compression, use the `gzip` directive (`on` or `off`) at the `http`, `server`, `location`, and even the `if` level (though that is not recommended). The following directives will help you to further configure the filter options:

Directive	Description
`gzip_buffers` Context: `http`, `server`, `location`	Defines the amount and size of buffers to be used for storing the compressed response. Syntax: `gzip_buffers amount size;` Default: `gzip_buffers 4 4k` (or `8k`, depending on the OS)
`gzip_comp_level` Context: `http`, `server`, `location`	Defines the compression level of the algorithm. The specified value ranges from `1` (low compression, faster for the CPU) to `9` (high compression, slower). Syntax: Numeric value. Default: `1`
`gzip_disable` Context: `http`, `server`, `location`	Disables Gzip compression for requests where the User-Agent HTTP header matches the specified regular expression. Syntax: Regular expression Default: None
`gzip_http_version` Context: `http`, `server`, `location`	Enables Gzip compression for the specified protocol version. Syntax: `1.0` or `1.1` Default: `1.1`
`gzip_min_length` Context: `http`, `server`, `location`	If the response body length is inferior to the specified value, it is not compressed. Syntax: Numeric value (size) Default: `0`

Directive	Description
`gzip_proxied` Context: `http, server, location`	Enables or disables Gzip compression for the body of responses received from a proxy (see reverse-proxying mechanisms in later chapters). The directive accepts the following parameters; some can be combined: • `off`/`any`: Disables or enables compression for all requests • `expired`: Enables compression if the *Expires* header prevents caching • `no-cache`/`no-store`/`private`: Enables compression if the *Cache-Control* header is set to no-cache, no-store, or private • `no_last_modified`: Enables compression in case the *Last-Modified* header is not set • `no_etag`: Enables compression in case the *ETag* header is not set • `auth`: Enables compression in case an *Authorization* header is set

`gzip_types`
Context: `http, server, location`
	Enables compression for types other than the default `text/html` MIME type.
	Syntax:
	`gzip_types    mime_type1 [mime_type2...];`
	`gzip_types *;`
	Default: `text/html` (cannot be disabled)

`gzip_vary` Context: `http, server, location`	Adds the Vary: Accept-Encoding HTTP header to the response. Syntax: `on` or `off` Default: `off`
`gzip_window` Context: `http, server, location`	Sets the size of the window buffer (`windowBits` argument) for Gzipping operations. This directive value is used for calls to functions from the Zlib library. Syntax: Numeric value (size) Default: `MAX_WBITS` constant from the Zlib library

Directive	Description
`gzip_hash` Context: `http, server, location`	Sets the amount of memory that should be allocated for the internal compression state (`memLevel` argument). This directive value is used for calls to functions from the Zlib library. Syntax: Numeric value (size) Default: `MAX_MEM_LEVEL` constant from the Zlib prerequisite library
`postpone_gzipping` Context: `http, server, location`	Defines a minimum data threshold to be reached before starting the Gzip compression. Syntax: Size (numeric value) Default: `0`
`gzip_no_buffer` Context: `http, server, location`	By default, Nginx waits until at least one buffer (defined by `gzip_buffers`) is filled with data before sending the response to the client. Enabling this directive disables buffering. Syntax: `on` or `off` Default: `off`

Gzip static

This module adds a simple functionality to the Gzip filter mechanism. When its `gzip_static` directive (`on`, `off`, or `always`) is enabled, Nginx will automatically look for a `.gz` file corresponding to the requested document before serving it. This allows Nginx to send pre-compressed documents instead of compressing documents on-the-fly at each request. Specifying `always` will force Nginx to serve the `gzip` version regardless of whether the client accepts `gzip` encoding.

 This module is not included in the default Nginx build.

If a client requests `/documents/page.html`, Nginx checks for the existence of a `/documents/page.html.gz` file. If the `.gz` file is found, it is served to the client. Note that Nginx does not generate `.gz` files itself, even after serving the requested files.

Gunzip filter

With the Gunzip filter module, you can decompress a gzip-compressed response sent from a backend in order to serve it *raw* to the client, for example, in case the client browser would not be able to process gzipped files (Microsoft Internet Explorer 6). Simply insert `gunzip on;` in a location block to employ this module. You can also set the buffer amount and size with `gunzip_buffers amount size;`, where `amount` is the amount of buffers to allocate, and `size` is the size of each allocated buffer.

Charset filter

With the Charset filter module, you can control the character set of the response body more accurately. Not only are you able to specify the value of the `charset` argument of the `Content-Type` HTTP header (such as `Content-Type: text/html; charset=utf-8`), but Nginx can also re-encode data to a specified encoding method automatically:

Directive	Description

`charset`
Context: `http, server,`
`location, if`
	This directive adds the specified encoding to the Content-Type header of the response. If the specified encoding differs from the `source_charset` one, Nginx re-encodes the document.
	Syntax: `charset encoding | off;`
	Default: `off`
	Example: `charset utf-8;`

`source_charset`
Context: `http, server,`
`location, if`
	Defines the initial encoding of the response; if the value specified in the `charset` directive differs, Nginx re-encodes the document.
	Syntax: `source_charset encoding;`

`override_charset`
Context: `http, server,`
`location, if`
	When Nginx receives a response from the proxy or FastCGI gateway, this directive defines whether or not the character encoding should be checked, and potentially overridden.
	Syntax: `on` or `off`
	Default: `off`

Directive	Description

`charset_types`
Context: `http, server, location`
	Defines the MIME types that are eligible for re-encoding.
	Syntax:
	`charset_types    mime_type1 [mime_type2...];`
	`charset_types    * ;`
	Default: `text/html, text/xml, text/plain,`
	`text/vnd.wap.wml, application/x-javascript,`
	and `application/rss+xml`

`charset_map` Context: `http`	Lets you define character re-encoding tables. Each line of the table contains two hexadecimal codes to be exchanged. You will find re-encoding tables for the `koi8-r` character set in the default Nginx configuration folder (`koi-win` and `koi-utf`). Syntax: `charset_map src_encoding dest_encoding {` `... }`

Memcached

Memcached is a daemon application that can be connected via sockets. Its main purpose, as the name suggests, is to provide an efficient distributed key/value memory caching system. The Nginx Memcached module provides directives, allowing you to configure access to the Memcached daemon:

Directive	Description
`memcached_pass` Context: `location, if`	Defines the hostname and port of the Memcached daemon. Syntax: `memcached_pass hostname:port;` Example: `memcached_pass localhost:11211;`
`memcached_bind` Context: `http, server, location`	Forces Nginx to use the specified local IP address for connecting to the Memcached server. This can come in handy if your server has multiple network cards connected to different networks. Syntax: `memcached_bind IP_address;` Example: `memcached_bind 192.168.1.2;`
`memcached_connect_timeout` Context: `http, server, location`	Defines the connection timeout in milliseconds (default: `60000`) Example: `memcached_connect_timeout 5000;`

Directive	Description
memcached_send_timeout Context: http, server, location	Defines the data writing operations timeout in milliseconds (default: 60000) Example: memcached_send_timeout 5,000;
memcached_read_timeout Context: http, server, location	Defines the data reading operations timeout in milliseconds (default: 60000) Example: memcached_read_timeout 5,000;
memcached_buffer_size Context: http, server, location	Defines the size of the read and write buffer in bytes (default: page size) Example: memcached_buffer_size 8k;
memcached_next_upstream Context: http, server, location	When the memcached_pass directive is connected to an upstream block (see Upstream module), this directive defines the conditions that should be matched in order to skip to the next upstream server. Syntax: Values selected among error timeout, invalid_response, not_found, or off Default: error timeout Example: memcached_next_upstream off;
memcached_gzip_flag Context: http, server, location	Checks for the presence of the specified flag in the memcached server response. If the flag is present, Nginx sets the Content-encoding header to gzip to indicate that it will be serving gzipped content. Syntax: Numeric flag Default: (none) Example: memcached_gzip_flag 1;

Additionally, you will need to define the $memcached_key variable that defines the key of the element that you are placing or fetching from the cache. You may, for instance, use set $memcached_key $uri or set $memcached_key $uri?$args.

Note that the Nginx Memcached module is only able to retrieve data from the cache; it does not store the results of requests. Storing data in the cache should be done by a server-side script. You just need to make sure to employ the same key naming scheme in both your server-side scripts and the Nginx configuration. As an example, we could decide to use `memcached` to retrieve data from the cache before passing the request to a proxy, if the requested URI is not found (see Chapter 7, *Apache and Nginx Together*, for more details about the Proxy module):

```
server {
    server_name example.com;
    [...]
    location / {
        set $memcached_key $uri;
        memcached_pass 127.0.0.1:11211;
        error_page 404 @notcached;
    }
    location @notcached {
        internal;
        # if the file is not found, forward request to proxy
        proxy_pass 127.0.0.1:8080;
    }
}
```

Image filter

This module provides image processing functionalities through the **GD Graphics Library** (also known as **gdlib**).

This module is not included in the default Nginx build.

Make sure to employ the following directives on a `location` block that filters image files only, such as `location ~* \.(png|jpg|gif|webp)$ { ... }`.

Directive	Description
`image_filter` Context: `location`	Lets you apply a transformation on the image before sending it to the client. There are five options available: • `off`: Turns off previously set `image_filter` • `test`: Makes sure that the requested document is an image file; returns a `415 Unsupported media type` HTTP error if the test fails • `size`: Composes a simple JSON response indicating information about the image, such as the size and type (for example; `{ "img": { "width":50, "height":50, "type":"png"}}`). If the file is invalid, a simple `{}` is returned • `resize width height`: Resizes the image to the specified dimensions • `crop width height`: Selects a portion of the image of the specified dimensions • `rotate 90│180│270`: Rotates the image by the specified angle (in degrees) Example: `image_filter resize 200 100;`
`image_filter_buffer` Context: `http, server, location`	Defines the maximum file size for images to be processed. Default: `image_filter_buffer 1m;`
`image_filter_jpeg_quality` Context: `http, server, location`	Defines the quality of output JPEG images. Default: `image_filter_jpeg_quality 75;`
`image_filter_webp_quality` Context: `http, server, location`	Defines the quality of output `webp` images. Default: `image_filter_webp_quality 80;`
`image_filter_transparency` Context: `http, server, location`	By default, PNG and GIF images keep their existing transparency during operations you perform using the Image Filter module. If you set this directive to `off`, all existing transparency will be lost, but the image quality will be improved. Syntax: `on` or `off` Default: `on`

image_filter_sharpen Context: http, server, location	Sharpens the image by specified percentage (value may exceed 100). Syntax: Numeric value Default: 0
image_filter_interlace Context: http, server, location	Enables interlacing of the output image. If the output image is a JPG file, the image is generated in *progressive JPEG* format. Syntax: on or off Default: off

When it comes to JPG images, Nginx automatically strips off metadata (such as **EXIF**) if it occupies more than five percent of the total space of the file.

XSLT

The Nginx XSLT module allows you to apply an XSLT transform on an XML file or response received from a backend server (proxy, FastCGI, and so on) before serving the client:

Directive	Description
xml_entities Context: http, server, location	Specifies the DTD file containing symbolic element definitions. Syntax: File path Example: xml_entities xml/entities.dtd;
xslt_stylesheet Context: location	Specifies the XSLT template file path with its parameters. Variables may be inserted in the parameters. Syntax: xslt_stylesheet template [param1] [param2...]; Example: xslt_stylesheet xml/sch.xslt param=value;

`xslt_types`
Context: `http, server, location`
	Defines additional MIME types to which the transforms may apply, other than `text/xml`.
	Syntax: MIME type
	Example:
	`xslt_types    text/xml text/plain;`
	`xslt_types *;`

`xslt_param` `xslt_string_param` Context: `http, server, location`	Both directives allow defining parameters for XSLT stylesheets. The difference lies in the way the specified value is interpreted: using `xslt_param`, XPath expressions in the value are processed; `xslt_string_param` should be used for plain character strings. Syntax: `xslt_param key value;`

About your visitors

The following set of modules provides extra functionality that will help you find out more information about the visitors, such as by parsing client request headers for browser name and version, assigning an identifier to requests presenting similarities, and so on.

Browser

The Browser module parses the User-Agent HTTP header of the client request in order to establish values for variables that can be employed later in the configuration. The three variables produced are:

- `$modern_browser`: If the client browser is identified as being a modern web browser, the variable takes the value defined by the `modern_browser_value` directive
- `$ancient_browser`: If the client browser is identified as being an old web browser, the variable takes the value defined by `ancient_browser_value`
- `$msie`: This variable is set to 1 if the client is using a Microsoft IE browser

To help Nginx recognize web browsers, distinguishing the old from the modern, you need to insert multiple occurrences of the `ancient_browser` and `modern_browser` directives:

```
modern_browser opera 10.0;
```

With this example, if the User-Agent HTTP header contains Opera 10.0, the client browser is considered modern.

Map

Just like the Browser module, the Map module allows you to create maps of values, depending on a variable:

```
map $uri $variable {
    /page.html    0;
    /contact.html    1;
    /index.html    2;
    default 0;
}
rewrite ^ /index.php?page=$variable;
```

The `map` directive can only be inserted within the `http` block. Following this example, `$variable` may have three different values. If `$uri` was set to `/page.html`, `$variable`, the value is now defined as 0; if `$uri` was set to `/contact.html`, `$variable` is now 1; if `$uri` was set to `/index.html`, `$variable`, the value now equals 2. For all other cases (`default`), `$variable` is set to 0. The last instruction rewrites the URL accordingly. Apart from `default`, the `map` directive accepts another special keyword: `hostnames`. It allows you to match hostnames using wildcards such as `*.domain.com`. Finally, it's possible to mark a map as `volatile`, which makes the map non-cacheable.

Two additional directives allow you to tweak the way Nginx manages the mechanism in memory:

- `map_hash_max_size`: Sets the maximum size of the hash table holding a map
- `map_hash_bucket_size`: The maximum size of an entry in the map

Regular expressions may also be used in patterns if you prefix them with ~ (case-sensitive) or ~* (case-insensitive):

```
map $http_referer $ref {
~google "Google";
    ~* yahoo "Yahoo";
    \~bing "Bing"; # not a regular expression due to the \ before the tilde
default $http_referer; # variables may be used
}
```

Geo

The purpose of this module is to provide functionality that is quite similar to the `map` directive, affecting a variable based on client data (in this case, the IP address). The syntax is slightly different, in the extent that you are allowed to specify IPv4 and IPv6 address ranges (in CIDR format):

```
geo $variable {
  default unknown;
  127.0.0.1   local;
  123.12.3.0/24  uk;
  92.43.0.0/16  fr;
}
```

Note that the preceding block is being presented to you just for the sake of the example and does not actually detect UK and French visitors; you'll want to use the GeoIP module if you wish to achieve proper geographical location detection. In this block, you may insert a number of directives that are specific to this module:

- `delete`: Allows you to remove the specified subnetwork from the mapping.
- `default`: The default value given to `$variable` in case the user's IP address does not match any of the specified IP ranges.
- `include`: Allows you to include an external file.
- `proxy`: Defines a subnet of trusted addresses. If the user IP address is among those trusted, the value of the `X-Forwarded-For` header is used as the IP address instead of the socket IP address.
- `proxy_recursive`: If enabled, this will look for the value of the `X-Forwarded-For` header, even if the client IP address is not trusted.
- `ranges`: If you insert this directive as the first line of your `geo` block, it allows you to specify IP ranges instead of CIDR masks. The following syntax is thus permitted: `127.0.0.1-127.0.0.255 LOCAL;`.

GeoIP

Although the name suggests some similarities with the previous one, this optional module provides accurate geographical information about your visitors by making use of the *MaxMind* (`https://www.maxmind.com/en/home`) GeoIP binary databases. You need to download the database files from the MaxMind website and place them in your Nginx directory.

This module is not included in the default Nginx build.

Then, all you have to do is specify the database path with either directive:

```
geoip_country country.dat; # country information db
geoip_city city.dat; # city information db
geoip_org geoiporg.dat; # ISP/organization db
```

The first directive enables several variables: `$geoip_country_code` (two-letter country code), `$geoip_country_code3` (three-letter country code), and `$geoip_country_name` (full country name). The second directive includes the same variables, but provides additional information: `$geoip_region`, `$geoip_city`, `$geoip_postal_code`, `$geoip_city_continent_code`, `$geoip_latitude`, `$geoip_longitude`, `$geoip_dma_code`, `$geoip_area_code`, and `$geoip_region_name`. The third directive offers information about the organization or ISP that owns the specified IP address, by filling up the `$geoip_org` variable.

 If you need the variables to be encoded in UTF-8, simply add the `utf8` keyword at the end of the `geoip_` directives.

UserID filter

This module assigns an identifier to clients by issuing cookies. The identifier can be accessed from the variables `$uid_got` and `$uid_set` further in the configuration:

Directive	Description
userid Context: `http, server, location`	Enables or disables issuing and logging of cookies. The directive accepts four possible values: • `on`: Enables v2 cookies and logs them • `v1`: Enables v1 cookies and logs them • `log`: Does not send cookie data, but logs incoming cookies • `off`: Does not send cookie data Default value: `userid off;`

Directive	Description
userid_service Context: http, server, location	Defines the IP address of the server issuing the cookie. Syntax: userid_service ip; Default: IP address of the server
userid_name Context: http, server, location	Defines the name assigned to the cookie. Syntax: userid_name name; Default value: The user identifier
userid_domain Context: http, server, location	Defines the domain assigned to the cookie. Syntax: userid_domain domain; Default value: None (the domain part is not sent)
userid_path Context: http, server, location	Defines the path part of the cookie. Syntax: userid_path path; Default value: /
userid_expires Context: http, server, location	Defines the cookie expiration date. Syntax: userid_expires date | max; Default value: No expiration date
userid_p3p Context: http, server, location	Assigns a value to the P3P header sent with the cookie. Syntax: userid_p3p data; Default value: None

Referer

A simple directive is introduced by this module: valid_referers. Its purpose is to check the Referer HTTP header from the client request and to possibly deny access based on the value. If the referrer is considered invalid, $invalid_referer is set to 1. In the list of valid referrers, you may employ three kinds of values:

- **None**: The absence of a referrer is considered to be a valid referrer
- **Blocked**: A masked referrer (such as XXXXX) is also considered valid
- **A server name**: The specified server name is considered to be a valid referrer

Following the definition of the $invalid_referer variable, you may, for example, return an error code if the referrer was found invalid:

```
valid_referers none blocked *.website.com *.google.com;
  if ($invalid_referer) {
  return 403;
}
```

Be aware that spoofing the Referer HTTP header is a very simple process, so checking the referer of client requests should not be used as a security measure.

Two more directives are offered by this module, referer_hash_bucket_size and referer_hash_max_size, respectively allowing you to define the bucket size and maximum size of the valid referrers' hash tables.

Real IP

This module provides one simple feature: it replaces the client IP address with the one specified in the X-Real-IP HTTP header for clients that visit your website behind a proxy or for retrieving IP addresses from the proper header if Nginx is used as a backend server (it essentially has the same effect as Apache's mod_rpaf; see Chapter 7, *Apache and Nginx Together*, for more details). To enable this feature, you need to insert the real_ip_header directive that defines the HTTP header to be exploited: either X-Real-IP or X-Forwarded-For. The second step is to define trusted IP addresses. In other words, the clients that are allowed to make use of those headers. This can be done thanks to the set_real_ip_from directive, which accepts both IP addresses and CIDR address ranges:

```
real_ip_header X-Forwarded-For;
set_real_ip_from 192.168.0.0/16;
set_real_ip_from 127.0.0.1;
set_real_ip_from unix:; # trusts all UNIX-domain sockets
```

Directive	Description
set_real_ip_from Context: http, server, location	Sets the trusted addresses that will trigger the real IP header replacement. Set this to the IP of the trusted reverse proxy (or proxies) in front of Nginx. This directive can be specified multiple times, and hostnames are allowed. The special value of unix: sets all UNIX sockets as trusted. Syntax: set_real_ip_from address | CIDR | unix:; Default: None
real_ip_header Context: http, server, location	Sets the header field that will be used as replacement for the IP address. The special value proxy_protocol changes the IP to the one from the Proxy protocol. Syntax: real_ip_header field | X-Real-Ip | X-Forwarded-For | proxy_protocol; Default: X-Real-Ip
real_ip_recursive Context: http, server, location	If set to on, the replacement IP will be set to the last non-trusted IP in the real_ip_header field. If set to off, will be replaced with the last IP in the real_ip_header field, whether trusted or not. Syntax: on or off Default: off

 This module is not included in the default Nginx build.

Split clients

The split clients module provides a resource-efficient way to split the visitor base into subgroups, based on the percentages that you specify. To distribute visitors into one group or another, Nginx hashes a value that you provide (such as the visitor's IP address, cookie data, query arguments, and so on) and decides which group the visitor should be assigned to. The following example configuration divides visitors up into three groups based on their IP address. If a visitor is assigned to the first 50 percent, the value of $variable will be set to group1:

```
split_clients "$remote_addr" $variable {
  50% "group1";
  30% "group2";
  20% "group3";
}
location ~ \.php$ {
  set $args "${query_string}&group=${variable}";
}
```

SSL and security

Nginx provides secure HTTP functionalities through the SSL module, but also offers an extra module, called **Secure Link**, that helps you protect your website and visitors in a totally different way.

SSL

The SSL module enables HTTPS support, HTTP over SSL/TLS in particular. It gives you the possibility to serve secure websites by providing a certificate, a certificate key, and other parameters, defined with the following directives:

Directive	Description
ssl Context: http, server	Enables HTTPS for the specified server. This directive is the equivalent of listen 443 ssl, or listen port ssl, more generally. Syntax: on or off Default: ssl off;
ssl_certificate Context: http, server	Sets the path of the PEM certificate. This directive can be specified multiple times to load certificates of different types. Syntax: File path

Directive	Description
ssl_certificate_key Context: http, server	Sets the path of the PEM secret key file. This directive can be specified multiple times to load certificates of different types. Syntax: File path
ssl_client_certificate Context: http, server	Sets the path of the client PEM certificate. Syntax: File path
ssl_crl Context: http, server	Orders Nginx to load a **CRL (Certificate Revocation List)** file, which allows checking the revocation status of certificates.
ssl_dhparam Context: http, server	Sets the path of the **Diffie-Hellman** parameters file. Syntax: File path.
ssl_protocols Context: http, server	Specifies the protocol that should be employed. Syntax: ssl_protocols [SSLv2] [SSLv3] [TLSv1] [TLSv1.1] [TLSv1.2] [TLSv1.3]; Default: ssl_protocols TLSv1 TLSv1.1 TLSv1.2 TLSv1.3;
ssl_ciphers Context: http, server	Specifies the ciphers that should be employed. The list of available ciphers can be obtained by running the following command from the shell: openssl ciphers. Syntax: ssl_ciphers cipher1[:cipher2...]; Default: ssl_ciphers ALL:!ADH:RC4+RSA:+HIGH:+MEDIUM:+LOW:+SSLv2:+EXP;
ssl_prefer_server_ciphers Context: http, server	Specifies whether server ciphers should be preferred over client ciphers. Syntax: on or off Default: off
ssl_verify_client Context: http, server	Enables verifying certificates transmitted by the client and sets the result in the $ssl_client_verify. The optional_no_ca value verifies the certificate if there is one, but does not require it to be signed by a trusted CA certificate. Syntax: on | off | optional | optional_no_ca Default: off
ssl_verify_depth Context: http, server	Specifies the verification depth of the client certificate chain. Syntax: Numeric value Default: 1

Directive	Description
ssl_session_cache Context: http, server	Configures the cache for SSL sessions. Syntax: off, none, builtin:size or shared:name:size Default: off (disables SSL sessions)
ssl_session_timeout Context: http, server	When SSL sessions are enabled, this directive defines the timeout for using session data. Syntax: Time value Default: 5 minutes
ssl_password_phrase Context: http, server	Specifies a file containing passphrases for secret keys. Each passphrase is specified on a separate line; they are tried one after the other when loading a certificate key. Syntax: Filename Default: (none)
ssl_buffer_size Context: http, server	Specifies buffer size when serving requests over SSL. Syntax: Size value Default: 16k
ssl_session_tickets Context: http, server	Enables TLS session tickets, allowing for the client to reconnect faster, skipping renegotiation. Syntax: on or off Default: on
ssl_session_ticket_key Context: http, server	Sets the path of the key file used to encrypt and decrypt TLS session tickets. By default, a random value is generated. Syntax: file name Default: (none)
ssl_trusted_certificate Context: http, server	Sets the path of a trusted certificate file (PEM format), used to validate authenticity of client certificates, as well as stapling of OCSP responses. More about SSL stapling can be found here: Syntax: Filename Default: (none)

 This module is not included in the default Nginx build.

Additionally, the following variables are made available:

- $ssl_cipher: Indicates the cipher used for the current request
- $ssl_ciphers: Returns list of client supported ciphers
- $ssl_curves: Returns list of client supported curves
- $ssl_client_serial: Indicates the serial number of the client certificate
- $ssl_client_s_dn and $ssl_client_i_dn: Indicates the value of the subject and issuer DN of the client certificate
- $ssl_protocol: Indicates the protocol at use for the current request
- $ssl_client_cert and $ssl_client_raw_cert: Returns client certificate data, which is raw data for the second variable
- $ssl_client_verify: Set to SUCCESS if the client certificate was successfully verified
- $ssl_session_id: Allows you to retrieve the ID of an SSL session
- $ssl_client_escaped_cert: Returns the client certificate in PEM format

Setting up an SSL certificate

Although the SSL module offers a lot of possibilities, in most cases, only a couple of directives are actually useful for setting up a secure website. This guide will help you configure Nginx to use an SSL certificate for your website (in the example, your website is identified by secure.website.com). Before doing so, ensure that you already have the following elements at your disposal:

- A .key file generated with the following command: openssl genrsa -out secure.website.com.key 1024 (other encryption levels work, too).
- A .csr file generated with the following command: openssl req -new -key secure.website.com.key -out secure.website.com.csr.
- Your website certificate file, as issued by the certificate authority, for example, secure.website.com.crt. (In order to obtain a certificate from the CA, you will need to provide your .csr file).
- The CA certificate file as issued by the CA (for example, gd_bundle.crt, if you purchased your certificate from https://godaddy.com/).

The first step is to merge your website certificate and the CA certificate together with the following command:

```
cat secure.website.com.crt gd_bundle.crt > combined.crt
```

You are then ready to configure Nginx to serve secure content:

```
server {
    listen 443;
    server_name secure.website.com;
    ssl on;
    ssl_certificate /path/to/combined.crt;
    ssl_certificate_key /path/to/secure.website.com.key;
    [...]
}
```

SSL stapling

SSL stapling, also called **OCSP (Online Certificate Status Protocol)** stapling, is a technique allowing clients to easily connect and resume sessions to an SSL/TLS server without having to contact the certificate authority, thus reducing SSL negotiation times. In normal OCSP transactions, the client contacts the certificate authority so as to check the revocation status of the server's certificate. In the case of high traffic websites, this can cause huge stress on CA servers. An intermediary solution was designed: stapling. The OCSP record is obtained from the CA by your server itself periodically, and **stapled** to exchanges with the client. The OCSP record is cached by your server for a period of up to 48 hours in order to limit communications with the CA.

Enabling SSL stapling should thus speed up communications between your visitors and your server. Achieving this in Nginx is relatively simple: all you really need is to insert three directives in your server block and obtain a full trusted certificate chain file (containing both the root and intermediate certificates) from your CA:

- `ssl_stapling on`: Enables SSL stapling within the server block
- `ssl_stapling_verify on`: Enables verification of OCSP responses by the server
- `ssl_trusted_certificate filename`: Where `filename` is the path of your full trusted certificate file (extension should be `.pem`)

Two optional directives also exist, allowing you to modify the behavior of this module:

- `ssl_stapling_file filename`: Where `filename` is the path of a cached OCSP record, overriding the record provided by the OCSP responder specified in the certificate file
- `ssl_stapling_responder url`: Where `url` is the URL of your CA's OCSP responder, overriding the URL specified in the certificate file.

If you are having issues connecting to the OCSP responder, make sure your Nginx configuration contains a valid DNS resolver (using the `resolver` directive).

Secure link

Totally independent from the SSL module, Secure Link provides a basic protection by checking the presence of a specific hash in the URL before allowing the user to access a resource:

```
location /downloads/ {
secure_link_md5        "secret";
secure_link $arg_hash,$arg_expires;
    if ($secure_link = "") {
      return 403;
    }
}
```

With such a configuration, documents in the `/downloads/` folder must be accessed via a URL containing a query string parameter, `hash=XXX` (note the `$arg_hash` in the example), where `XXX` is the MD5 hash of the secret you defined through the `secure_link_md5` directive. The second argument of the `secure_link` directive is a UNIX timestamp defining the expiration date. The `$secure_link` variable is empty if the URI does not contain the proper hash or if the date has expired. Otherwise, it is set to 1.

 This module is not included in the default Nginx build.

Other miscellaneous modules

The remaining three modules (which all need to be enabled at compile time) are optional and provide additional advanced functionalities.

Stub status

The Stub status module was designed to provide information about the current state of the server, such as the amount of active connections, the total handled requests, and more. To activate it, place the `stub_status` directive in a `location` block. All requests matching the `location` block will produce the status page:

```
location = /nginx_status {
    stub_status on;
    allow 127.0.0.1; # you may want to protect the information
    deny all;
}
```

 This module is not included in the default Nginx build.

An example result produced by Nginx:

```
Active connections: 1
server accepts handled requests
 10 10 23
Reading: 0 Writing: 1 Waiting: 0
```

It's interesting to note that there are several server monitoring solutions, such as *Monitorix*, that offer Nginx support through the Stub status page by calling it at regular intervals and parsing the statistics.

Degradation

The HTTP Degradation module configures your server to return an error page when your server runs low on memory. It works by defining a memory amount that is to be considered low, and then specifying the locations for which you wish to enable the degradation check:

```
degradation sbrk=500m; # to be inserted at the http block level
degrade 204; # in a location block, specify the error code (204 or 444) to
return in case the server condition has degraded
```

Google-perftools

This module interfaces the Google performance tools profiling mechanism for the Nginx worker processes. The tool generates a report based on performance analysis of the executable code. More information can be discovered from the official website of the project at https://code.google.com/archive/search?q=gperftools.

 This module is not included in the default Nginx build.

In order to enable this feature, you need to specify the path of the report file that will be generated using the google_perftools_profiles directive:

```
google_perftools_profiles logs/profiles;
```

WebDAV

WebDAV is an extension of the well-known HTTP protocol. While HTTP was designed for visitors to download resources from a website (in other words, reading data), WebDAV extends the functionality of web servers by adding write operations, such as creating files and folders, moving and copying files, and more. The Nginx WebDAV module implements a small subset of the WebDAV protocol:

Directive	Description
dav_methods Context: http, server, location	Selects the DAV methods you want to enable. Syntax: dav_methods [off | [PUT] [DELETE] [MKCOL] [COPY] [MOVE]]; Default: off
dav_access Context: http, server, location	Defines access permissions at the current level. Syntax: dav_access [user:r|w|rw] [group:r|w|rw] [all:r|w|rw]; Default: dav_access user:rw;

Directive	Description
create_full_put_path Context: http, server, location	This directive defines the behavior when a client requests to create a file in a directory that does not exist. If set to on, the directory path is created. If set to off, the file creation fails. Syntax: on or off Default: off
min_delete_depth Context: http, server, location	This directive defines a minimum URI depth for deleting files or directories when processing the DELETE command. Syntax: Numeric value Default: 0

 This module is not included in the default Nginx build.

Third-party modules

The Nginx community has been growing larger over the past few years, and many additional modules have been written by third-party developers. These can be downloaded from the official wiki website at http://wiki.nginx.org/nginx3rdPartyModules.

The currently available modules offer a wide range of new possibilities, among which are:

- An *Access Key* module to protect your documents in a similar fashion to Secure Link, by Mykola Grechukh
- A *Fancy Indexes* module that improves the automatic directory listings generated by Nginx, by Adrian Perez de Castro
- The *Headers More* module that improves flexibility with HTTP headers, by Yichun Zhang (agentzh)
- Many more features for various parts of the web server

To integrate a third-party module into your Nginx build, you need to follow these three simple steps:

1. Download the `.tar.gz` archive associated with the module you wish to download.

2. Extract the archive with the following command:

   `tar xzf module.tar.gz`

3. Configure your Nginx build with the following command:

   `./configure --add-module=/module/source/path [...]`

Once you finished building and installing the application, the module is available just like a regular Nginx module, with its directives and variables.

If you are interested in writing Nginx modules yourself, Evan Miller published an excellent walkthrough: *Emiller's Guide to Nginx Module Development*. The complete guide may be consulted from his personal website at `http://www.evanmiller.org/`.

Summary

All throughout this chapter, we have been discovering modules that help you improve or fine-tune the configuration of your web server. Nginx fiercely stands up to other concurrent web servers in terms of functionality, and its approach to virtual hosts and the way they are configured will probably convince many administrators to make the switch.

Three additional modules were left out, though. Firstly, the FastCGI module will be approached in the next chapter, as it will allow us to configure a gateway to applications such as PHP or Python. Secondly, the proxy module that lets us design complex setups will be described in `Chapter 7`, *Apache and Nginx Together*. Finally, the Upstream module is tied to both, so it will be detailed in parallel.

5

PHP and Python with Nginx

The 2000s have been the decade of server-side technologies. Over the past 15 years or so, an overwhelming majority of websites have migrated from simple static HTML content to highly and fully dynamic pages, taking the web to an entirely new level in terms of interaction with visitors. Software solutions emerged quickly, including open source ones, and some became mature enough to process high-traffic websites. In this chapter, we will study the ability of Nginx to interact with these applications. We have selected two for different reasons. The first one is obviously PHP. As of June 2015, W3Techs (a website specializing in web technology surveys) reveals that PHP empowers over 80% of websites designed with a server-side language. The second language in our selection is Python, due to the way it is installed and configured to work with Nginx. The mechanism we will discover effortlessly applies to other applications, such as Perl or Ruby on Rails.

This chapter covers the following topics:

- Discovering the CGI and FastCGI technologies
- The Nginx FastCGI and similar modules
- Setting up PHP and PHP-FPM
- Setting up Python and Django
- Configuring Nginx to work with PHP and Python

Introduction to FastCGI

Before we begin, you should know that (as the name suggests) FastCGI is actually a variation of CGI. Therefore, explaining CGI first is in order. The improvements introduced by FastCGI are detailed in the following sections.

Understanding the CGI mechanism

The original purpose of a web server was merely to respond to requests from clients by serving files located on a storage device. The client sends a request to download a file and the server processes the request and sends the appropriate response: **200 OK** if the file can be served normally, 404 if the file was not found, and other variants, as illustrated in the following diagram:

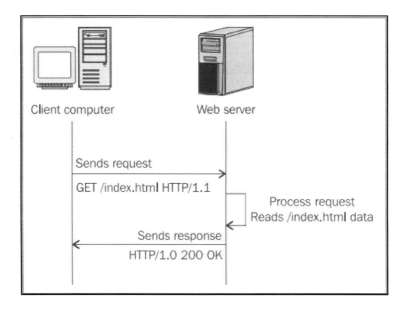

This mechanism has been in use since the beginning of the World Wide Web and it still is. However, as stated before, static websites are being progressively abandoned at the expense of dynamic ones that contain scripts that are processed by applications such as PHP and Python among others. The web serving mechanism thus evolved into the following:

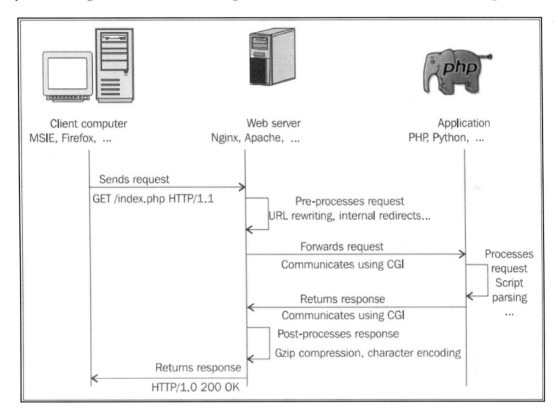

When a client attempts to visit a dynamic page, the web server receives the request and forwards it to a third-party application. The application processes the script independently and returns the produced response to the web server, which then forwards the response back to the client.

In order for the web server to communicate with that application, the CGI protocol was invented in the early 1990s.

Common Gateway Interface

As stated in RFC 3875 (CGI protocol v1.1), designed by the **Internet Society** (**ISOC**):

The Common Gateway Interface (CGI) allows an HTTP server and a CGI script to share responsibility for responding to client requests. [...]. The server is responsible for managing connection, data transfer, transport, and network issues related to the client request, whereas the CGI script handles the application issues such as data access and document processing.

Common Gateway Interface (**CGI**) is the protocol that describes the way information is exchanged between the web server (Nginx) and the gateway application (PHP, Python, and so on). In practice, when the web server receives a request that should be forwarded to the gateway application, it simply executes the command corresponding to the desired application, for example, `/usr/bin/php`. Details about the client request (such as the `User Agent` and other request information) are passed either as command-line arguments or in environment variables, while actual data from `POST` or `PUT` requests is transmitted through the standard input. The invoked application then writes the processed document contents to the standard output, which is recaptured by the web server.

While this technology seems simple and efficient enough at first sight, it comes with a few major drawbacks, which are discussed as follows:

- A unique process is spawned for each request. Memory and other context information are lost from one request to another.
- Starting up a process can be resource-consuming for the system. Massive numbers of simultaneous requests (each spawning a process) could quickly clutter a server.
- Designing an architecture where the web server and the gateway application are located on different computers seems difficult, if not impossible.

Fast Common Gateway Interface (FastCGI)

The issues mentioned in the *Common Gateway Interface* section render the CGI protocol relatively inefficient for servers that are subject to heavy load. The will to find solutions led open market in the mid-90s to develop an evolution of CGI: **Fast Common Gateway Interface** (**FastCGI**). It has become a major standard over the past 15 years and most web servers now offer the functionality, even proprietary server software such as Microsoft IIS.

Although the purpose remains the same, FastCGI offers significant improvements over CGI with the establishment of the following principles:

- Instead of spawning a new process for each request, FastCGI employs persistent processes that come with the ability to handle multiple requests.
- The web server and the gateway application communicate with the use of sockets such as TCP or POSIX local IPC sockets. Consequently, the web server and backend processes may be located on two different computers on a network.
- The web server forwards the client request to the gateway and receives the response within a single connection. Additional requests may also follow without needing to create additional connections. Note that, on most web servers, including Nginx and Apache, the implementation of FastCGI does not (or at least not fully) support *multiplexing*.
- Since FastCGI is a socket-based protocol, it can be implemented on any platform with any programming language.

Throughout this chapter, we will be setting up PHP and Python via FastCGI. Additionally, you will find the mechanism to be relatively similar in the case of other applications, such as Perl or Ruby on Rails.

Designing a FastCGI-powered architecture is actually not as complex as one might imagine. As long as you have the web server and the backend application running, the only difficulty that remains is to establish the connection between both parties. The first step in that perspective is to configure the way Nginx will communicate with the FastCGI application. FastCGI compatibility with Nginx is introduced by the FastCGI module, which is included in default Nginx builds (including those that are installed via software repositories). This section details the directives that are made available by the module.

uWSGI and SCGI

Before reading the rest of the chapter, you should know that Nginx offers two other CGI-derived module implementations:

- The uWSGI module allows Nginx to communicate with applications through the uwsgi protocol, itself derived from **Web Server Gateway Interface** (**WSGI**). The most commonly used (the unique) server implementing the uwsgi protocol is the unoriginally named uWSGI server. Its latest documentation can be found at http://uwsgi-docs.readthedocs.io/en/latest/. This module will prove useful to Python adepts, seeing as the uWSGI project was designed mainly for Python applications.

- **SCGI**, which stands for **Simple Common Gateway Interface**, is a variant of the CGI protocol, much like FastCGI. Younger than FastCGI since its specification was first published in 2006, SCGI was designed to be easier to implement and as its name suggests: simple. It is not related to a particular programming language. SCGI interfaces and modules can be found in a variety of software projects such as Apache, IIS, Java, Cherokee, and a lot more.

There are no major differences in the way Nginx handles the FastCGI, uWSGI, and SCGI protocols: each of these has its respective module, containing similarly named directives. The following table lists a couple of directives from the FastCGI module, which are detailed in the following sections, and their uWSGI and SCGI equivalents:

FastCGI module	uWSGI equivalent	SCGI equivalent
`fastcgi_pass`	`uwsgi_pass`	`scgi_pass`
`fastcgi_cache`	`uwsgi_cache`	`scgi_cache`
`fastcgi_temp_path`	`uwsgi_temp_path`	`scgi_temp_path`

Directive names and syntaxes are identical. In addition, the Nginx development team has been maintaining all three modules in parallel. New directives or directive updates are always applied to all of them. As such, the following sections will be documenting Nginx's implementation of the FastCGI protocol (since it is the most widely used), but they also apply to uWSGI and SCGI.

Main directives

The FastCGI, uWSGI, and SCGI modules are included in the default Nginx build. You do not need to enable them manually at compile time. The directives listed in the following table allow you to configure the way Nginx *passes* requests to the FastCGI/uWSGI/SCGI application. Note that you will find `fastcgi_params`, `uwsgi_params`, and `scgi_params` files in the Nginx configuration folder; these define directive values that are valid for most situations:

Directive	Description

`fastcgi_pass`
Context: `location, if`
	This directive specifies that the request should be passed to the FastCGI server, by indicating its location:
	• For TCP sockets, the syntax is: `fastcgi_pass hostname:port;`
	• For Unix domain sockets, the syntax is: `fastcgi_pass unix:/path/to/fastcgi.socket;`
	• You may also refer to upstream blocks (read the following sections for more information): `fastcgi_pass myblock;`
	Examples:
	`fastcgi_pass    localhost:9000;`
	`fastcgi_pass    127.0.0.1:9000;`
	`fastcgi_pass    unix:/tmp/fastcgi.socket;`
	`# Using an   upstream block`
	`upstream fastcgi   {`
	`  server   127.0.0.1:9000;`
	`  server   127.0.0.1:9001;`
	`}`
	`location ~*   \.php$ {`
	`    fastcgi_pass   fastcgi;`
	`}`

`fastcgi_param`
Context: `http, server, location`
	This directive allows you to configure the request passed to FastCGI. Two parameters are strictly required for all FastCGI requests: `SCRIPT_FILENAME` and `QUERY_STRING`.
	Example:
	`fastcgi_param   SCRIPT_FILENAME`
	`/home/website.com/www$fastcgi_script_name;`
	`fastcgi_param   QUERY_STRING $query_string;`
	As for `POST` requests, additional parameters are required: `REQUEST_METHOD`, `CONTENT_TYPE`, and `CONTENT_LENGTH`:
	`fastcgi_param   REQUEST_METHOD $request_method;`
	`fastcgi_param   CONTENT_TYPE $content_type;`
	`fastcgi_param   CONTENT_LENGTH $content_length;`
	The `fastcgi_params` file that you will find in the Nginx configuration folder already includes all of the necessary parameter definitions, except for `SCRIPT_FILENAME`, which you need to specify for each of your FastCGI configurations.
	If the parameter name begins with `HTTP_`, it will override potentially existing HTTP headers of the client request.
	You may optionally specify the `if_not_empty` keyword, forcing Nginx to transmit the parameter only if the specified value is not empty.
	Syntax: `fastcgi_param PARAM value [if_not_empty];`

Directive	Description
`fastcgi_bind` Context: `http`, `server`, `location`	This directive binds the socket to a local IP address, allowing you to specify the network interface you want to use for FastCGI communications. Syntax: `fastcgi_bind IP_address[:port]` `[transparent] | off;`
`fastcgi_pass_header` Context: `http`, `server`, `location`	This directive specifies the additional headers that should be passed to the FastCGI server. Syntax: `fastcgi_pass_header headername;` Example: `fastcgi_pass_header   Authorization;`
`fastcgi_hide_header` Context: `http`, `server`, `location`	This directive specifies the headers that should be hidden from the FastCGI server (headers that Nginx does not forward). Syntax: `fastcgi_hide_header headername;` Example: `fastcgi_hide_header   X-Forwarded-For;`
`fastcgi_index` Context: `http`, `server`, `location`	The FastCGI server does not support automatic directory indexes. If the requested URI ends with a /, Nginx appends the value `fastcgi_index`. Syntax: `fastcgi_index filename;` Example: `fastcgi_index   index.php;`
`fastcgi_ignore_client_abort` Context: `http`, `server`, `location`	This directive lets you define what happens if the client aborts their request to the web server. If the directive is turned `on`, Nginx ignores the abort request and finishes processing the request. If it's turned `off`, Nginx does not ignore the abort request. It interrupts the request treatment and aborts related communication with the FastCGI server. Syntax: `on` or `off` Default: `off`
`fastcgi_intercept_errors` Context: `http`, `server`, `location`	This directive defines whether or not Nginx should process errors returned by the gateway or directly return error pages to the client. Error processing is done via the `error_page` directive of Nginx. Syntax: `on` or `off` Default: `off`

Directive	Description
`fastcgi_read_timeout` Context: `http`, `server`, `location`	This directive defines the timeout for the response from the FastCGI application. If Nginx does not receive the response after this period, the `504 Gateway Timeout` HTTP error is returned. Syntax: Numeric value (in seconds) Default: `60`
`fastcgi_connect_timeout` Context: `http`, `server`, `location`	This directive defines the backend server connection timeout. This is different than the read/send timeout. If Nginx is already connected to the backend server, the `fastcgi_connect_timeout` is not applicable. Syntax: Time value (in seconds) Default: `60`
`fastcgi_send_timeout` Context: `http`, `server`, `location`	This is the timeout for sending data to the backend server. The timeout isn't applied to the entire response delay but rather between two write operations. Syntax: Time value (in seconds) Default value: `60`

`fastcgi_split_path_info`
Context: `location`
	A directive particularly useful for URLs of the following form:
	`http://website.com/page.php/param1/param2/`
	The directive splits the path information according to the specified regular expression:
	`fastcgi_split_path_info ^(.+\.php)(.*)$;`
	This affects two variables:
	• `$fastcgi_script_name`: The filename of the actual script to be executed, for example; `page.php`
	• `$fastcgi_path_info`: The part of the URL that is after the script name, example; `/param1/param2/`)
	These can be employed in further parameter definitions:
	`fastcgi_param SCRIPT_FILENAME /home/website.com/www$fastcgi_script_name;`
	`fastcgi_param PATH_INFO $fastcgi_path_info;`
	Syntax: Regular expression

`fastcgi_store` Context: `http`, `server`, `location`	This directive enables a simple *cache store* where responses from the FastCGI application are stored as files on the storage device. When the same URI is requested again, the document is directly served from the cache store instead of forwarding the request to the FastCGI application. This directive enables or disables the cache store. Syntax: `on` or `off`

Directive	Description
`fastcgi_store_access` Context: `http, server, location`	This directive defines the access permissions applied to the files created in the context of the cache store. Syntax: `fastcgi_store_access` `[user:r|w|rw] [group:r|w|rw] [all:r|w|rw];` Default: `fastcgi_store_access user:rw;`
`fastcgi_temp_path` Context: `http, server, location`	This directive sets the path of temporary and cache store files. Syntax: File path Example: `fastcgi_temp_path /tmp/nginx_fastcgi;`
`fastcgi_max_temp_file_size` Context: `http, server, location`	Set this directive to `0` to disable the use of temporary files for FastCGI requests or to specify a maximum file size. Default value: 1 GB Syntax: Size value Example: `fastcgi_max_temp_file_size 5m;`
`fastcgi_temp_file_write_size` Context: `http, server, location`	This directive sets the write buffer size when saving temporary files to the storage device. Syntax: Size value Default value: `2 * proxy_buffer_size`
`fastcgi_send_lowat` Context: `http, server, location`	This option allows you to make use of the `SO_SNDLOWAT` flag for TCP sockets under FreeBSD only. This value defines the minimum number of bytes in the buffer for output operations. Syntax: Numeric value (size) Default value: `0`

`fastcgi_pass_request_body`
`fastcgi_pass_request_headers`
Context: `http, server, location`
	This directive defines whether or not, respectively, the request body and extra request headers should be passed on to the *backend* server.
	Syntax: `on` or `off`
	Default: `on`

Directive	Description
`fastcgi_ignore_headers` Context: `http, server, location`	This directive prevents Nginx from processing one or more of the following headers from the backend server response: • `X-Accel-Redirect` • `X-Accel-Expires` • `Expires` • `Cache-Control` • `X-Accel-Limit-Rate` • `X-Accel-Buffering` • `X-Accel-Charset` Syntax: `fastcgi_ignore_headers header1 [header2...];`

`fastcgi_next_upstream`
Context: `http, server, location`
	When `fastcgi_pass` is connected to an upstream block, this directive defines cases where requests should be abandoned and re-sent to the next upstream server of the block. The directive accepts a combination of values among the following:
	• `error`: An error occurred while communicating or attempting to communicate with the server
	• `timeout`: A timeout occured during transfers or connection attempts
	• `invalid_header`: The backend server returned an empty or invalid response
	• `http_500, http_503, http_403, http_404, http_429`: If such HTTP errors occur, Nginx switches to the next upstream server
	• `non-idempotent`: Allows retrying non-idempotent requests (`LOCK`, `POST`, `PATCH`)
	• `off`: Forbids using the next upstream server
	Examples:
	`fastcgi_next_upstream   error timeout http_504;`
	`fastcgi_next_upstream   timeout invalid_header;`

`fastcgi_next_upstream_timeout` Context: `http, server, location`	Defines the timeout to be used in conjunction with `fastcgi_next_upstream`. Setting this directive to `0` disables it. Syntax: Time value (in seconds)
`fastcgi_next_upstream_tries` Context: `http, server, location`	Defines the maximum number of upstream servers tried before returning an error message, to be used in conjunction with `fastcgi_next_upstream`. Syntax: Numeric value (default: `0`)

Directive	Description
`fastcgi_catch_stderr` Context: `http, server, location`	This directive allows you to intercept some of the error messages sent to `stderr` (**standard error** stream) and store them in the Nginx error log. Syntax: `fastcgi_catch_stderr filter;` Example: `fastcgi_catch_stderr "PHP Fatal error:";`
`fastcgi_keep_conn` Context: `http, server, location`	When set to `on`, Nginx will conserve the connection to the FastCGI server, thus reducing overhead. Syntax: `on` or `off` (default: `off`) Note that there is no equivalent directive in the uWSGI and SCGI modules.
`fastcgi_force_ranges` Context: `http, server, location`	When set to `on`, Nginx will enable byte-range support on responses from the FastCGI backend. Syntax: `on` or `off` (default: `off`)
`fastcgi_limit_rate` Context: `http, server, location`	Allows you to limit the rate at which Nginx downloads the response from the FastCGI backend. Syntax: numeric value (bytes per second)

FastCGI caching and buffering

Once you have correctly configured Nginx to work with your FastCGI application, you may optionally make use of the following directives, which will help you improve the overall server performance by setting up a cache system. Additionally, FastCGI buffering allows you to buffer responses from the FastCGI backend instead of synchronously forwarding them to the client:

Directive	Description
`fastcgi_cache` Context: `http, server, location`	This directive defines a cache zone. The identifier given to the zone is to be reused in further directives. Syntax: `fastcgi_cache zonename;` Example: `fastcgi_cache cache1;`

Directive	Description
`fastcgi_cache_key` Context: `http, server, location`	This directive defines the *cache key*. In other words, it is what differentiates one cache entry from another. If the cache key is set to `$uri`, as a result all requests with a similar `$uri` will correspond to the same cache entry. This is not enough for most dynamic websites; you also need to include query string arguments in the cache key so that `/index.php` and `/index.php?page=contact` do not point to the same cache entry. Syntax: `fastcgi_cache_key key;` Example: `fastcgi_cache "$scheme$host$request_uri $cookie_user";`
`fastcgi_cache_methods` Context: `http, server, location`	This directive defines the HTTP methods eligible for caching. `GET` and `HEAD` are included by default and cannot be disabled. You may, for example, enable caching of `POST` requests. Syntax: `fastcgi_cache_methods METHOD;` Example: `fastcgi_cache_methods POST;`
`fastcgi_cache_min_uses` Context: `http, server, location`	This directive defines the minimum number of hits before a request is eligible for caching. By default, the response of a request is cached after one hit (the next requests with the same cache key will receive the cached response). Syntax: Numeric value Example: `fastcgi_cache_min_uses 1;`
`fastcgi_cache_max_range_offset` Context: `http, server, location`	Sets an offset in bytes for byte-range requests. If the range is beyond the offset, the range request will be passed to the FastCGI server and the response will not be cached. Syntax: Numeric value Example: `fastcgi_cache_min_uses 16k;`

Directive	Description
`fastcgi_cache_path` Context: `http`, `server`, `location`	This directive indicates the directory for storing cached files, as well as other parameters. Syntax: `fastcgi_cache_path path [levels=numbers] keys_zone=name:size [inactive=time] [max_size=size] [loader_files=number] [loader_sleep=time] [loader_threshold=time];` The additional parameters are: • `levels`: Indicates the depth of subdirectories (1:2 indicates that subfolders will be created down to two levels) • `keys_zone`: Selects the zone you previously declared with the `fastcgi_cache` directive, and indicates the size to occupy in memory • `inactive`: If a cached response is not used within the specified time frame, it's removed from the cache (default: 10 minutes) • `max_size`: Defines the maximum size of the entire cache • `loader_files`, `loaded_sleep`, `loader_threshold`: Configures the cache loader; the number of files it processes in one read cycle (`loader_files`|`manager_files`, default: 100 files), the pause time between read cycles (`loader_sleep`|`manager_sleep`, default: 50ms), and the maximum duration of a read cycle (`loader_threshold`|`manager_threshold`, default: 200ms). Example: `fastcgi_cache_path /tmp/nginx_cache levels=1:2 zone=zone1:10m inactive=10m max_size=200M;`

Directive	Description
`fastcgi_cache_use_stale` Context: `http, server, location`	This directive defines whether or not Nginx should serve stale cached data in certain circumstances (in respect of the gateway). If you use `fastcgi_cache_use_stale timeout`, and if the gateway times out, then Nginx will serve cached data. Syntax: `fastcgi_cache_use_stale [updating] [error] [timeout] [invalid_header] [http_500];` Example: `fastcgi_cache_use_stale error timeout;`

`fastcgi_cache_valid`
Context: `http, server, location`
	This directive allows you to customize the caching time for different kinds of response code. You may cache responses associated to `404` error codes for 1 minute, and on the opposite cache, `200 OK` responses for 10 minutes or more. This directive can be inserted more than once, demonstrated as follows:
	`fastcgi_cache_valid    404 1m;`
	`fastcgi_cache_valid    500 502 504 5m;`
	`fastcgi_cache_valid    200 10;`
	Syntax: `fastcgi_cache_valid code1 [code2...] time;`

`fastcgi_no_cache` Context: `http, server, location`	You may want to disable caching for requests that meet certain conditions. The directive accepts a series of variables. If at least one of these variables has a value (not an empty string, and not 0), this request will not be stored in the cache. Syntax: `fastcgi_no_cache $variable1 [$variable2] [...];` Example: `fastcgi_no_cache $args_nocaching;`

Directive	Description
`fastcgi_cache_bypass` Context: `http, server, location`	This directive functions in a similar manner to `fastcgi_no_cache`, except that it tells Nginx whether or not the request should be loaded from cache, if it can be (as opposed to deciding whether to store the request result in cache). Syntax: `fastcgi_cache_bypass $variable1 [$variable2] [...];` Example: `fastcgi_cache_bypass $cookie_bypass_cache;`
`fastcgi_cache_background_update` Context: `http, server, location`	This directive works in conjunction with `fastcgi_cache_use_stale updating` by allowing Nginx to immediately serve a stale cached response while creating a subrequest to the backend to update the cache. Defaults: `off` Syntax: `fastcgi_cache_background_update on|off;` Example: `fastcgi_cache_background_update on;`

`fastcgi_cache_lock`
`fastcgi_cache_lock_timeout`
`fastcgi_cache_lock_age`
Context: `http, server, location`
	If set to `on`, `fastcgi_cache_lock` prevents repopulating existing cache elements for the duration specified by `fastcgi_cache_lock_age` (`fastcgi_cache_lock_timeout` achieving the same result, except the response isn't cached).
	Example:
	`fastcgi_cache_lock    on;`
	`fastcgi_cache_lock_timeout    10s;`

`fastcgi_cache_revalidate` Context: `http, server, location`	When enabled, Nginx revalidates expired cache items when instructed to do so by the `If-modified-since` and `If-none-match` headers. Syntax: `fastcgi_cache_revalidate on | off;` Default: `off`

Directive	Description

`fastcgi_buffering`
`fastcgi_request_buffering`
Context: `http, server, location`
	Enables or disables buffering of responses (or client requests, in the case of `fastcgi_request_buffers`) sent by a FastCGI backend. When disabled, Nginx forwards responses to the client synchronously. When enabled, responses are stored in buffers until the backend finishes sending the entire content, then sent to the client.
	Syntax: `fastcgi_buffering on | off;`
	Default: `on`

`fastcgi_buffers` Context: `http, server, location`	This directive sets the number and size of buffers that will be used for reading the response data from the FastCGI application. Syntax: `fastcgi_buffers amount size;` Default: 8 buffers, 4k or 8k each, depending on platform Example: `fastcgi_buffers 8 4k;`
`fastcgi_buffer_size` Context: `http, server, location`	This directive sets the size of the buffer for reading the beginning of the response from the FastCGI application, which usually contains simple header data. The default value corresponds to the size of one buffer, as defined by the previous directive (`fastcgi_buffers`). Syntax: Size value Example: `fastcgi_buffer_size 4k;`

Here is a full Nginx FastCGI cache configuration example, making use of most of the cache-related directives described in the preceding table:

```
fastcgi_cache phpcache;
fastcgi_cache_key "$scheme$host$request_uri"; # $request_uri includes the
request arguments (such as /page.php?arg=value)
fastcgi_cache_min_uses 2; # after 2 hits, a request receives a cached
response
fastcgi_cache_path /tmp/cache levels=1:2 keys_zone=phpcache:10m
```

```
    inactive=30m max_size=500M;
    fastcgi_cache_use_stale updating timeout;
    fastcgi_cache_valid 404 1m;
    fastcgi_cache_valid 500 502 504 5m;
```

Since these directives are valid for pretty much any virtual host configuration, you may want to save these in a separate file (`fastcgi_cache`), that you include in the appropriate place:

```
server {
    server_name website.com;
    location ~* \.php$ {
        fastcgi_pass 127.0.0.1:9000;
        fastcgi_param SCRIPT_FILENAME
/home/website.com/www$fastcgi_script_name;
        fastcgi_param PATH_INFO $fastcgi_script_name;
        include fastcgi_params;
        include fastcgi_cache;
    }
}
```

PHP with Nginx

We are now going to configure PHP to work together with Nginx via FastCGI. Why FastCGI in particular, as opposed to the other two alternatives, SCGI and uWSGI? The answer came with the release of PHP version 5.3.3. As of this version, all releases come with an integrated FastCGI process manager allowing you to easily connect applications implementing the FastCGI protocol. The only requirement is for your PHP build to have been configured with the `--enable-fpm` argument. If you are unsure whether your current setup includes the necessary components, worry not: a section of this chapter is dedicated to building PHP with everything we need. Alternatively, the package `php-fpm` or `php5-fpm` can be found in most repositories.

Architecture

Before starting the setup process, it's important to understand the way PHP will interact with Nginx. We have established that FastCGI is a communication protocol running through sockets, which implies that there is a client and a server. The client is obviously Nginx. As for the server, well, the answer is actually more complicated than just "PHP."

By default, PHP supports the FastCGI protocol. The PHP binary processes scripts and is able to interact with Nginx via sockets. However, we are going to use an additional component to improve the overall process management: the FastCGI Process Manager, also known as **PHP-FPM**:

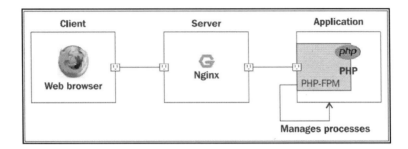

PHP-FPM takes FastCGI support to an entirely new level. Its numerous features are detailed in the next section.

PHP-FPM

The process manager, as its name suggests, is a script that manages PHP processes. It awaits and receives instructions from Nginx and runs the requested PHP scripts under the environment that you configure. In practice, PHP-FPM introduces a number of possibilities such as:

- Automatically *daemonizing* PHP (turning it into a background process)
- Executing scripts in a *chrooted* environment
- Improved logging, IP address restrictions, pool separation, and many more

Setting up PHP and PHP-FPM

In this section, we will detail the process of downloading and compiling a recent version of PHP. You will need to go through this particular step if you are currently running an earlier version of PHP (<5.3.3).

Downloading and extracting

At the time of writing these lines, the latest stable version of PHP is 5.6.10. Download the tarball via the following command:

```
[user@local ~]$ wget
http://php.net/get/php-7.2.0.tar.gz/from/www.php.net/mirror
```

Once downloaded, extract the PHP archive with the `tar` command:

```
[user@local ~]$ tar xzf php-7.2.0.tar.gz
```

Requirements

There are two main requirements for building PHP with PHP-FPM: the `libevent` and `libxml` development libraries. If these are not already installed on your system, you will need to install them with your system's package manager.

For Red Hat-based systems and other systems using `yum` as the package manager:

```
[root@local ~]# yum install libevent-devel libxml2-devel
```

For Ubuntu, Debian, and other systems that use `apt-get` or `aptitude`:

```
[root@local ~]# aptitude install libxml2-dev libevent-dev
```

Building PHP

Once you have installed all of the dependencies, you may start building PHP. As with other applications and libraries that were previously installed, you will basically need three commands: `configure`, `make`, and `make install`. Be aware that this will install a new instance of the application. If you already have PHP set up on your system, the new instance will not override it, but instead will be installed in a different location that is revealed to you during the `make install` command execution.

The first step (`configure`) is critical here as you will need to enable the PHP-FPM options in order for PHP to include the required functionality. There are numerous configuration arguments that you can pass to the `configure` command; some are necessary to enable important features such as database interaction, regular expressions, file compression support, web server integration, and so on. All of the possible configure options are listed when you run this command:

```
[user@local php-7.2.0]$ ./configure --help
```

A minimal command may also be used, but be aware that many features will be missing. If you wish to include other components, additional dependencies may be needed, but they are not documented here. In all cases, the `--enable-fpm` switch should be included:

```
[user@local php-7.2.0]$ ./configure --enable-fpm [...]
```

The next step is to build the application and install it at the same time:

```
[user@local php-7.2.0]$ make && make install
```

This process may take a while depending on your system specifications. Take note of (some of) the information given to you during the build process. If you did not specify the location of the compiled binaries and configuration files, they will be revealed to you at the end of this step.

Post-install configuration

Begin by configuring your newly installed PHP, for example, by copying the `php.ini` of your previous setup over the new one.

 Due to the way Nginx forwards script files and request information to PHP, a security breach might be caused by the use of the `cgi.fix_pathinfo=1` configuration option. It is highly recommended that you set this option to `0` in your `php.ini` file. For more information about this particular security issue, please consult the following article:
http://cnedelcu.blogspot.in/2010/05/nginx-php-via-fastcgi-important.html

The next step is to configure PHP-FPM. Open up the `php-fpm.conf` file, which is located in `/usr/local/php/etc/` by default. We cannot detail all aspects of the PHP-FPM configuration here (they are largely documented in the configuration file itself anyway), but there are important configuration directives that you shouldn't miss:

- Edit the user(s) and group(s) used by the worker processes and optionally the UNIX sockets
- Address(es) and port(s) on which PHP-FPM will be listening
- Number of simultaneous requests that will be served
- IP address(es) allowed to connect to PHP-FPM

Running and controlling

Once you have made the appropriate changes to the PHP-FPM configuration file, you may start it with the following command (the file paths may vary depending on your build configuration):

```
[user@local ~]# /usr/local/php/sbin/php-fpm -c /usr/local/php/etc/php.ini -
-pid /var/run/php-fpm.pid --fpm-config=/usr/local/php/etc/php-fpm.conf -D
```

The preceding command includes several important arguments:

- `-c /usr/local/php/etc/php.ini` sets the path of the PHP configuration file
- `--pid /var/run/php-fpm.pid` sets the path of the PID file, which can be useful to control the process via an init script
- `--fpm-config=/usr/local/php/etc/php-fpm.conf` forces PHP-FPM to use the specified configuration file
- `-D` daemonize PHP-FPM (ensures it runs in the background)

Other command-line arguments can be obtained by running `php-fpm -h`.

> Stopping PHP-FPM can be done via the `kill` or `killall` commands. Alternatively, you may use an init script to start and stop the process, provided the version of PHP you installed came with one.

Nginx configuration

If you have managed to configure and start PHP-FPM correctly, you are ready to tweak your Nginx configuration file to establish the connection between both parties. The following server block is a simple, valid template on which you can base your own website configuration:

```
server {
    server_name .website.com; # server name, accepting www
    listen 80; # listen on port 80
    root /home/website/www; # our root document path
    index index.php; # default request filename: index.php

    location ~* \.php$ { # for requests ending with .php
        # specify the listening address and port that you configured
previously
        fastcgi_pass 127.0.0.1:9000;
        # the document path to be passed to PHP-FPM
```

```
        fastcgi_param SCRIPT_FILENAME $document_root$fastcgi_script_name;
        # the script filename to be passed to PHP-FPM
        fastcgi_param PATH_INFO $fastcgi_script_name;
        # include other FastCGI related configuration settings
        include fastcgi_params;
    }
}
```

After saving the configuration file, reload Nginx using one of the following commands:

```
/usr/local/nginx/sbin/nginx -s reload
Or:
service nginx reload
```

Create a simple script at the root of your website to make sure PHP is being correctly interpreted:

```
[user@local ~]# echo "<?php phpinfo(); ?>" >/home/website/www/index.php
```

Fire up your favorite web browser and load http://localhost/ (or your website URL). You should see something similar to the following screenshot, which is the PHP server information page:

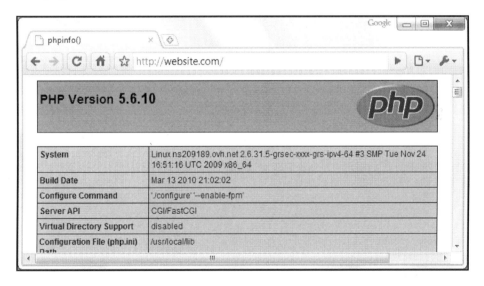

Note that you may run into the occasional 403 forbidden HTTP error, if the file and directory access permissions are not properly configured. If that is the case, make sure that you specified the correct user and group in the php-fpm.conf file and that the directory and files are readable by PHP.

Python and Nginx

Python is a popular object-oriented programming language available on many platforms, from Unix-based systems to Windows. It is also available for Java and the Microsoft .NET platform. If you are interested in configuring Python to work with Nginx, it's likely that you already have a clear idea of what Python does. We are going to use Python as a server-side web programming language, with the help of the Django framework.

Django

Django is an open source web development framework for Python that aims at making web development simple and easy, as its slogan states:

> *The Web framework for perfectionists with deadlines.*

More information is available on the project website at `https://www.djangoproject.com/`.

Among other interesting features, such as a dynamic administrative interface, a caching framework, and unit tests, Django comes with a FastCGI manager. It's going to make things much simpler for us from the perspective of running Python scripts through Nginx.

Setting up Python and Django

We will now install Python and Django on your Linux operating system, along with its prerequisites. The process is relatively smooth and mostly consists of running a couple of commands that rarely cause trouble.

Python

Python should be available on your package manager repositories. To install it, run the following commands. For Red Hat-based systems and other systems using `yum` as the package manager, use:

```
[root@local ~]# yum install python python-devel
```

For Ubuntu, Debian, and other systems that use `apt` or `aptitude`, use:

```
[root@local ~]# aptitude install python python-dev
```

The package manager will resolve dependencies by itself.

Django

In order to install Django, we will use a different approach (although you could skip this entirely and just install it from your usual repositories). We will be downloading the framework with PIP, a tool which simplifies the installation of Python packages. Therefore, the first step is to install PIP: for Red Hat-based systems and other systems using yum as the package manager, execute the following command:

```
[root@local ~]# yum install python-pip
```

For Ubuntu, Debian, and other systems that use Apt or Aptitude, use:

```
[root@local ~]# apt-get install python-pip
```

The package manager will resolve dependencies by itself. Once PIP is installed, run the following command to download and install Django 1.8.2, the latest stable version to date:

```
[root@website.com ~]# pip install Django==1.8.2
[...]
[root@website.com ~]# pip install -e django-trunk/
```

Finally, there is one last component required to run the Python FastCGI manager: the flup library. This provides the actual FastCGI protocol implementation. For Red Hat-based systems and other systems using yum as the package manager (EPEL repositories must be enabled, otherwise you will need to build from source), use:

```
[root@local ~]# yum install python-flup
```

For Ubuntu, Debian, and other systems that use Apt or Aptitude, use:

```
[root@local ~]# aptitude install python-flup
```

Starting the FastCGI process manager

The process of beginning to build a website with the Django framework is as simple as running the following command:

```
[root@website.com ~]# django-admin startproject mysite
```

Once that part is done, you will find a manage.py Python script that comes with the default project template. Open the newly created mysite directory containing manage.py, and run the following command:

```
[root@website.com mysite]# python manage.py runfcgi method=prefork
host=127.0.0.1 port=9000 pidfile=/var/run/django.pid
```

If everything was correctly configured, and the dependencies are properly installed, running this command should produce no output, which is often a good sign. The FastCGI process manager is now running in the background waiting for connections. You can verify that the application is running with the ps command (for example, by executing ps aux | grep python). If you don't see any running process, try changing the previous command slightly by selecting a different port. All we need to do now is to set up the virtual host in the Nginx configuration file.

Nginx configuration

The Nginx configuration is similar to the PHP one:

```
server {
    server_name .website.com;
listen 80;
# Insert the path of your Python project public files below
    root /home/website/www;
    index index.html;

    location / {
        fastcgi_pass 127.0.0.1:9000;
        fastcgi_param SCRIPT_FILENAME  $document_root$fastcgi_script_name;
        fastcgi_param PATH_INFO $fastcgi_script_name;
        include fastcgi_params;
    }
}
```

Summary

Whether you use PHP, Python, or any other CGI application, you should now have a clear idea of how to get your scripts processed behind Nginx. There are all sorts of implementations on the web for mainstream programming languages and the FastCGI protocol. Due to its efficiency, it is starting to replace server-integrated solutions such as Apache's mod_php, mod_wsgi, among others.

If you are unsure about connecting Nginx directly to those server applications, because you already have a well-functioning system architecture in place (for example, Apache with mod_php), you may want to consider the option offered in chapter 7, Running *Nginx and Apache together.*

6
Nginx as an Application Server

The web has traditionally consisted of, relatively speaking, simple websites. The past few years have seen that change, though. The modern web consists as much of complex SaaS applications as it does of personal blogs, news sites, and so on. As the web evolves, so does the list of technologies used to power these applications. No longer is it enough to just be a fast static file server with a FastCGI interface. These days we need to consider technologies such as web sockets, as well the expanded complexity of web application architectures and the demands they put on the front line of our web stack.

Thankfully, Nginx was originally built, not only as a fast static file server but also as a reverse proxy. This means that Nginx was always intended to sit in front of other backend servers, and farm out requests to different servers on the internal network and serve up the response to the end user.

In this chapter, we will take a look at the basics of how to do this with Nginx, but also at some of the more advanced things Nginx can do to make our life easier.

The reverse proxy mechanism

Running Nginx as an application server is somewhat like the **FastCGI architecture** described in the previous chapter; we are going to be running Nginx as a frontend server, and for the most part, reverse proxy requests to our backend servers.

In other words, it will be in direct communication with the outside world whereas our backend servers, whether Node.js, Apache, and so on, will only exchange data with Nginx:

There are now two web servers running and processing requests:

- Nginx positioned as a frontend server (in other words, as reverse proxy), receives all the requests coming from the outside world. It filters them, either serving static files directly to the client or forwarding dynamic content requests to our backend server.
- Our backend backend server only communicates with Nginx. It may be hosted on the same computer as the frontend, in which case, the listening port must be edited to leave port 80 available to Nginx. Alternatively, you can employ multiple backend servers on different machines and load balance between themselves.

To communicate and interact with each other, neither processes will be using FastCGI. Instead, as the name suggests, Nginx acts as a simple proxy server, it receives HTTP requests from the client (acting as HTTP server) and forwards them to the backend server (acting as HTTP client). There is thus no new protocol or software involved. The mechanism is handled by the proxy module of Nginx, as detailed later in this chapter.

Nginx proxy module

Similar to the previous chapter, the first step towards establishing the new architecture will be to discover the appropriate module. The default Nginx build comes with the proxy module, which allows forwarding of HTTP requests from the client to a backend server. We will be configuring multiple aspects of the module:

- Basic address and port information of the backend server
- Caching, buffering, and temporary file options
- Limits, timeout, and error behavior
- Other miscellaneous options

All these options are available via directives which we will learn to configure throughout this section.

Main directives

The first set of directives will allow you to establish a basic configuration such as the location of the backend server, information to be passed, and how it should be passed:

Directive	Description

proxy_pass
Context: `location, if`
	Specifies that the request should be forwarded to the backend server by indicating its location:
	• For regular HTTP forwarding, the syntax is `proxy_pass http://hostname:port;`
	• For Unix domain sockets, the syntax is `proxy_pass http://unix:/path/to/file.socket;`
	• You may also refer to upstream blocks `proxy_pass http://myblock;`
	• Instead of `http://`, you can use `https://` for secure traffic. Additional URI parts as well as the use of variables are allowed.
	Examples:
	• `proxy_pass http://localhost:8080;`
	• `proxy_pass http://127.0.0.1:8080;`
	• `proxy_pass http://unix:/tmp/nginx.sock;`
	• `proxy_pass https://192.168.0.1;`
	• `proxy_pass http://localhost:8080/uri/;`
	• `proxy_pass http://unix:/tmp/nginx.sock:/uri/;`
	• `proxy_pass http://$server_name:8080;`
	Using an upstream block:
	<pre>upstream backend {
	    server 127.0.0.1:8080;
	    server 127.0.0.1:8081;
	}
	location ~* .php$
	{
	    proxy_pass http://backend;
	}</pre>

Directive	Description
`proxy_method` Context: `http`, `server`, `location`	Allows the overriding of the HTTP method of the request to be forwarded to the backend server. If you specify `POST`, for example, all requests forwarded to the backend server will be `POST` requests. Syntax: `proxy_method method;` Example: `proxy_method POST;`
`proxy_hide_header` Context: `http`, `server`, `location`	By default, as Nginx prepares the response received from the backend server to be forwarded back to the client, it ignores some of the headers, such as `Date`, `Server`, `X-Pad`, and `X-Accel-*`. With this directive, you can specify an additional header line to be hidden from the client. You may insert this directive multiple times with one header name for each. Syntax: `proxy_hide_header header_name;` Example: `proxy_hide_header Cache-Control;`
`proxy_pass_header` Context: `http`, `server`, `location`	Related to the previous directive, this directive forces some of the ignored headers to be passed on to the client. Syntax: `proxy_pass_header headername;` Example: `proxy_pass_header Date;`

`proxy_pass_request_body`
`proxy_pass_request_headers`
Context: `http`, `server`, `location`
	Defines whether or not, respectively, the request body and extra request headers should be passed on to the backend server.
	Syntax: `on` or `off`;
	Default: `on`

Directive	Description
proxy_redirect Context: http, server, location	Allows you to rewrite the URL appearing in the Location HTTP header on redirections triggered by the backend server. Syntax: off, default, or the URL of your choice off: Redirections are forwarded *as it is*. default: The value of the proxy_pass directive is used as the hostname and the current path of the document is appended. Note that the proxy_redirect directive must be inserted after the proxy_pass directive as the configuration is parsed sequentially. URL: Replace a part of the URL by another. Additionally, you may use variables in the rewritten URL. Examples: • proxy_redirect off; • proxy_redirect default; • proxy_redirect http://localhost:8080/ http://example.com/; • proxy_redirect http://localhost:8080/wiki/ /w/; • proxy_redirect http://localhost:8080/ http://$host/;

Directive	Description
`proxy_next_upstream` Context: `http, server, location`	When `proxy_pass` is connected to an upstream block, this directive defines the cases where requests should be abandoned and resent to the next upstream server of the block. The directive accepts a combination of values among the following: • `error`: An error occurred while communicating or attempting to communicate with the server • `timeout`: A timeout occurs during transfers or connection attempts • `invalid_header`: The backend server returned an empty or invalid response • `http_500, http_502, http_503, http_504, http_40:` In case such HTTP errors occur, Nginx switches to the next upstream • `off`: Forbids you from using the next upstream server Examples: • `proxy_next_upstream error timeout http_504;` • `proxy_next_upstream timeout invalid_header;`
`proxy_next_upstream_timeout` Context: `http, server, location`	Defines the timeout to be used in conjunction with `proxy_next_upstream`. Setting this directive to `0` disables it. Syntax: Time value (in seconds)
`proxy_next_upstream_tries` Context: `http, server, location`	Defines the maximum number of upstream servers tried before returning an error message, to be used in conjunction with `proxy_next_upstream`. Syntax: Numeric value (default: `0`)

Caching, buffering, and temporary files

Ideally, as much as possible, you should reduce the amount of requests being forwarded to the backend server. The following directive will help you build a caching system, as well as control buffering options and the way Nginx handles temporary files:

Directive	Description
proxy_buffer_size Context: http, server, location	Sets the size of the buffer for reading the beginning of the response from the backend server, which usually contains simple header data. The default value corresponds to the size of 1 buffer, as defined by the previous directive (proxy_buffers). Syntax: Numeric value (size) Example: proxy_buffer_size 4k;
proxy_buffering, proxy_request_buffering Context: http, server, location	Defines whether or not the response from the backend server should be buffered (or client requests, in the case of proxy_request_buffering). If set to on, Nginx will store the response data in memory using the memory space offered by the buffers. If the buffers are full, the response data will be stored as a temporary file. If the directive is set to off, the response is directly forwarded to the client. Syntax: on or off Default: on
proxy_buffers Context: http, server, location	Sets the amount and size of buffers that will be used for reading the response data from the backend server. Syntax: proxy_buffers amount size; Default: 8 buffers, 4k or 8k each depending on platform Example: fastcgi_buffers 8 4k;
proxy_busy_buffers_size Context: http, server, location	When the backend-received data accumulated in buffers exceeds the specified value, buffers are flushed and data is sent to the client. Syntax: Numeric value (size) Default: 2 * proxy_buffer_size
proxy_cache Context: http, server, location	Defines a cache zone. The identifier given to the zone is to be reused in further directives. Syntax: proxy_cache zonename; Example: proxy_cache cache1;

Directive	Description
`proxy_cache_key` Context: `http, server, location`	This directive defines the cache key, in other words, it differentiates one cache entry from another. If the cache key is set to `$uri`, as a result, all requests with this `$uri` will work as a single cache entry. But that's not enough for most dynamic websites. You also need to include the query string arguments in the cache key, so that `/index.php` and `/index.php?page=contact` do not point to the same cache entry. Syntax: `proxy_cache_key key;` Example: `proxy_cache_key` `"$scheme$host$request_uri $cookie_user";`

`proxy_cache_path`
Context: `http`
	Indicates the directory for storing cached files, as well as other parameters.
	Syntax: `proxy_cache_path path`
	`[use_temp_path=on|off] [levels=numbers`
	`keys_zone=name:size inactive=time`
	`max_size=size];`
	The additional parameters are:
	• `use_temp_path`: Set this flag to `on` if you want to use the path defined via the `proxy_temp_path` directive
	• `levels`: Indicates the depth level of subdirectories (usually *1:2* is enough)
	• `keys_zone`: Lets you make use of the zone you previously declared with the `proxy_cache` directive and indicates the size to occupy in memory
	• `inactive`: If a cached response is not used within the specified time frame, it is removed from the cache
	• `max_size`: Defines the maximum size of the entire cache
	Example: `proxy_cache_path /tmp/nginx_cache`
	`levels=1:2 zone=zone1:10m inactive=10m`
	`max_size=200M;`

Directive	Description
proxy_cache_methods Context: http, server, location	Defines the HTTP methods eligible for caching. GET and HEAD are included by default and cannot be disabled. Syntax: proxy_cache_methods METHOD; Example: proxy_cache_methods OPTIONS;
proxy_cache_min_uses Context: http, server, location	Defines the minimum amount of hits before a request is eligible for caching. By default, the response of a request is cached after one hit (next requests with the same cache key will receive the cached response). Syntax: Numeric value Example: proxy_cache_min_uses 1;
proxy_cache_valid Context: http, server, location	This directive allows you to customize the caching time for different kinds of response codes. You may cache responses associated with 404 error codes for 1 minute, and on the opposite cache, 200 OK responses for 10 minutes or more. This directive can be inserted more than once: • proxy_cache_valid 404 1m; • proxy_cache_valid 500 502 504 5m; • proxy_cache_valid 200 10; Syntax: proxy_cache_valid code1 [code2...] time;
proxy_cache_use_stale Context: http, server, location	Defines whether or not Nginx should serve stale cached data in certain circumstances (in regard to the gateway). If you use proxy_cache_use_stale timeout, and if the gateway times out, then Nginx will serve cached data. Syntax: proxy_cache_use_stale [updating] [error] [timeout] [invalid_header] [http_500]; Example: proxy_cache_use_stale error timeout;

Directive	Description
`proxy_max_temp_file_size` Context: `http, server, location`	Set this directive to `0` to disable the use of temporary files for requests eligible to proxy forwarding or specify a maximum file size. Syntax: Size value Default value: 1 GB Example: `proxy_max_temp_file_size 5m;`
`proxy_temp_file_write_size` Context: `http, server, location`	Sets the write buffer size when saving temporary files to the storage device. Syntax: Size value Default value: `2 * proxy_buffer_size`
`proxy_temp_path` Context: `http, server, location`	Sets the path of temporary and cache store files. Syntax: `proxy_temp_path path [level1 [level2...]]` Examples: • `proxy_temp_path /tmp/nginx_proxy;` • `proxy_temp_path /tmp/cache 1 2;`

Limits, timeouts, and errors

The following directives will help you define timeout behavior, as well as various limitations regarding communications with the backend server:

Directive	Description
`proxy_connect_timeout` Context: `http, server, location`	Defines the backend server connection timeout. This is different from the read/send timeout. If Nginx is already connected to the backend server, the `proxy_connect_timeout` is not applicable. Syntax: `Time value` (in seconds) Example: `proxy_connect_timeout 15;`
`proxy_read_timeout` Context: `http, server, location`	The timeout for reading data from the backend server. This timeout isn't applied to the entire response delay but between two read operations instead. Syntax: `Time value` (in seconds) Default value: `60` Example: `proxy_read_timeout 60;`

Directive	Description
proxy_send_timeout Context: http, server, location	This timeout is for sending data to the backend server. The timeout isn't applied to the entire response delay but between two write operations instead. Syntax: Time value (in seconds) Default value: 60 Example: proxy_send_timeout 60;
proxy_ignore_client_abort Context: http, server, location	If set to on, Nginx will continue processing the proxy request, even if the client aborts its request. In the other case (off), when the client aborts its request, Nginx also aborts its request to the backend server. Default value: off
proxy_intercept_errors Context: http, server, location	By default, Nginx returns all error pages (HTTP status code 400 and higher) sent by the backend server directly to the client. If you set this directive to on, the error code is parsed and can be matched against the values specified in the error_page directive. Default value: off
proxy_send_lowat Context: http, server, location	An option allowing you to make use of the SO_SNDLOWAT flag for TCP sockets under BSD-based operating systems only. This value defines the minimum number of bytes in the buffer for output operations. Syntax: Numeric value (size) Default value: 0
proxy_limit_rate Context: http, server, location	Allows you to limit the rate at which Nginx downloads the response from the backend proxy. Syntax: Numeric value (bytes per second)

SSL-related directives

If you are going to be working with SSL backend servers, the following directives will be useful to you.

Directive	Description
`proxy_ssl_certificate` Context: `http, server, location`	Sets the path of a PEM file that contains a certificate for authentication to an SSL backend. Syntax: File path Default value: None
`proxy_ssl_certificate_key` Context: `http, server, location`	Sets the path of the secret key file (PEM format) for authentication to an SSL backend. Syntax: File path Default value: None
`proxy_ssl_ciphers` Context: `http, server, location`	Sets the ciphers for SSL communication with the backend server. Run the following shell command to get the list of available ciphers on your server: `openssl ciphers`. Syntax: Cipher names Default value: `DEFAULT`
`proxy_ssl_crl` Context: `http, server, location`	Sets the path of the **CRL (Certificate Revocation List)** file in PEM format, allowing Nginx to verify the revocation state of the backend server's SSL certificate. Syntax: File path Default value: –
`proxy_ssl_name` Context: `http, server, location`	Use this directive to override the server name when verifying the revocation state of the backend server's SSL certificate. Syntax: Character string Default value: `equal to $proxy_host`
`proxy_ssl_password_file` Context: `http, server, location`	Sets the path of a file containing passphrases (one per line) which are tried in turn when loading the certificate key. Syntax: File path Default value: –

Directive	Description
`proxy_ssl_server_name` Context: `http, server, location`	If you set this directive to `on` (as it is `off` by default) your server name will be communicated to the backend server as per the SNI (Server Name Indication) protocol. Syntax: `on` or `off` Default value: `off`
`proxy_ssl_session_reuse` Context: `http, server, location`	This directive instructs Nginx to reuse existing SSL sessions when communicating with the backend (thus reducing overhead). The official documentation recommends disabling this if the following errors start to show up in server logs: `SSL3_GET_FINISHED:digest check failed` Syntax: `on` or `off` Default value: `on`
`proxy_ssl_protocols` Context: `http, server, location`	Sets the protocols to be used when communicating with SSL backends. Syntax: `proxy_ssl_protocols [SSLv2] [SSLv3] [TLSv1] [TLSv1.1] [TLSv1.2];` Default value: `TLSv1 TLSv1.1 TLSv1.2`
`proxy_ssl_trusted_certificate` Context: `http, server, location`	Sets the path of your trusted CA certificates (in PEM format). Syntax: `file path` Default value: –
`proxy_ssl_verify` Context: `http, server, location`	If set to `on`, Nginx will verify the certificate of the SSL backend server. Syntax: `on` or `off` Default value: `off`
`proxy_ssl_verify_depth` Context: `http, server, location`	If the `proxy_ssl_verify` directive is set to `on`, this sets the certificate chain verification depth. Syntax: `Numeric value` Default value: `1`

Other directives

Finally, the last set of directives available in the proxy module is uncategorized and is as follows:

Directive	Description
`proxy_headers_hash_max_size` Context: `http`, `server`, `location`	Sets the maximum size for the proxy header's hash tables. Syntax: Numeric value Default value: `512`
`proxy_headers_hash_bucket_size` Context: `http`, `server`, `location`	Sets the bucket size for the proxy header's hash tables. Syntax: Numeric value Default value: `64`
`proxy_force_ranges` Context: `http`, `server`, `location`	When set to `on`, Nginx will enable byte-range support on responses from the backend proxy. Syntax: `on` or `off` Default value: `off`
`proxy_ignore_headers` Context: `http`, `server`, `location`	Prevents Nginx from processing one of the following four headers from the backend server response: `X-Accel-Redirect`, `X-Accel-Expires`, `Expires`, and `Cache-Control`. Syntax: `proxy_ignore_headers header1 [header2...];`
`proxy_set_body` Context: `http`, `server`, `location`	Allows you to set a static request body for debugging purposes. Variables may be used in the directive value. Syntax: String value (any value) Example: `proxy_set_body test;`
`proxy_set_header` Context: `http`, `server`, `location`	This directive allows you to redefine header values to be transferred to the backend server. It can be declared multiple times. Syntax: `proxy_set_header Header Value;` Example: `proxy_set_header Host $host;`
`proxy_store` Context: `http`, `server`, `location`	Specifies whether or not the backend server response should be stored as a file. Stored response files can be reused for serving other requests. Possible values: `on`, `off`, or a path relative to the document root (or alias). You may also set this to `on` and define the `proxy_temp_path` directive. Examples: • `proxy_store on;` • `proxy_temp_path /temp/store;`
`proxy_store_access` Context: `http`, `server`, `location`	This directive defines file access permissions for the stored response files. Syntax: `proxy_store_access [user:[r|w|rw]][group:[r|w|rw]][all:[r|w|rw]];` Example: `proxy_store_access user:rw group:rw all:r;`
`proxy_http_version` Context: `http`, `server`, `location`	Sets the HTTP version to be used for communicating with the proxy backend. HTTP `1.0` is the default value, but if you are going to enable keepalive connections, you might want to set this directive to `1.1`. Syntax: `proxy_http_version 1.0	1.1;`
`proxy_cookie_domain` `proxy_cookie_path` Context: `http`, `server`, `location`	Applies an on-the-fly modification to the domain or path attributes of a cookie (case insensitive). Syntaxes: • `proxy_cookie_domain off	domain replacement;` • `proxy_cookie_path off	domain replacement;`

Variables

The proxy module offers several variables that can be inserted in various locations, for example, in the `proxy_set_header` directive or in the logging-related directives such as `log_format`. The available variables are:

- `$proxy_host`: Contains the hostname of the backend server used for the current request.
- `$proxy_port`: Contains the port of the backend server used for the current request.
- `$proxy_add_x_forwarded_for`: This variable contains the value of the X-Forwarded-For request header, followed by the remote address of the client. Both values are separated by a comma. If the X-Forwarded-For request header is unavailable, the variable only contains the client remote address.
- `$proxy_internal_body_length`: Length of the request body (set with the `proxy_set_body` directive or 0).

Nginx and microservices

Now that we've explored the proxy module in depth, it's time to have a look at what a modern web application architecture might look like. There are entire books dedicated to this topic but we only really need to know how Nginx can enable various setups, and the Nginx part doesn't differ too much between different setups.

For any given task that we need our application to do we have two options, we can either proxy to a backend server like Node.js and have that handle the work, or we can implement it directly in Nginx. Which option you go with depends on a lot of factors, but the two main factors to consider are speed and complexity.

Proxying to a complex backend server has an overhead cost but usually allows you to code reusability and to use package managers such as Packagist and NPM. Conversely, implementing a feature in Nginx puts us closer to the user so we have less overhead but the development itself also becomes more difficult.

Most setups will choose to proxy to a backend for simplicity. An example of a feature implemented in Nginx would be Cloudflare and their proxy/CDN service. Since they deal with a huge scale of requests and response time is critical to them, they have implemented their security filtering (web application firewall) directly in Nginx using a module to add Lua support in the Nginx config file.

Cloudflare has hundreds of developers, including people who have worked on the core part of Nginx code before, so don't expect to quite reach their level, but there are also simpler scenarios where Nginx can implement part of the application logic.

For example, it's possible to use **Server Side Includes** (**SSIs**) to instruct Nginx to fill in part of a page with information fetched directly from a cache server such as Memcached or Redis, bypassing the backend server.

A simple example of application logic in Nginx is to move out cache from inside our backend server to Nginx itself. In the following example, we're checking Memcached for a cached version of a page and only if we don't find it, do we proxy to our application backend:

```
# Check cache and use PHP as a fallback.
location ~* \.php$ {
    default_type text/html;
    charset utf-8;

    if ($request_method = GET) {
        set $memcached_key $request_uri;

        memcached_pass memcached;
        error_page 404 502 = @nocache;
    }

    if ($request_method != GET) {
        fastcgi_pass backend;
    }
}

location @nocache {
    fastcgi_pass backend;
}
```

When we go into more advanced logic, using just the standard Nginx configuration format gets a bit complicated. Thankfully, Nginx has recently shipped a custom JavaScript-based scripting language called **nginScript** that we can use to more efficiently implement logic.

nginScript

nginScript (pronounced engine script) is essentially a subset of ECMA 5.1 JavaScript with a few ECMA 6.0 extensions implemented. It is available in two versions, `ngx_http_js_module` for standard HTTP usage and `ngx_stream_js_module` for TCP stream usage. Make sure one or both of these are included in your Nginx compile, if you're not sure, you can check by using `nginx -V | grep js_module` in a terminal or by seeing if your main configuration file is loading either module dynamically.

nginScript works by implementing handlers that are passed two arguments, the client request and the client response. This allows you full access to the HTTP request to access and manipulate data. Additionally, nginScript allows you to assign nginScript function output to normal Nginx variables that can be used with the standard directives:

```
js_include http.js;

js_set $foo foo; // Function implemented in http.js
js_set $summary summary; // Function implemented in http.js

server {
    listen 8000;

    location / {
        add_header X-Foo $foo;
        js_content bar; // Function implemented in http.js
    }

    location /summary {
        return 200 $summary;
    }
}
```

We'll have a closer look at what the `http.js` file might look like later on, for now, let's quickly have a look at what parts of JavaScript are supported and which are not.

Supported features

The following are the JavaScript supported features. They can be classified into General, String methods, Object methods, and Array methods:

General:

- Boolean values, numbers, strings, objects, arrays, functions, and regular expressions
- ES5.1 operators, ES7 exponentiation operators
- ES5.1 statements are `var`, `if`, `else`, `switch`, `for`, `for in`, `while`, `do while`, `break`, `continue`, `return`, `try`, `catch`, `throw`, and `finally`
- ES6 number and math properties and methods
- ES5.1 function methods are `call`, `apply`, and `bind`
- ES5.1 RegExp methods are `test`, and `exec`
- ES5.1 Date methods
- ES5.1 JSON objects
- ES5.1 global functions are `isFinite`, `isNaN`, `parseFloat`, `parseInt`, `decodeURI`, `decodeURIComponent`, `encodeURI`, and `encodeURIComponent`
- Error objects are `Error`, `EvalError`, `InternalError`, `RangeError`, `ReferenceError`, `SyntaxError`, `TypeError`, and `URIError`
- File system methods (Node.js-style) are `fs.readFile`, `fs.readFileSync`, `fs.appendFile`, `fs.appendFileSync`, `fs.writeFile`, and `fs.writeFileSync`

String methods:

- **ES5.1**: `fromCharCode`, `concat`, `slice`, `substring`, `substr`, `charAt`, `charCodeAt`, `indexOf`, `lastIndexOf`, `toLowerCase`, `toUpperCase`, `trim`, `search`, `match`, `split`, and `replace`
- **ES6**: `fromCodePoint`, `codePointAt`, `includes`, `startsWith`, `endsWith`, and **repeat non-standard**: `fromUTF8`, `toUTF8`, `fromBytes`, and `toBytes`

Object methods:

- **ES5.1**: `create` (support without properties list), `keys`, `defineProperty`, `defineProperties`, `getOwnPropertyDescriptor`, `getPrototypeOf`, `hasOwnProperty`, `isPrototypeOf`, `preventExtensions`, `isExtensible`, `freeze`, `isFrozen`, `seal`, `isSealed`

Array methods:

- **ES5.1**: `isArray`, `slice`, `splice`, `push`, `pop`, `unshift`, `shift`, `reverse`, `sort`, `join`, `concat`, `indexOf`, `lastIndexOf`, `forEach`, `some`, `every`, `filter`, `map`, `reduce`, `reduceRight`
- **ES6**: `of`, `fill`, `find`, `findIndex`
- **ES7**: `includes`

Unsupported features

Some of the features that are not supported are:

- ES6 `let` and `const` declarations
- Labels
- Arguments array
- Eval function
- `setTimeout`, `setInterval`, `setImmediate` functions
- Non-integer fractions (`.235`), binary literals (`0b0101`)

Main directives

nginScript adds three new directives we can use to interface between the Nginx configuration and the JavaScript part:

Directive	Description
`js_include` Context: `http`	Includes a nginScript file that implements the various handlers. Each handler is passed two arguments. A client request with the following properties: • `uri`: current URI in a request, read-only • `method`: request method, read-only • `httpVersion`: HTTP version, read-only • `remoteAddress`: client address, read-only • `headers{}`: request headers object, read-only • `args{}`: request arguments object, read-only • `variables{}`: nginx variables object, read-only • `log(string)`: function for writing a string to the error log A client response with the following properties: • `status`: response status, writable • `headers{}`: response headers object • `contentType`: the response "Content-Type" header field value, writable • `contentLength`: the response "Content-Length" header field value, writable • `sendHeader()`: function for sending the HTTP header to the client • `send(string)`: function for sending a part of the response body to the client • `finish()`: function for finishing sending a response to the client Syntax: `file` Default value: –

Directive	Description
`js_content` Context: `location, limit_except`	Sets a function as a content handler. This directive is used to send the client response to the user directly from Nginx. Syntax: `function` Default value: –
`js_set` Context: `http`	Sets an nginScript function as callback for a specific variable. Syntax: `$variable function` Default value: –

Handler example

Let's have a quick look at what an example handler could look like to give you an idea of the syntax:

```
function foo(req, res) {
    req.log("hello from foo() handler");
    return "foo";
}

function summary(req, res) {
    var a, s, h;

    s = "JS summary\n\n";

    s += "Method: " + req.method + "\n";
    s += "HTTP version: " + req.httpVersion + "\n";
    s += "Host: " + req.headers.host + "\n";
    s += "Remote Address: " + req.remoteAddress + "\n";
    s += "URI: " + req.uri + "\n";

    s += "Headers:\n";
    for (h in req.headers) {
        s += " header '" + h + "' is '" + req.headers[h] + "'\n";
    }

    s += "Args:\n";
    for (a in req.args) {
        s += " arg '" + a + "' is '" + req.args[a] + "'\n";
    }

    return s;
```

```
    }

function bar(req, res) {
    res.headers.foo = 1234;
    res.status = 200;
    res.contentType = "text/plain; charset=utf-8";
    res.contentLength = 15;
    res.sendHeader();
    res.send("nginx");
    res.send("java");
    res.send("script");

    res.finish();
}
```

Nginx Unit

Where nginScript allows us to implement logic in Nginx itself, Unit helps us manage the potentially complex ecosystem of backend services.

A typical microservice architecture usually consists of many distributed services, to just mention a few potentials:

- Frontend servers
- Backend servers, potentially multiple languages
- Database servers
- Caching servers
- Search daemon servers
- Job servers and workers

Managing these servers, keeping Nginx configuration updated as well as managing load balancing and IPs quickly becomes a pain.

This is where Nginx Unit comes in. Unit is an open source application server designed to lessen the pain of managing a highly distributed architecture. This includes managing configurations of programming languages, networking and dynamically managing the proxying and load balancing to backends.

Essentially, Nginx Unit provides a programmatic way to manage (parts of) your backend infrastructure, providing an API for changing your backend configuration or even changing PHP versions.

Nginx Unit is currently a beta product so not yet fully featured. Currently, it supports the following languages:

- PHP (5 and 7)
- Python (2.7 and 3)
- Go

With the following are coming soon:

- JavaScript/Node.js
- Java
- Ruby

What makes Nginx Unit worth keeping an eye on is how it integrates with Nginx and takes care of the network management. With Unit, it becomes possible to abstract your backend infrastructure behind a single IP:

```
upstream unit_backend {
    server 127.0.0.1:8300;
}

server {
    location / {
        root /var/www/static-data;
    }

    location ~ \.php$ {
        proxy_pass http://unit_backend;
        proxy_set_header Host $host;
    }
}
```

If a new server gets deployed, simply have the deploy script call the Unit API to add itself to the pool of servers and Unit will automatically add it to the load balancing. This is a far cleaner approach than managing the backend IPs inside the Nginx config file.

Nginx Unit can be found at http://unit.nginx.org/.

Summary

In this chapter, we had a look at how reverse proxying works and how Nginx fits into the modern picture of microservices and complex web applications; both in the sense of enabling the microservice architecture but also in the sense of building application logic directly into Nginx.

This chapter should have given you an idea of the possibilities that Nginx provides as an application server, and hopefully clarified the complexity/speed trade-off of implementing logic in Nginx.

7
Apache and Nginx Together

A lot of the administrators interested in Nginx are people who have encountered issues with the former: slowdowns, complexity to configure, lack of responsivity at times, and a variety of other problems. Consequently, the first idea that comes to mind is to replace **Apache** with another web server, such as Nginx. However, there is an alternative that is not often considered, as it sounds a little far-fetched at first: running both Nginx and Apache at the same time. When you look into it, this solution offers a great deal of advantages, especially for administrators looking for a quick and efficient solution to the aforementioned issues.

The topics covered in the chapter are:

- How Nginx and Apache benefit from each other
- Configuring Apache and Nginx
- Improving the reverse proxy architecture

How Nginx and Apache benefit from each other

As we've seen in the previous chapters, Nginx works well as a reverse proxy to many modern web environments, such as Node.js and PHP, interfacing directly with those environments with no middleman in between. However, there are also many older technologies that focused on deep integration into Apache HTTPd, and removing Apache from the equation can be non-trivial.

If possible, removing Apache HTTPd is usually the desired approach, for the simple fact that it gives you fewer things to maintain and keep updated. However, given the immense amount of modules for Apache, it's impossible for all of them to be ported, so even if this is not possible, using Nginx and Apache together can still bring benefits for us.

The main purpose of setting up Nginx as a frontend server and giving Apache a backend role is to improve the serving speed. As we established, a lot of requests coming from clients are for static files, and static files are served much faster by Nginx. The overall performance sharply improves on both the client side and the server side.

The good aspect of this approach is how easy it is to set up, as nearly no modification is required when it comes to Apache configuration. All it takes is a simple port change, but that isn't even necessary if you set up Nginx and Apache on different servers. Your setup works as-is, which is particularly useful if you've already spent hours configuring Apache to work with server-side preprocessors, such as PHP, Python, Java, or others.

Adding Nginx as a reverse proxy in front of Apache takes some work, but in a reverse-proxy scenario, it is mostly about telling Nginx which requests it can serve directly and which it needs to proxy to Apache. This is also required if replacing Apache, so in the end, this approach won't add much extra work during setup.

Last but not the least, and this will be further discussed in the last section of this chapter, there may be some issues with control panel software, such as Parallels Plesk, cPanel, and others. These panels are very useful for administrators, as they automate some of the most bothersome tasks, such as adding virtual hosts to the Apache configuration, creating email accounts, configuring the DNS daemon, and many more. The two main issues are:

- These control panels allow you to apply changes on the web server configuration, and based on your changes, they automatically generate valid configuration files for the server. Unfortunately, so far these control panels only offer compatibility with Apache; they do not generate Nginx configuration files. So any changes that you make will have no effect.
- Whether you completely replace Apache with Nginx or go for the reverse proxy mechanism, Nginx usually ends up running on port 80 (and 443 for HTTPS). The control panel software generating configuration files is unaware of this fact and might be stubborn. When generating configuration files, it will systematically reset the Apache port to 80, creating conflicts with Nginx.

Both issues will be discussed again later in the chapter.

An example case

To understand how Nginx can make a difference, let's examine what resources a typical website loads when you first visit it:

Media type	File/request count	Total size	Total gzipped size
HTML source code	1	157.6 KB	52.5 KB
JavaScript (`.js`) code files and libraries	6	382.1 KB	112.3 KB
CSS (`.css`) files	3	256.8 KB	42.8 KB
Flash animations (`.swf`)	2	61.4 KB	61.4 KB
Images linked from CSS files (`.png`, `.gif`)	18	43.0 KB	43.0 KB
Regular images (`.gif`, `.jpg`)	11	73.3 KB	73.3 KB
TOTAL	41	974.2 KB	385.3 KB

These figures reflect a snapshot taken at the time of writing these lines, as visited by a US-based visitor. Results may differ slightly according to your geographical location, date of visit, and other criteria.

The amount of data that your browser needs to download is relatively low. After all, the 385.3 KB (make that 400-450 KB, including cookie data and other overheads) can be transferred in less than a second with the fast internet connections that are now being offered in many countries.

A much bigger problem, in our case, is the amount of requests that the server will have to handle. For all of the first-time visitors, and for any web browser that does not use cached data to load this page, a minimum of **41** HTTP requests will be processed by the web server.

In some dated Apache setups, a massive amount of modules and other components are loaded into the memory of the main Apache process, which means that each request will occupy a rather heavy process until the user finishes downloading the file. In practice, this results in excessive memory and CPU overhead. On the other hand, Nginx has proven to be both lightweight and stable while serving a larger amount of requests (using less RAM and CPU time, in comparison to Apache).

Configuring Apache and Nginx

After having reviewed the proxy module, which allows us to establish our reverse proxy configuration architecture, it's now time to put all these principles into practice. There are basically two main parts involved in the configuration: one relating to Apache and one relating to Nginx. The order in which you decide to apply those modifications does not make any difference whatsoever.

Note that while we have chosen to describe the process specifically for Apache, this method can be applied to any other HTTP server. The only point that differs is the exact configuration sections and directives that you will need to edit. Otherwise, the principle of reverse proxy can be applied regardless of the server software you are using.

Reconfiguring Apache

There are two main aspects of your Apache configuration that will need to be edited in order to allow both Apache and Nginx to work together and at the same time. But let us first clarify where we are coming from and where we are going.

Configuration overview

At this point, you probably have the following architecture set up on your server:

- A web server application running on port 80, such as Apache
- A dynamic server-side script-processing application, such as PHP, communicating with your web server via CGI, FastCGI, or as a server module

The new configuration we are going towards will resemble the following:

- Nginx running on port 80
- Apache (or another web server) running on a different port, accepting requests coming from local sockets only
- The script-processing application configuration (PHP or Python, for instance) will remain unchanged

As you can tell, only two main configuration changes will be applied to Apache (or any other web server that you might be running). Firstly, change the listening-port number in order to avoid conflicts with Nginx. Secondly (although this is optional), you may want to disallow requests coming from the outside and only allow requests forwarded by Nginx. Both configuration steps are detailed in the next sections.

Resetting the port number

Depending on how your web server was set up (manual build or automatic configuration from server panel managers, such as cPanel or Plesk), you may find yourself with a lot of configuration files to edit. The main configuration file is often found in `/etc/httpd/conf/` or `/etc/apache2/`, and there might be more, depending on how your configuration is structured. Some server panel managers create extra configuration files for each virtual host.

There are three main elements you need to replace in your Apache configuration:

- The `Listen` directive is set to listen on port `80` by default. You will have to replace that port with another, such as `8080`. This directive is usually found in the main configuration file, but on some setups the directive appears in a separate file called `ports.conf`.
- You must make sure that the following configuration directive is present in the main configuration file: `NameVirtualHost A.B.C.D:8080`, where `A.B.C.D` is the IP address of the main network interface which server communications go through.
- The port you just selected needs to be reported in all your virtual host configuration sections.

The virtual host sections must be transformed from the following template:

```
<VirtualHost A.B.C.D:80>
  ServerName   example.com
  ServerAlias  www.example.com
  [...]
</VirtualHost>
```

They should be transformed to the following:

```
<VirtualHost A.B.C.D:8080>
  ServerName   example.com:8080
  ServerAlias  www.example.com
  [...]
</VirtualHost>
```

In this example, `A.B.C.D` is the IP address of the virtual host and `example.com` is the virtual host's name. The port must be edited on the first two lines.

Accepting local requests only

There are many ways by which you can restrict Apache to only accept local requests and deny access to the outside world. But first, why would you want to do that? As an extra layer positioned between the client and Apache, Nginx provides a certain comfort in terms of security. Visitors no longer have direct access to Apache, which decreases the potential risk—no one would be able to exploit possible new vulnerabilities. Generally speaking, the principle of least privilege should apply.

The first method consists of changing the listening network interface in the main configuration file. The `Listen` directive of Apache lets you specify a port, but also an IP address. However, by default, no IP address is selected, which results in communications coming from all interfaces. All you have to do is replace the `Listen 8080` directive with `Listen 127.0.0.1:8080`; Apache should then only listen on the local IP address. If you do not host Apache on the same server, you will need to specify the IP address of the network interface that can communicate with the server hosting Nginx.

An alternative would be to establish per-virtual-host restrictions:

```
<VirtualHost A.B.C.D:8080>
  ServerName   example.com:8080
  ServerAlias  www.example.com
  [...]
  order deny,allow
  allow from 127.0.0.1
  allow from 192.168.0.1
  deny all
</VirtualHost>
```

Using the `allow` and `deny` Apache directives, you are able to restrict the allowed IP addresses accessing your virtual hosts. This allows for a finer configuration, which can be useful if some of your websites cannot be fully served by Nginx.

Once all of your changes are done, don't forget to reload the server to make sure the new configuration is applied, such as with `service httpd reload` or `/etc/init.d/httpd reload`.

Configuring Nginx

There are only a couple of simple steps to establish a working configuration of Nginx, although it can be tweaked more accurately, as seen in the next section.

Enabling proxy options

The first step is to enable proxying of requests in your location blocks. Since the `proxy_pass` directive cannot be placed at the `http` or server level, you need to include it in every single place that you want forwarded. Usually, a `location / {` fallback block suffices, since it encompasses all requests, except those that match `location` blocks containing a `break` statement.

The following is a simple example using a single static backend hosted on the same server:

```
server {
  server_name .example.com;
  root /home/example.com/www;
  [...]
  location / {
      proxy_pass http://127.0.0.1:8080;
  }
}
```

In the following example, we make use of an `upstream` block, allowing us to specify multiple servers:

```
upstream apache {
    server 192.168.0.1:80;
    server 192.168.0.2:80;
    server 192.168.0.3:80 weight=2;
    server 192.168.0.4:80 backup;
}

 server {
    server_name .example.com;
    root /home/example.com/www;
    [...]
    location / {
```

```
        proxy_pass http://apache;
    }
}
```

So far, with such a configuration, all requests are proxies by your backend server(s). We are now going to separate the content into two categories:

- **Dynamic files**: Files that require processing before being sent to the client, such as PHP, Perl, and Ruby scripts, will be served by Apache
- **Static files**: All other content that does not require additional processing, such as images, CSS files, static HTML files, and media, will be served directly by Nginx

Therefore, we need to somehow separate the dynamic from the static content to be provided by either server.

Separating content

In order to establish this separation, we can simply use two different location blocks: one that will match the dynamic file extensions, and another one encompassing all the other files. This example passes requests for .php files to the proxy:

```
server {
    server_name .example.com;
    root /home/example.com/www;
    [...]
    location ~* .php.$ {
      # Proxy all requests with an URI ending with .php*
      # (includes PHP, PHP3, PHP4, PHP5...)
        proxy_pass http://127.0.0.1:8080;
    }
    location / {
        # Your other options here for static content
        # for example cache control, alias...
        expires 30d;
    }
}
```

This method, although simple, will cause trouble with websites using URL rewriting. Most *Web 2.0* websites now use links that hide file extensions, such as http://example.com/articles/us-economy-strengthens/; some even append artificial extensions, such as .html:
http://example.com/us-economy-strengthens.html.

If you find yourself in this situation, you will want to employ one of the solutions described as follows:

- The cleaner method is to convert your Apache rewrite rules for Nginx (with Apache, rewrite rules are usually found in the `.htaccess` file at the root of the website), in order for Nginx to know the actual file extension of the request and proxy it to Apache correctly.
- If you do not wish to port your Apache rewrite rules, you can use the `try_files` directive to try serving the requested URI, and redirect the request to Apache in case the URI doesn't match any file accessible to Nginx. Or, simply let Apache handle `404` responses via the `error_page` directive.

The more appropriate method is with `try_files`; we attempt to serve the requested URI directly, or a corresponding folder by appending a `/`, and if all fails, we forward the request to Apache:

```
server {
    server_name .example.com;
    root /home/example.com/www;
    [...]
location / {
    # Try serving requested file, or forward to Apache
    try_files $uri $uri/ @proxy;

        # Insert configuration for static files here
        expires 30d;
        [...]
    }
location @proxy {
    # Forwards requests to Apache
        proxy_pass http://127.0.0.1:8080;
    }
}
```

Here is an implementation of this mechanism, using the `error_page` directive:

```
server {
    server_name .example.com;
    root /home/example.com/www;
    [...]
    location / {
        # Your static files are served here
        expires 30d;
        [...]
        # For 404 errors, submit the query to the @proxy
```

```
            # named location block
            error_page 404 @proxy;
        }
    location @proxy {
        # Forwards requests to Apache
            proxy_pass http://127.0.0.1:8080;
        }
    }
```

Alternatively, make use of the `if` directive from the rewrite module:

```
    server {
        server_name .example.com;
        root /home/example.com/www;
        [...]
        location / {
          # If the requested file extension ends with .php,
          # forward the query to Apache
          if ($request_filename ~* .php.$) {
            break; # prevents further rewrites
            proxy_pass http://127.0.0.1:8080;
          }
          # If the requested file does not exist,
          # forward the query to Apache
          if (!-f $request_filename) {
            break; # prevents further rewrites
            proxy_pass http://127.0.0.1:8080;
          }
          # Your static files are served here
          expires 30d;
        }
    }
```

There is no major performance difference between either solution, as each will transfer the same amount of requests to the backend server. For optimal performance, you should work on porting your Apache rewrite rules to Nginx.

Advanced configuration

For now, we have only made use of one directive offered by the proxy module. There are many more features that we can employ to optimize our design. The following table in this section lists a handful of settings that are valid for most of your reverse proxy configurations, although they need to be verified individually. Since they can be employed multiple times, you can also place them in a separate configuration file that you will include in your location blocks.

Start by creating a `proxy.conf` text file, which you will place in the Nginx configuration directory. Insert the directives described in the following table. Then, for each location of your `if` blocks that forward requests to a backend server or upstream block, insert the following line after the `proxy_pass` directive:

```
include proxy.conf;
```

The following are suggested values for some of the settings:

Setting	Description
`proxy_set_header Host $host;`	The `Host` HTTP header in the request forwarded to the backend server defaults to the proxy hostname, as specified in the configuration file. This setting lets Nginx use the original `Host` from the client request instead.
`proxy_set_header X-Real-IP $remote_addr;`	Since the backend server receives a request from Nginx, the IP address it communicates with is not that of the client. Use this setting to forward the actual client IP address into a new header, `X-Real-IP`.
`proxy_set_header X-Forwarded-For $proxy_add_x_forwarded_for;`	Similar to the previous header, except that if the client already uses a proxy on his/her own end, the actual IP address of the client should be contained in the `X-Forwarded-For` request header. Using `$proxy_add_x_forwarded_for` ensures that both the IP address of the communicating socket and possibly the original IP address of the client (behind a proxy) get forwarded to the backend server.
`client_max_body_size 10m;`	Limits the maximum size of the request body to `10m` (megabytes). Actually, this setting is referenced here to make sure that you adjust the value to the same level as your backend server. Otherwise, a request that is correctly received and processed by Nginx may not be successfully forwarded to the backend.

Setting	Description
`client_body_buffer_size 128k;`	Defines the minimum size of the memory buffer that will hold a request body. Past this size, the content is saved in a temporary file. Adjust it according to the expected size of requests your visitors will be sending, similar to `client_max_body_size`.
`proxy_connect_timeout 15;`	If you are working with a backend server on a local network, make sure to keep this value reasonably low (15 seconds here, but it depends on the average load). The maximum value for this directive is 75 seconds, anyway.
`proxy_send_timeout 15;`	Make sure you define a timeout for write operations (timeout between two write operations during a communication to the backend server).
`proxy_read_timeout 15;`	Similar to the previous directive, except for read operations.

Many other directives may be configured here. However, default values are appropriate for most setups.

Improving the reverse proxy architecture

There are a few more additional steps that you may be interested in if you want to perfect your reverse proxy architecture. Three main issues are discussed here: the issue of IP addresses and how to ensure that the backend server retrieves the correct one, how to handle HTTPS requests with such a setup, and finally, a quick word about server control panels (cPanel, Plesk, and others).

Forwarding the correct IP address

Nowadays, a good portion of websites make use of the visitor's IP address for all kinds of reasons:

- Storing the IP address of a visitor posting a comment on a blog or a discussion forum
- Geo-targeted advertising or other services
- Limiting services to specific IP address ranges

Therefore, it is important for those websites to ensure that the web server correctly receives the IP address of the visitor.

As explained before, since Apache—or more generally, the backend server—uses the IP address of the socket it communicates with, the IP that will appear in our design will always be the IP of the server hosting Nginx. In the previous section, we discovered a possible solution is inserting the `proxy_set_header X-Real-IP $remote_addr;` directive in the configuration in order to forward the client IP address in the `X-Real-IP` header.

Unfortunately, that is not enough, as some web applications are not configured to make use of the `X-Real-IP` header. The client remote address needs to be somehow replaced by that value. When it comes to Apache, a module was written to do just that: `mod_rpaf`. Details on how to install and configure it are not discussed here; you may find more documentation over at the official website: `http://stderr.net/apache/rpaf/`

Alternatively, you could edit the source code of your backend application to take this particular header into consideration. In PHP, the following piece of code would retrieve the correct IP address:

```
$ip_address = $_SERVER["X_REAL_IP"];
```

SSL issues and solutions

If your website is going to serve secure web pages, you need to somehow allow visitors to connect to your infrastructure via **SSL** on port 443. Two solutions are possible at this point: either you do not make use of Nginx at all and keep your Apache SSL configuration unmodified, or you configure Nginx to accept communications on port 443.

The first solution is clearly the simplest—do not change the port of your virtual hosts, as configured in Apache. Your website should still be fully accessible from the outside, unless your backend server is hosted on another computer on the local network.

The alternative is to configure Nginx to accept secure connections via the SSL module, as described in `Chapter 5`, *PHP and Python with Nginx*. Once your `server` block is correctly configured, you can establish a proxied configuration to forward secure requests to your Apache server. Note that if your backend server is hosted on the same machine, you will need to edit the configuration in order to avoid port conflicts between the frontend and backend.

Server control panel issues

A lot of server administrators rely on control panel software to simplify many aspects of their work: managing hosted domains, email accounts, network settings, and much more. Advanced software solutions, such as Parallels Plesk or cPanel, are able to generate configuration files for many server applications (web, email, database, and so on) on-the-fly. Unfortunately, most of them only support Apache as a unique web server application; Nginx is often left behind.

If you followed the steps of the reverse proxy configuration process, you noticed that at some point, the Apache configuration files had to be manually edited. We replaced the listening port and edited or inserted some configuration directives. Obviously, when the control panel software generates configuration files, it is unaware of the manual changes we made. Therefore, it erases our modifications. When you restart Apache, you are greeted with error messages and conflicts.

At this point, there is no solution other than to apply the changes again after each configuration rebuild. With the growing popularity of Nginx, developers will hopefully implement full Nginx support in their software, or at least allow those configuration settings, which are required to use Nginx as a reverse proxy, to be edited.

 Facing the growing popularity of Nginx, web-control-panel developers are indeed starting to take steps towards full or partial support of Nginx. As of version 11, Parallels Plesk now offers support for Nginx as a frontend server.

Summary

Configuring Nginx as a reverse proxy for our architecture introduces a lot of advantages in terms of loading speeds and server load, as well as architecture reliability, since you can use multiple backends. However, a few obstacles might stand in your way, especially if you are running control panel software solutions to manage your services. Moreover, you do not get to make the most of Nginx, as you are not using it for all your requests.

If you are seeking to find an even more efficient solution, you may want to look into completely replacing Apache by Nginx. The next chapter will detail this process step-by-step, from virtual hosts, to rewrite rules, to FastCGI.

8
From Apache to Nginx

Every experienced system administrator will tell you the same story. When your web infrastructure works fine and client requests are served at a good speed, the last thing you want to do is modify the architecture that you have spent days, weeks, or even months putting together. In reality, as your website grows more popular, problems pertaining to scalability tend to occur inevitably (and these problems are not as well documented as mainstream ones), regardless of the effort you originally involved in your initial server configuration. Eventually, you have to start looking for solutions. To that extent, there are multiple reasons why you would want to completely adopt Nginx at the expense of your previous web server application. Whether you have decided that Nginx could be more efficient as a unique server rather than working as a reverse proxy, or simply because you want to get rid of Apache once and for all, this chapter will guide you through the complete process of replacing the latter with the former.

This chapter covers:

- A quick comparison between Apache and Nginx
- A detailed guide to porting your Apache configuration
- How to port your Apache rewrite rules to Nginx
- Rewrite rule walkthroughs for a few popular web applications

Nginx versus Apache

This section will provide answers to the main questions that you might ask about Nginx—how does it stand apart from the other servers? How does it compare to Apache? Whether you were using Apache before or considered it as a replacement for your current web server, why would you decide to adopt Nginx at the expense of the web server that empowers almost 40% of internet websites worldwide?

Features

With the reverse proxy configuration that was elaborated in the previous chapter, the presence or absence of specific features wasn't much of a problem. This is because Nginx would simply have to differentiate between static and dynamic content, and in consequence serve static file requests and forward dynamic file requests to a backend server. However, when you start to consider Nginx as a possible full replacement for your current web server, you had better make sure that you know what's in the box. If your projected architecture requires specific components, the first thing you would usually do is check the application features. The table listed in the following section lists a few of the major features and describes how Nginx performs in comparison to Apache.

Core and functioning

This section lists various features of Nginx and Apache:

Features	Nginx	Apache
HTTP request management (how the web server processes client requests)	**Event-driven architecture**: In this architecture, requests are accepted using asynchronous sockets and aren't processed in separate threads, in order to reduce memory and CPU overhead.	**Synchronous sockets, threads, and processes**: In this, each request is in a separate thread or process and uses synchronous sockets.
Programming language (the language the web server is written in)	**C**: The C language is notably low-level and offers more accurate memory management.	**C and C++**: Although Apache was written in C, many modules were designed with C++.
Portability (operating systems that are currently supported)	**Multiplatform**: Nginx runs under Windows, GNU/Linux, Unix, BSD, macOS, and Solaris.	**Multiplatform**: Apache runs under Windows, GNU/Linux, Unix, BSD, macOS, Solaris, Novell NetWare, OS/2, TPF, OpenVMS, eCS, AIX, z/OS, HP-UX, and more.

Year of birth	**2002**: While Nginx is younger than Apache, it was intended for a more modern era.	**1994**: Apache is one of the numerous open source projects initiated in the 90s that contributed to making the World Wide Web what it is today.

General functionality

This section mainly focuses on differences between Apache and Nginx rather than listing features that have already been covered in previous chapters:

Feature	Nginx	Apache
HTTPS support: This specifies whether the web server can deliver secure web pages.	**Supported as module**: If you require HTTPS support, you need to make sure you compile Nginx with the proper module.	**Supported as module**: Apache comes with HTTPS support via a module included by default.
Virtual Hosting: This specifies whether the web server can host multiple websites on the same computer.	**Supported natively**: Nginx natively supports virtual hosting, but is not configured by default to accept per-virtual-host configuration files (more details are provided further in this chapter).	**Supported natively**: Apache natively supports virtual hosting and offers the possibility of including one configuration file per folder (`.htaccess`).
CGI Support: This specifies whether the web server supports CGI-based protocols.	**FastCGI, uWSGI, SCGI**: Nginx supports FastCGI, uWSGI, and SCGI (as well as HTTP proxying) via modules that are included by default at compile time.	**CGI, FastCGI**: Most CGI protocols are exploitable via modules that can be loaded into Apache.
Module system: This specifies how the web server handles the modules.	**Static module system**: Modules are built-in; they must be included at compile time.	**Dynamic module system**: Modules can be loaded and unloaded dynamically from configuration files.

Generally speaking, Apache has a lot to offer, notably a much larger number of modules available. Most of its functionality is modularized, including its core engine. At this time, the official Apache module website references over 500 modules for various version branches, versus a little more than 100 for Nginx.

Flexibility and community

This is another criterion for establishing an honest comparison between two applications of the likes of Nginx and Apache. In today's information technology industry, you cannot simply take into account the raw functionality of a server application without considering questions such as:

- Where am I going to get help if I get stuck?
- Am I going to find documentation about specific features offered by either server?
- Are there going to be more modules in the future?
- Is the project still active and being updated by its developers?
- Has the security of either server been tested by a large enough number of administrators?

These questions generally answer themselves when the server gets popular enough. In the case of Apache, saying that it is a mainstream application would be an understatement. Documentation is easily found, developers have released hundreds of modules over the years, and it has received regular updates over the past 20 years. What about Nginx, where does it stand on those matters? That is definitely a sensitive issue. To begin with, there are some solid websites, centralizing information, such as the official documentation reference at Nginx.org. If you have a problem with Apache, a simple search engine query suffices to find multiple articles, answering the exact question you have been asking yourself. If you have an overly specific problem with Nginx though, you will likely have to resort to newsgroups, mailing lists, or web forums. On the updates and security side though, Nginx is frequently updated by its author, *Igor Sysoev*, and his team. Those updates rarely need to include critical security fixes as the server has been built on solid and reliable foundations from the start. Although it doesn't serve as many websites as Apache does, Nginx still empowers some of the most popular online platforms such as Facebook, SourceForge, WordPress, ImageShack, and many more. This contributes to conferring it undeniable legitimacy on it in the domain of high-performance web servers.

Performance

While features and community-related matters are important in general, the aspect that can make all the difference is performance. Administrators naturally tend to favor the server that will provide optimal comfort for the end user, characterized by minimal page load times and maximum download speeds. Chapter 2, *Basic Nginx Configuration*, provided a first approach to HTTP server performance testing. The same tests can be applied to Apache in order to establish direct performance comparisons. In fact, many admin bloggers and technicians have already done so, and the general trend is unquestionably in favor of Nginx on all aspects, such as the following:

- The **RPS** (**requests per second**) rate is generally much higher with Nginx, sometimes twice as high as with Apache. In other words, Nginx is able to serve twice as many pages as Apache in the same lapse of time.
- Response times are lower on Nginx. As the request count grows, Apache becomes slower and slower to serve pages.
- Apache tends to use slightly more bandwidth than Nginx for serving the same requests. This can be interpreted in two ways—either Apache generates more traffic overhead, or it is able to transfer data at a faster rate by better occupying the available bandwidth (it's still debatable as to which of these assumptions is the most valid).

In conclusion on the field of performance, Nginx wins hands down. It's clearly the main reason why so many have switched to the lightweight Russian web server.

Usage

The reason why Nginx is so far ahead of Apache performance wise, is because it was written for precisely this purpose. Originally, *Igor Sysoev* created Nginx to empower an extremely high-traffic Russian website (https://www.rambler.ru/), which received hundreds of millions of requests every day. This was probably not part of the original plans of the Apache designers when they initiated the project back in the early 90s. More generally, it is said that Nginx was designed to address the **C10k problem**. This expression designates a common observation according to which the current state of computer technology and network scalability only allows a computer (from the mainstream industry) to maintain up to 10,000 simultaneous network connections, due to the operating system and software limitations.

While that number isn't representative anymore due to the progress of the technology, at the time, the issue was considered very seriously and it triggered the development of major web servers such as Lighttpd, Cherokee, and, last but not least, Nginx.

Conclusion

There is one famous quote going around the Nginx community that summarizes the situation pretty accurately:

> *"Apache is like Microsoft Word, it has a million options but you only need six. Nginx does those six things, and it does five of them 50 times faster than Apache."*

> – *Chris Lea, https://chrislea.com/*

Other notable testimonies helped build the reputation of Nginx over time:

> *"I currently have Nginx doing reverse proxy of over tens of millions of HTTP requests per day (that's a few hundred per second) on a single server. At peak load, it uses about 15 MB RAM and 10 percent of my CPU on my particular configuration (FreeBSD 6). Under the same kind of load, Apache falls over (after using 1,000 or so processes and god knows how much RAM), Pound falls over (too many threads, and using 400 MB+ of RAM for all the thread stacks), and Lighty leaks more than 20 MB per hour (and uses more CPU, but not significantly more)."*

> – *Bob Ippolito, MochiMedia.com*

If you are in the market for high-scale projects with limited resources at your disposal, Nginx is as a great solution. Apache is a good option to get your projects started when your knowledge of web servers and hosting is limited, but as soon as you meet success, you, your server, and your visitors may eventually find it to be inconsistent.

Porting your Apache configuration

That's it. You've had enough of Apache. You finally decided to make a complete switch to Nginx. There are quite a few steps ahead of you now, the first of which is to adapt your previous configuration to ensure that your existing websites work 1:1 after the switch.

Directives

This first section will summarize some of the common Apache configuration directives and attempt to provide equivalent or replacement solutions from Nginx. The list follows the order of the default Apache configuration file:

Apache directive	Nginx equivalent
`ServerTokens`: Apache allows you to configure the information transmitted in request headers regarding the server OS and software name and versions.	`server_tokens`: In Nginx, you may enable or disable transmission of server information by using the `server_tokens` directive from the main HTTP module.
`ServerRoot`: Lets you define the `root` folder of the server, which will contain the configuration and logs folder.	`--prefix` build-time option: With Nginx, this option is defined at compile time with the `--prefix` switch of the configure script or at execution time with the -p command line option.
`PidFile`: Defines the path of the application PID file.	`pid`: The precisely equivalent directive is PID.
`TimeOut`: This directive defines three elements: • The maximum execution time of a GET request • The maximum allowed delay between two TCP packets in POST and PUT requests • The maximum allowed delay between two TCP ACK packets	**Multiple directives:** There are multiple directives allowing a similar behavior: • `send_timeout`: Defines the maximum allowed delay between two read operations by the client • `client_body_timeout`: Defines the timeout for reading the client request body • `client_header_timeout`: Defines the timeout for reading client request headers
`KeepAlive`, `MaxKeepAliveRequests`, `KeepAliveTimeout`: These three directives control the keepalive behavior of Apache.	`keepalive_timeout`, `keepalive_requests`: These two directives are the direct equivalents of the Apache ones, except that, if you want to completely disable keepalives, set `keepalive_timeout` or `keepalive_requests` to 0.
`Listen`: Defines the interface and port on which Apache will listen for connections.	`listen`: In Nginx, this directive is only defined at the virtual host level (`server` block).

Apache directive	Nginx equivalent
`LoadModule`: With this directive, Apache offers the possibility of loading modules dynamically.	`--with_****_module`: Nginx cannot load modules dynamically; these need to be included at compile time. Once incorporated in Nginx, they cannot be disabled.
`Include`: File inclusion directive supports wildcards.	`include`: The `include` directive of Nginx is identical.
`User`, `Group`: Allows you to define the user and group under which the daemon will be running.	`user`: The `user` directive of Nginx lets you specify both the user and the group.
`ServerAdmin`, `ServerSignature`: Lets you specify the email address of the server administrator and a signature message to be displayed on error and diagnostic pages.	No equivalent, as of Version 1.8. Error pages do not show the email address of the server administrator or other information. Look into the `error_page` directive to customize your site's error pages.
`UseCanonicalName`: Defines how Apache constructs self-referential URLs.	No direct equivalent. Although there is no direct equivalent for this Apache directive, the construction of self-referential URLs can be defined via module-specific settings (proxy, FastCGI, and so on).
`DocumentRoot`: Defines the `root` folder from which Apache will serve files. The directive can be used at the server and virtual host levels.	`root`: The `root` directive can be inserted to define the document root at all levels: `http`, `server`, `location`, and `if` blocks.
`DirectoryIndex`, `IndexOptions`, `IndexIgnore`: Define directory index and file listing options.	`index`, `autoindex`, `random_index`, `fancyindex` (third party):Nginx also offers a good variety of options for managing indexes.
`AccessFileName`: Defines the filename of `.htaccess` files that are included dynamically on page execution.	No equivalent. Nginx, as of version 1.8, has no such feature as `.htaccess` files. Read the further sections for more information.
`TypesConfig`, `DefaultType`: Defines MIME type options.	`types`, `default_type`: Equivalent directives exist in Nginx, although with a different syntax.

Apache directive	Nginx equivalent
`HostNameLookups`: Allows looking up of hostnames for client IP addresses for logging or access control purposes.	No equivalent; as of Nginx 1.8, there is no equivalent functionality.
`ErrorLog`, `LogLevel`, `LogFormat`, `CustomLog`: Logging activation and format settings.	`access_log`, `log_format`: Nginx also allows a large variety of options, but they are combined in fewer directives.
`Alias`, `AliasMatch`, `ScriptAlias`: Directory aliasing options.	`alias`: The `alias` equivalent directive is offered by Nginx, but nothing for the other two.

Modules

As we have learned earlier in `Chapter 1`, *Downloading and Installing Nginx*, modules in Nginx cannot be loaded dynamically and must be included at compile time. Additionally, they cannot be disabled at runtime since they are completely compiled and integrated in the main binary. Consequently, you should carefully consider your choice of modules when you build Nginx.

 If you are worried about the impact on performance of the modules you selected, you should be aware that the only noticeable differences will come from filter modules. This name is given to modules that apply a filter to the content of requests and/or responses, and therefore they are always activated. Examples of filter modules are Addition, Charset, Gzip, SSI, and more. In the case of non-filter modules (such as Autoindex, FastCGI, Stub Status, and others), if none of their directives are used, the module handler is never executed.

The following table lists some modules that Apache and Nginx have in common. Note that there might be equivalent modules, but they do not necessarily provide the exact same functionality and directives are likely to be different in all cases. You should check the documentation of these modules in their respective chapters:

Apache module	Nginx module	Status	Configure switch
`mod_auth_basic`	`auth_basic`	Included by default	`--without-http_auth_basic_module`

Apache module	Nginx module	Status	Configure switch
`mod_autoindex`	`autoindex`	Included by default	`--without-http_autoindex_module`
`mod_charset_lite`	`charset`	Included by default	`--without-http_charset_module`
`mod_dav`	`Dav`	Optional	`--with-http_dav_module`
`mod_deflate`	`gzip`	Included by default	`--without-http_gzip_module`
`mod_expires`	`headers`	Included by default	Cannot be disabled
`mod_fcgid`	`fastcgi`	Included by default	`--without-http_fastcgi_module`
`mod_headers`	`Headers`	Included by default	Cannot be disabled
`mod_include`	`Ssi`	Included by default	`--without-http_ssi_module`
`mod_log_config`	`Log`	Included by default	Cannot be disabled
`mod_proxy`	`proxy`	Included by default	`--without-http_proxy_module`
`mod_rewrite`	`rewrite`	Included by default	`--without-http_rewrite_module`
`mod_ssl`	`Ssl`	Optional	`--with-http_ssl_module`

Apache module	Nginx module	Status	Configure switch
mod_status	stub_status	Optional	--with-http_stub_status_module
mod_substitute	Sub	Optional	--with-http_sub_module
mod_uid	userid	Included by default	--without-http_userid_module

Virtual hosts and configuration sections

Just like Nginx allows you to define configuration settings at various levels (http, server, location, if), Apache also has its own sections. The section list is described as follows together with a configuration example.

Configuration sections

The following table provides a translation of Apache sections into Nginx configuration blocks. Some Apache sections have no direct Nginx equivalent, but for most cases, identical behavior can be reproduced in a slightly different syntax.

Apache section	Nginx section	Description
(default)	http	The settings placed at the root of the Apache configuration files correspond to the settings placed at the root of the Nginx configuration file and also those placed in the http block (as opposed to other blocks such as mail or imap used for mail server proxying functionality).
<VirtualHost>	server	Apache settings placed in the <VirtualHost> sections should be placed in the server blocks of the Nginx configuration file.
<Location> <LocationMatch>	location	The behavior of <Location> and <LocationMatch> (regular expressions) can be reproduced with the Nginx location block.

None	if	Nginx offers a dynamic conditional structure with the if block. There is no exact equivalent in Apache. The closest equivalence is the `RewriteCond` directive from the Rewrite module.
`<Directory>` `<DirectoryMatch>` `<Files>` `<FilesMatch>`	None	Apache allows you to apply settings to specific locations of the local file system while Nginx only offers per-URI settings.
`<IfDefine>`	None	Applies a set of directives on startup if the specified condition is `true`. This feature is not available on Nginx.
`<IfModule>`	None	Applies a set of directives on startup if the specified module is loaded. Since Nginx does not support dynamic module loading, this feature is not available.
`<Proxy>` `<ProxyMatch>`	None	Applies a set of directives to proxied resources by specifying a wildcard URI or a regular expression. This section has no equivalent on Nginx.

Creating a virtual host

In Apache, virtual hosts are optional. You are allowed to define server settings at the root of the configuration file:

```
Listen 80
ServerName example.com
ServerAlias www.example.com
DocumentRoot "/home/example.com/www"
[...]
```

However, this behavior is useful only if you are going to host one website on the server, or if you want to define default settings for incoming requests that do not match other virtual host access rules. In Nginx, however, all the websites you will be hosting must be placed in a server block which allows the creation of a virtual host, equivalent to the `<VirtualHost>` section in Apache. The following table describes the translation of an Apache `<VirtualHost>` section to an Nginx server block:

Apache virtual host	Nginx virtual host equivalent
`<VirtualHost 12.34.56.78:80>`	`server {`
`ServerName example.com:80` `ServerAlias www.example.com`	`listen 12.34.56.78:80;` `server_name example.com www.example.com;`
`UseCanonicalName Off`	No equivalent
`SuexecUserGroup user group`	No equivalent
`ServerAdmin "admin@example.com"`	No equivalent
`DocumentRoot` `/home/example.com/www`	`root /home/example.com/www;`

`CustomLog`
`/home/example.com/logs/access_log`
`cust`
	`access_log/home/example.com/logs/access_log`
	`cust;`
	Note that the `cust` format must be declared
	beforehand with `log_format`

`ErrorLog` `/home/example.com/logs/error_log`	`error_log /home/example.com/logs/error_log;`

`<Location /documents/>`
`Options +Indexes`
`</Location>`
	`location /documents/ {`
	`autoindex on;`
	`}`

`<IfModule mod_ssl.c>`
`SSLEngine off`
`</IfModule>`
	There is no equivalent for `IfModule.ssl off;`

`<Directory /home/example.com/www>`
`<IfModule mod_fcgid.c>`
`<Files ~ (.php)>`
`SetHandler fcgid-script`
`FCGIWrapper /usr/bin/php-cgi .php`
`Options +ExecCGI`
`allow from all`
`</Files>`
`</IfModule>`
`Options -Includes -ExecCGI`
`</Directory>`
	There is no equivalent to the `Directory` section. The `location` block only applies per-URI settings. The `location` block applies settings for all requests relative to the virtual host `root` folder. We use it to apply settings to the `.php` files.
	`location ~ .php    {`
	Insert your FCGI settings:
	`    fastcgi_pass    127.0.0.1:9000;`
	`    fastcgi_param    SCRIPT_FILENAME`
	`/home/example.com/ www$fastcgi_script_name;`
	`    fastcgi_param    PATH_INFO`
	`$fastcgi_script_name;`
	`    include    fastcgi_params; # Your additional`
	`FastCGI settings`
	`}`
	Other directives have no direct equivalent or are not necessary with Nginx.

`</VirtualHost>`	`}`

This translation guide is valid for regular virtual hosts, serving non-secure web pages. There are a few differences when creating a secure virtual host using **SSL**. The following table focuses on SSL-related directives, although directives from the previous table can still be used:

Apache virtual host	Nginx virtual host
`<VirtualHost 12.34.56.78:443>`	`server {`

`ServerName example.com:443`
`ServerAlias www.example.com`
	`listen 12.34.56.78:443;`
	`server_name example.com`
	`www.example.com;`

`SSLEngine on`
`SSLVerifyClient none`
`SSLCertificateFile`
`/home/example.com/cert/certchL9435`
	`ssl on;`
	`ssl_verify_client off;`
	`ssl_certificate`
	`/home/example.com/cert/cert.pem;`
	`ssl_certificate_key`
	`/home/example.com/cert/cert.key;`

`<Directory /home/example.com/www>`
`SSLRequireSSL`
`</Directory>`
	There is no equivalent required with Nginx

`</VirtualHost>`	`}`

.htaccess files

This section approaches the tricky problem of `.htaccess` files and the underlying thematic of shared hosting. There is indeed no such mechanism in Nginx, which, among other factors, renders shared hosting difficult to achieve.

Reminder on Apache .htaccess files

`.htaccess` files are small independent configuration files that webmasters are allowed to place in every single folder of their website. Upon receiving a request to access a particular folder, Apache checks for the presence of such a file and applies it to the request context. This allows webmasters to apply separate settings at multiple levels. Take a look at the following screenshot:

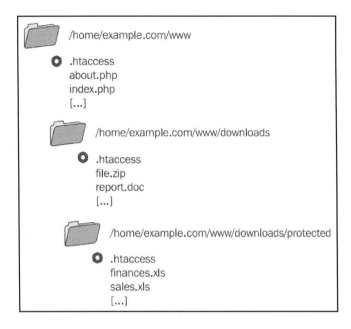

In the context of a client request for `/downloads/protected/finances.xls`, all three `.htaccess` files would be applied in the following order:

- `/home/example.com/www/.htaccess`
- `/home/example.com/www/downloads/.htaccess`
- `/home/example.com/www/downloads/protected/.htaccess`

The settings precedence is given to the last `.htaccess` file read—if the same setting is defined in `/www/.htaccess` and `/www/downloads/.htaccess`, the latter file has priority over the former.

Nginx equivalence

Unfortunately, there is no such mechanism in Nginx. We can, however, find replacement solutions by making the most of directives that we have at our disposal. There are three major uses for `.htaccess` files in Apache:

- Creating access and authentication rules for specific directories
- Defining rewrite rules at the top level (usually not folder-specific)
- Setting flags for modules such as `mod_php`, `mod_perl`, or `mod_python`

When it comes to the latter, the use of flags is only achievable when the preprocessors are set up as Apache modules. If your server runs PHP through CGI or FastCGI, flags will not be recognized and will generate a 500 Internal Server Error. In our case, connecting Nginx to such applications can only be done via FastCGI or HTTP; consequently flags are not allowed.

Depending on the way you declare your virtual hosts, there are two solutions for implementing an .htaccess-like behavior or at least something remotely similar. The first solution, if you are going to list all virtual hosts from a unique configuration file, is to insert an include directive in the server block that refers to an extra configuration file located in the /www/ folder. Do not forget that this configuration file should be hidden and not downloadable by clients:

```
server {
    listen 80;
    server_name .example.com;
    root /home/example.com/www;
    [...]
    # Include extra configuration files
    location / {
        include /home/example.com/www/.ngconf*;
    }
    # Deny access if someone tries to download the file
    location ~ .ngconf {
        return 404;
    }
}
```

This will include any file with a name starting with .ngconf from the /www/ folder of the virtual host. Note the * in the include directive. If you specify a filename without a wildcard, Nginx will consider the configuration to be invalid if the file is missing. If you use the wildcard, the absence of such a file does not generate any error. The .ngconf file would then include directives related to the virtual host itself:

```
autoindex off; # Disable directory listing
location /downloads/ {
    autoindex on; # Allow directory listing in /downloads/
}
[...]
```

This solution seems relatively secure for web hosting providers, as this only allows webmasters to define location-related settings (preventing important changes such as using a different port, different hostname, and more). However, be aware that, if a webmaster creates invalid `.ngconf` files, Nginx will refuse to reload until the issue is fixed. This could be solved by testing configuration files with the `nginx -t` command in a shell script. Alternatively, you could decide to place virtual host declarations within separate files located in the `root` folder of each virtual host. In this case, you would only need the following directive in the main Nginx configuration file:

```
include /home/*/www/.ngconf;
```

The `.ngconf` file then needs to contain the complete virtual host declaration, including the port and server name. This solution should only be considered for servers that you entirely manage by yourself; you should never allow external webmasters to have so much control over your server. That being said, there is still one major difference between Apache and Nginx:

- Apache applies settings from `.htaccess` files every time a client request is processed
- Nginx applies settings from `.ngconf` files only when you reload the configuration (such as `service nginx reload`)

At this moment, there is no work-around for this last issue; Nginx does not allow on-the-fly configuration changes.

 Administrators of web servers primarily running PHP scripts might be interested in the `htscanner` from **PECL package**. This extension offers the possibility to process `.htaccess`-like files containing PHP settings. For more details, please refer to the official page of the package at `http://pecl.php.net/package/htscanner`.

Rewrite rules

The most common source of worries during an HTTP server switch is the rewrite rules. Unfortunately, Nginx is not directly compatible with the Apache rewrite rules in two regards:

- Usually, rewrite rules are placed within .htaccess files, as discussed in the previous section. Nginx offers no such mechanism, so rewrite rules will have to be placed in a different location.
- The syntax of the rewrite instructions and conditions is quite different and will need to be adapted. Thankfully, the regular expression syntax does not change.

This section will explore some of the issues encountered when porting rules to Nginx, and then will provide some prewritten rules for a couple of major web applications.

General remarks

Before studying practical examples, let us begin with a couple of important remarks regarding rewrite rules in Nginx.

On the location

With all that has been said and written about Nginx, we can safely say that it's not the most appropriate web server for web hosting companies that do shared hosting. The lack of .htaccess files renders it practically impossible to host websites that have their own server settings, among which are rewrite rules. While a replacement solution has been offered in the previous section, it's not optimal as it requires a configuration reload after each change; to crown it all, reloading is only possible if the entire configuration contains no error.

The consequence of this first issue is that you will have to relocate the rewrite rules. They will have to be placed directly in the server or location blocks of your virtual host, regardless of which file contains the virtual host configuration. With Apache, rewrite rules would be located somewhere such as /home/example.com/www/.htaccess; whereas, with Nginx, you will need to incorporate them in the virtual host configuration file (for example, /usr/local/nginx/conf/nginx.conf).

On the syntax

There are two major Apache directives that are important when it comes to porting rewrite rules to Nginx. Other directives have no equivalent, are not supported on purpose, or their behavior is already incorporated in the Nginx equivalent directives:

- `RewriteCond`: This allows you to define conditions that should be matched for the request URI to be rewritten
- `RewriteRule`: This performs the actual request URI rewrite by specifying a regular expression pattern, the rewritten URI, and a set of flags

The first of those directives, `RewriteCond`, is equivalent to Nginx's `if`. It is used for verifying conditions before applying a rewrite rule. The following example ensures that the requested file does not exist (`!-f` flag) before rewriting the URI:

```
RewriteCond %{REQUEST_FILENAME} !-f
RewriteRule . /index.php [L]
```

The Nginx equivalent, using `if` and `rewrite`, would be as follows:

```
if (!-f $request_filename) {
    rewrite . /index.php last;
}
```

It gets a little more complicated when you want to rewrite under multiple conditions. The Nginx `if` statement only allows one condition and does not allow imbrications of `if` blocks. The difficulty arises when trying to reproduce a behavior such as the following one:

```
RewriteCond %{REQUEST_FILENAME} !-f # File must not exist
RewriteCond %{REQUEST_FILENAME} !-d # Directory must not exist
RewriteRule . /index.php [L] # Rewrites URL
```

There is a simple logical workaround for this particular issue—we will be using multiple `if` blocks, in which we affect a variable. After the two initial `if` blocks, a third comes in to check if the variable was affected by the first two:

```
set $check "";
# If the specified file does not exist, set $check to "A"
if (!-f $request_filename) {
    set $check "A";
}
# If the specified directory does not exist, set $check to $check+B
if (!-d $request_filename) {
    set $check "${check}B";
}
```

```
# If $check was affected in both if blocks, perform the rewrite
if ($check = "AB") {
    rewrite . /index.php last
}
```

Note that, for those two particular rewrite conditions (-f to test file existence, -d to test folder existence), Nginx already offers a solution that combines both tests: -e. So a quicker solution would have been:

```
if (!-e $request_filename) {
    rewrite . /index.php last;
}
```

In addition to testing for file and folder existence, -e also checks whether the specified filename corresponds to an existing symbolic link. For more information on the rewrite module in general, please refer to Chapter 4, *Module Configuration*.

RewriteRule

The RewriteRule Apache directive is the direct equivalent to rewrite in Nginx. However, there is a subtle difference: URIs in Nginx begin with the / character. Nevertheless, the translation remains simple:

```
RewriteRule ^downloads/(.*)$ download.php?url=$1 [QSA]
```

The preceding Apache rule is transformed into the following:

```
rewrite ^/downloads/(.*)$ /download.php?url=$1;
```

Note that the [QSA] flag tells Apache to append the query arguments to the rewritten URL. However, Nginx does that by default. To prevent Nginx from appending query arguments, insert a trailing ? to the substitution URL:

```
rewrite ^/downloads/(.*)$ /download.php?url=$1?;
```

The RewriteRule Apache directive allows additional flags; these can be matched against those offered by Nginx, described in Chapter 4, *Module Configuration*. The following sections walk you through examples of Nginx rules in famous web applications.

WordPress

WordPress is probably a familiar name to you. As of July 2015, the immensely popular open source blogging application was being used by over 60 million websites worldwide. Powered by PHP and MySQL, it's compatible with Nginx *out-of-the-box*. Well, this statement would be entirely true if it weren't for rewrite rules. The web application comes with a .htaccess file to be placed at the root of the website:

```
# BEGIN WordPress
<IfModule mod_rewrite.c>
RewriteEngine On
RewriteBase /
RewriteCond %{REQUEST_FILENAME} !-f
RewriteCond %{REQUEST_FILENAME} !-d
RewriteRule . /index.php [L]
</IfModule>
# END WordPress
```

This first example is relatively easy to understand and to translate to Nginx. In fact, most of the rewriting process consists of three steps:

1. Checking whether the requested URI corresponds to an existing file, in which case, it is served normally (the request URI is not rewritten).
2. Checking whether the requested URI corresponds to a folder, in which case, it is served normally (the request URI is not rewritten).
3. Rewrite to index.php; WordPress will then analyze the original URI by itself from within the PHP script (by checking the $_SERVER["REQUEST_URI"] variable).

Since there are not a lot of complex rules to take care of and the URI is analyzed by the PHP script itself, the translation to Nginx is rather easy. Here is a full example of an Nginx virtual host, stripped of all unrelated directives for the sake of the example:

```
server {
    listen 80;
    server_name blog.example.com;
    root /home/example.com/blog/www;
    index index.php;
    location / {
    # If requested URI does not match any existing file,
    # directory or symbolic link, rewrite the URL to index.php
        try_files $uri $uri/ index.php;
    }
    # All PHP requests are passed on to PHP-FPM via FastCGI
```

```
     # For more information, consult chapter 5
     location ~ .php$ {
         fastcgi_pass 127.0.0.1:9000;
         fastcgi_param SCRIPT_FILENAME
/home/example.com/blog/www$fastcgi_script_name;
         fastcgi_param PATH_INFO $fastcgi_script_name;
         include fastcgi_params; # include extra FCGI params
     }
 }
```

MediaWiki

As its name suggests, MediaWiki is the web engine that empowers the famous Wikipedia online open encyclopedia. It is currently open source software and anyone can download and install it on their local server. The application can also be used as a **CMS** (**Content Management Software**), and large companies such as Novell have found it to be a reliable solution. Contrary to WordPress, MediaWiki does not come with a prewritten .htaccess file for prettying up URLs. Instead, the official MediaWiki website offers a wide variety of methods, which are all documented in the form of wiki articles. Webmasters can implement solutions that go as far as modifying the main Apache configuration file. However, there are simpler solutions that require no such measures. No particular Apache solution has been retained here, as three simple Nginx rewrite rules suffice to do the trick:

- The first one redirects default requests (for example, / as request URI) to /wiki/Main_Page
- The second one rewrites all the URIs of the /wiki/abcd form into the actual URL /w/index.php?title=abcd, without forgetting to append the rest of the parameters to the request URL
- The third one ensures that requests to /wiki get redirected to the home page /w/index.php

The following is a full virtual host configuration example, including the rewrite rules:

```
server {
    listen 80;
    server_name wiki.example.com;
root /home/example.com/wiki/www;
    location / {
        index index.php;
    # Permanent redirection to main page
        rewrite ^/$ /wiki/Main_Page permanent;
    }
# Rewrite /wiki/anything URIs to /w/index.php?title=anything
```

```
rewrite ^/wiki/([^?]*)(?:?(.*))? /w/index.php?title=$1&$2;
# Rewrite /wiki to /w/index.php
    rewrite ^/wiki /w/index.php;
    # Your usual FastCGI configuration here
    location ~ .php$ {
        fastcgi_pass    127.0.0.1:9000;
        fastcgi_index   index.php;
        fastcgi_param   SCRIPT_FILENAME
/home/example.com/wiki/www$fastcgi_script_name;
        include fastcgi_params;
    }
}
```

vBulletin

Discussion forums started blooming in the 2000s and a lot of popular web applications have appeared, such as vBulletin, phpBB, or InVision Board. Most of these forum software platforms have jumped on the bandwagon and now boast full SEO-friendly URL support. Unfortunately, rewrite rules often come in the form of `.htaccess` files. Indeed, the vBulletin developers have chosen to provide rewrite rules for Apache 2 and IIS, unsurprisingly forgetting Nginx. Let's teach them a lesson. The following table describes a solution for converting their Apache rewrite rules to Nginx:

Apache rule	Nginx rule
`RewriteEngine on`	Not necessary.
`RewriteCond %{REQUEST_FILENAME} -s [OR]` `RewriteCond %{REQUEST_FILENAME} -l [OR]` `RewriteCond %{REQUEST_FILENAME} -d` `RewriteRule ^.*$ - [NC,L]`	Do not rewrite if the requested URI corresponds to an existing file, folder, or link on the `system.if (-e $request_filename) { break; }`.
`RewriteRule ^threads/.* showthread.php [QSA]`	`rewrite ^/threads/.*$ /showthread.php last;`
`RewriteRule ^forums/.* forumdisplay.php [QSA]`	`rewrite ^/forums/.*$ /forumdisplay.php last;`
`RewriteRule ^members/.* member.php [QSA]`	`rewrite ^/members/.*$ /members.php last;`

Apache rule	Nginx rule
`RewriteRule ^blogs/.* blog.php [QSA]`	`rewrite ^/blogs/.*$ /blog.php last;`
`ReWriteRule ^entries/.* entry.php [QSA]`	`rewrite ^/entries/.*$ /entry.php last;`

`RewriteCond %{REQUEST_FILENAME} -s [OR]`
`RewriteCond %{REQUEST_FILENAME} -l [OR]`
`RewriteCond %{REQUEST_FILENAME} -d`
`RewriteRule ^.*$ - [NC,L]`
	For some reason, the same set of rules appears twice in the `.htaccess` file provided by vBulletin. You do not need to insert the Nginx equivalent a second time.

`RewriteRule ^(?:(.*?)(?:/|$))(.*|$)$ $1.php?r=$2 [QSA]`	`rewrite ^/(?:(.*?)(?:/|$))(.*|$)$ /$1.php?r=$2 last;`

Summary

Switching from Apache to Nginx may seem complex at first. There are many steps involved in the process, and you may face unsolvable problems if you are not confident and well prepared. You need to be aware of the current limitations of Nginx: no on-the-fly configuration changes, and thus no `.htaccess` files or any such similar feature. Nginx does not have as many modules as Apache does, at least not yet. Last but not least, you have to convert all your rewrite rules for your websites so they're functional under Nginx. So yes, it does take quite a bit of work. But this is a small price to pay to get a server that will ensure long-term stability and scalability. You and your visitors will not regret it, as it generally comes with improved loading and response speeds.

Introduction to Load Balancing and Optimization

9

As much as Nginx will help your servers hold the load, there are always limits to what a single machine can process: an aging hard drive or limited bandwidth will eventually induce a bottleneck, resulting in longer request-serving times, which in turn leads to the disappointment of your visitors.

As your websites grow more popular and your single machine begins to suffer, you will be tempted to simply get a bigger and more expensive server. But this would not be a cost-efficient approach in the long run, and remember that the more strain a server is exposed to, the more likely it is to suffer from hardware failure.

In this chapter, we will investigate two concepts, the first of which is load balancing: the art of distributing a load across several servers and managing this distribution efficiently. The second part will explore the subject of thread pools: a new mechanism relieving servers under heavy loads (more specifically, loads induced by blocking operations) by serving requests in a slightly different manner.

This chapter covers the following topics:

- An introduction to load balanced architectures
- Common concepts and issues of load balancing
- Dealing with the session affinity problem
- A demonstration of load balancing with MySQL
- Optimizing your setup with the help of thread pools

Introduction to load balancing

All of the most visited websites in the world are built over carefully planned server architectures: fast page loads and download speeds are a requirement for long-term traffic growth. The concept of load balancing has the potential to solve problems pertaining to scalability, availability, and performance. After a quick description of the concept, we will elaborate on how Nginx offers to implement such an architecture.

Understanding the concept of load balancing

To put it simply, the concept of load balancing consists of distributing the workload (CPU load, hard disk load, or other forms) across several servers, in a manner that is completely transparent to your visitors.

In the case of a single-server architecture, client requests are received and processed by one machine. A machine has a limited capacity of operation; for example, a web server that is able to respond to 1,000 HTTP requests per second. If the server receives more than 1,000 requests per second, the 1,001st client request received in that second will not be served in a timely manner. And from then on, page-serving speeds would begin to increase, resulting in a degraded experience for your visitors:

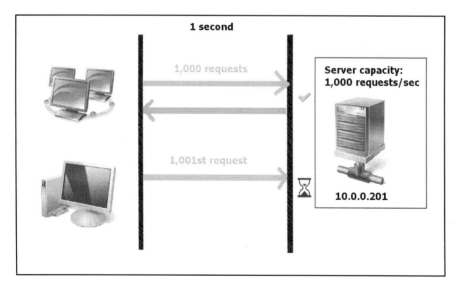

Distributing a load across several servers increases the overall request-serving capacity: with two servers at your disposal, you could theoretically allow 2,000 HTTP requests to be served per second. With three servers, you could serve 3,000 requests, and so on.

There are several techniques available for achieving load balancing, the simplest of which is **DNS load balancing**. When a person wishes to visit your website, their web browser will resolve your domain name (`example.com`) into an IP address (`1.2.3.4`). To achieve DNS load balancing, simply associate multiple IP addresses to your domain. Upon visiting your website, the operating system of your visitors will select one of these IP addresses following a **simple round-robin** algorithm, thus ensuring that on a global scale, all of your servers receive more or less the same amount of traffic:

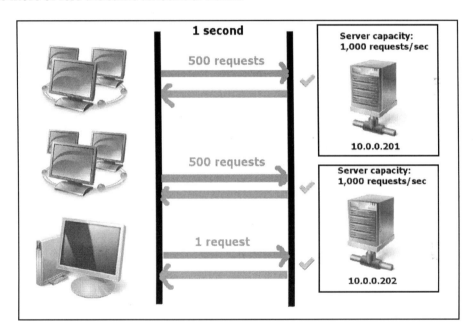

Albeit simple to implement, this load-balancing method cannot always be applied to high traffic websites, because it has several major issues:

- What if the IP address selected by a visitor's operating system points to a server that is temporarily unavailable?
- What if your architecture is made of several types of servers, some of which are capable of handling more requests than others?

- What if a visitor connects to a particular server and logs in to their user account, only to get switched to another server 10 minutes later, losing their session data?
- The last of these issues is also known as the **session affinity** problem and is further detailed in the next section.

Session affinity

Session affinity is an expression that designates the persistent assignment of a client to a particular server in a load-balanced infrastructure. We use the word *session* to describe a set of requests performed by a client to a server. When a visitor browses a website, they often visit more than one page: they log in to their account, they add a product to their shopping cart, they check out, and so on. Until they close their web browser (or a tab), all of their subsequent page views are part of a session, which is most of the time stateful: the server conserves data relative to the operations performed during the visit. In our example, that server would remember the contents of the shopping cart and the login credentials.

If at some point during the session the visitor were to switch servers and connect to **Server B**, they would lose any session information contained on **Server A**. The visitor would then lose the contents of their shopping cart, as well as their login credentials (they would get logged out):

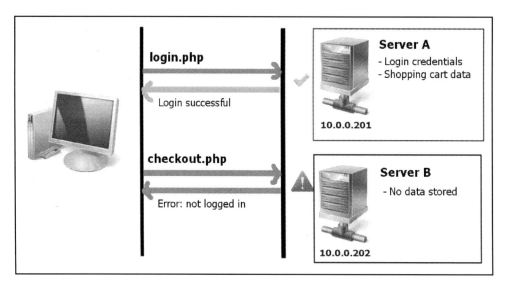

For that reason, it is of utmost importance to maintain session affinity: in other words, to ensure that a visitor remains assigned to a particular server at all times. The DNS load-balancing method does not ensure session affinity, but fortunately, Nginx will help you achieve it.

The upstream module

The implementation of load balancing in Nginx is particularly clever, as it allows you to distribute a load at several levels of your infrastructure. It isn't limited to proxying HTTP requests across backend servers: it also offers to distribute requests across FastCGI backends (FastCGI, uWSGI, SCGI, and more), or even distribute queries to Memcached servers. Any directive that ends with _pass, such as proxy_pass, fastcgi_pass, or memcached_pass, accepts a reference to a group of servers.

The first step is to declare this group of servers with the help of the *upstream* block, which must be placed within the http block. Within the upstream block, declare one or more servers with the server directive:

```
http {
    upstream MyUpstream {
        server 10.0.0.201;
        server 10.0.0.202;
        server 10.0.0.203;
    }
[...]
}
```

Alternatively, you can also use include inside your upstream block to load servers from an external file:

```
http {
    upstream MyUpstream {
        include myUpstreamServers.txt
    }
[...]
}
```

Now that your server group is declared, you can reference it in your virtual host configuration. For example, you can distribute incoming HTTP requests across the server group simply by proxying them:

```
server {
    server_name example.com;
    listen 80;
    root /home/example.com/www;
# Proxy all requests to the MyUpstream server group
proxy_pass http://MyUpstream;
    [...]
}
```

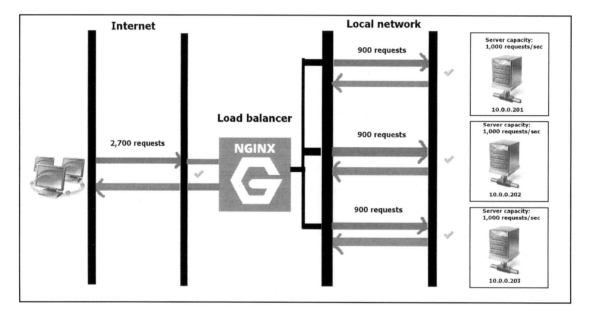

In this most basic state of configuration, requests are distributed across the three servers of the MyUpstream group according to a simple round-robin algorithm, without maintaining session affinity.

Request distribution mechanisms

Nginx offers several ways to solve the problems we mentioned earlier. The first and simplest of them is the `weight` flag, which can be enabled in the definition of your server group:

```
upstream MyUpstream {
    server 10.0.0.201 weight=3;
    server 10.0.0.202 weight=2;
    server 10.0.0.203;
}
```

By default, servers have a weight of 1, unless you specify otherwise. Such a configuration enables you to give more importance to particular servers: the higher their weight, the more requests they will receive from Nginx. In this example, for every six HTTP requests received, Nginx will systematically distribute:

- Three requests to the `10.0.0.201` server (`weight=3`)
- Two requests to the `10.0.0.202` server (`weight=2`)
- One request to the `10.0.0.203` server (`weight=1`)

For every 12 requests, Nginx will distribute:

- Six requests to the `10.0.0.201` server (`weight=3`)
- Four requests to the `10.0.0.202` server (`weight=2`)
- Two requests to the `10.0.0.203` server (`weight=1`)

Nginx also includes a mechanism that will verify the state of servers in a group. If a server doesn't respond in time, the request will be re-sent to the next server in the group. There are several flags that can be assigned to servers in an upstream block that will allow you to better control this mechanism:

- `fail_timeout=N`, where `N` is the number of seconds before a request is considered to have failed.
- `max_fails=N`, where `N` is the number of attempts that should be performed on a server before Nginx gives up and switches to the next server. By default, Nginx only tries once. If all servers become unresponsive, Nginx will wait for `fail_timeout` to expire before resetting all server fail counts and trying again.

- `max_conns=N`, where `N` is the number of maximum concurrent connections that can be sent to that server. By default, Nginx will not limit concurrent connections.
- `backup` marks the server as backup server, instructing Nginx to use it only in the case of failure from another server (it is not used otherwise).
- `down` marks the server as permanently unavailable, instructing Nginx not to use it anymore.

Finally, Nginx offers plenty of options to achieve session affinity. They come under the form of directives that should be inserted within the upstream block. The simplest of them is `ip_hash`: this directive instructs Nginx to calculate a hash from the first 3 bytes of the client IPv4 address (or the full IPv6 address), and, based on that hash, keep the client assigned to a particular server. As long as the client IP address remains the same, Nginx will always forward requests to the same server in the upstream group:

```
upstream {
    server 10.0.0.201 weight=3;
    server 10.0.0.202 weight=2;
    server 10.0.0.203;
    ip_hash;
}
```

Some administrators may deem this method too unreliable, considering the fact that a majority of internet service providers across the globe still provide dynamic IP addresses, renewed on a 24-hour basis. So why not use your own distribution key? Instead of the client IP address, you could separate requests based on the criteria of your choice, thanks to the `hash` directive. Since the directive allows variables, you could decide to separate requests based on a cookie value:

```
upstream {
    server 10.0.0.201;
    server 10.0.0.202;
    hash $cookie_username;
}
```

Based on the data contained in the `username` cookie, your visitors will be assigned to the first or the second server in the upstream group.

Using Nginx as a TCP load balancer

Until recently, the open source version of Nginx would only allow load balancing in the context of HTTP requests. In the meantime, the commercial subscription Nginx Plus took the concept one step further: using Nginx as TCP load balancer. This would pave the way to much broader possibilities: you could then set up Nginx to distribute the load across any form of networked servers—database servers, email servers, literally everything that communicates via TCP. In May 2015, the authors decided that TCP load balancing should be part of the open source version. As of Nginx 1.9.0, the stream module is included in the source code readily available on `http://nginx.org/`.

The stream module

The way TCP load balancing works in Nginx is remarkably similar to HTTP load balancing. However, since the module which brings forth the new set of directives is not included in the default build, you will need to run the `configure` command with the following flag before building the program:

```
--with-stream
```

The stream module offers a new block called **stream,** which must be placed at the root of the configuration file (outside of the `http` block). In this block, you must declare two sets of directives:

- `server` declares a TCP server listening on a particular port, and optionally, a network interface, with or without SSL
- `upstream` defines a server group in a similar manner as seen previously

In your server blocks, the requests will be sent to the server group with the `proxy_pass` directive

An example of MySQL load balancing

If you already understand how HTTP load balancing works in Nginx, the following example will look spectacularly simple to you. We will configure Nginx to receive MySQL connections and balance them across two backend servers:

```
stream {
  upstream MyGroup {
    # use IP address-based distribution
    hash $remote_addr;
    server 10.0.0.201 weight=2;
    server 10.0.0.202;
    server 10.0.0.203 backup; # use as backup only
  }
  server {
    # listen on the default MySQL port
    listen 3306;
    proxy_pass MyGroup; # forward requests to upstream
  }
}
```

That's all there is to it. All directives and options offered by the upstream module are still there, but keep in mind that you won't be able to use HTTP-based variables (such as cookies) to achieve session affinity. The stream module comes with a lot more options and flags, but they are not detailed here, as this falls outside the scope of an HTTP server; additional documentation can be found at http://nginx.org/.

Thread pools and IO mechanisms

Before making important financial decisions, such as investing in an additional server or two, you should look to optimize your current setup to make the most of your existing infrastructure.

Relieving worker processes

In the case of websites that require heavy I/O operations, such as file uploads or downloads, the asynchronous architecture of Nginx can present a certain disadvantage: while the master process is able to absorb incoming connections asynchronously, worker processes can be blocked for relatively long periods of time by certain tasks (the most common of which is reading data from hard disk drives or network drives).

Consider a simplified configuration with two worker processes; each HTTP request received by Nginx gets assigned to either process. Within a process, operations are performed sequentially: receiving and parsing the request, reading the requested file from its storage location, and finally, preparing and sending the response to the client. If for some reason you were to serve files stored on a network drive with a latency of about 100 ms, both of your worker processes would be spending most of their time waiting for the files. As a result, your server would only be able to serve 18 to 20 requests per second:

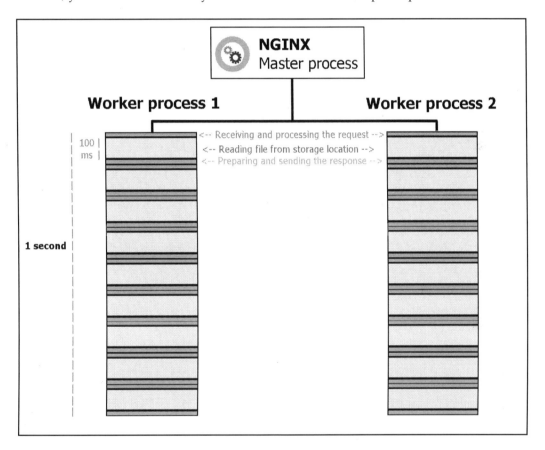

This isn't just a problem that occurs for network drives: even regular hard disk drives can take a certain time to fetch a file if it isn't in the cache; 10 milliseconds isn't insignificant when you multiply it by 1,000!

The solution that has been made available as of Nginx 1.7.11 is called **thread pools**. The basic principle behind this solution is that instead of reading files synchronously within the worker process, Nginx delegates the operation to a thread. This immediately liberates the worker process, which can then move on to the next request in the queue. Whenever the thread finishes performing the operation, the worker process finalizes and sends the response to the client. It is a pretty simple concept to understand, and thankfully, it's just as simple to configure.

AIO, Sendfile, and DirectIO

In order to enable support for thread pools, Nginx must be built with the `--with-threads` parameter; this functionality doesn't come by default. The first step of the configuration is to define a thread pool with the `thread_pool` directive, at the root of your configuration file.

Syntax: `thread_pool name threads=N [max_queue=Q];`

In this syntax, `name` is the name you wish to give to the thread pool, `N` is the number of threads that should be spawned, and `Q` the maximum number of operations allowed in the queue. By default, a thread pool exists with the name `default`, coming with 32 threads and a maximum queue of 65,536 operations.

In `location` blocks that require it, simply insert the `aio` directive and specify the thread pool name:

```
thread_pool MyPool threads=64;
[...]
location /downloads/ {
    aio threads=MyPool;
}
```

Alternatively, insert `aio threads` without a pool name if you want to use the default thread pool. It is also possible to use both `sendfile` and `aio` in the same location:

```
location /downloads/ {
aio threads;
directio 8k;
sendfile on;
}
```

If the file requested by the client is over `8k` (the value specified with the `directio` directive), `aio` will be used. Otherwise, the file will be sent via `sendfile`.

Summary

Before adapting your infrastructure to increasingly high traffic, you should always look for solutions offered by your current set of tools. If traffic causes your server to become unresponsive because of blocking operations, such as slow disk reads, you should give thread pools a try. If this turns out to be insufficient, load balancing is the next-best thing. Thankfully, as we have discovered in this chapter, implementing a load-balanced architecture is made particularly easy by Nginx; you can even use it to distribute the load of other server applications, such as MySQL, email, and more.

Now that we have seen a basic yet comprehensive approach to the most advanced mechanisms offered by Nginx, we will continue by exploring four real life case studies.

10
Case Studies

The chapters you have read until now have introduced the many facets of Nginx, from static web page serving to advanced features such as load balancing. You have learned to set up Nginx on your server and to configure it to fit the needs of your websites; you've also discovered the numerous advanced modules, bringing forth complex functionality.

We will now make use of the knowledge acquired so far by studying a couple of real-life examples: first, we will set up a complete WordPress site from scratch, approaching all aspects of the configuration, including optimization and caching. We will then enable HTTPS support as well as HTTP/2, and discover how to handle clients that visit your website from a mobile device.

The last part of the chapter will be dedicated to setting up ownCloud—an open source solution that allows you to store documents on your server and retrieve them from a variety of platforms. We will also secure access to your ownCloud drive by setting up a self-signed certificate.

This chapter covers:

- An in-depth guide to setting up a WordPress site
- Obtaining and setting up an SSL certificate to enable HTTPS support
- Enabling and testing HTTP/2 on your server
- Basic handling of mobile clients
- Creating a secure cloud drive with ownCloud

Deploying a WordPress site

As stated in Chapter 8, *From Apache to Nginx*, WordPress is currently the most popular content management system on the entire web. According to a recent survey from BuiltWith.com trends (https://trends.builtwith.com/), its market share totals 53%, leaving its competitors far behind: Joomla only captures 9% of the market, followed by Drupal with just a little over 2%. For a lot of web server administrators, setting up WordPress sites or blogs has become a common task, whether it is for personal or professional use.

Preparing your server and obtaining WordPress

In this section, we will be getting your server ready for downloading and installing the WordPress application. There will be a few configuration files to go through to make sure WordPress runs smoothly.

System requirements

The first step you need to go through to set up a WordPress site on a fresh new server is to make sure you have the necessary components installed and up to date: it is recommended that you run at least PHP 7.1 and MySQL Server 5.7. If you haven't done so yet, running the following commands will provide a basic working environment with minimal PHP extensions. Under a Debian-based Linux operating system:

```
# apt-get install mysql-server php7.1-fpm php7.1-mysql php7.1-gd php7.1-dev
php7.1-opcache
```

If your server runs a Red Hat-based OS, such as Fedora:

```
# yum install mysql-server php71-fpm php71-mysqlnd php71-gd php71-devel
php71-opcache
```

If you have an older version installed on your system, it is recommended that you upgrade to the latest available version using the apt-get update && apt-get upgrade or yum upgrade commands.

PHP configuration

After making sure your server components meet the minimum requirements, you should edit some of the settings, if you want WordPress to run smoothly. There are two main aspects of the PHP configuration you should look into. First, the default PHP configuration file (`php.ini`) contains directives that you will probably want to update:

- `cgi.fix_pathinfo`: Set this value to `0` for security reasons, as we have seen in `Chapter 5`, *PHP and Python with Nginx*.
- `post_max_size`: By default, the maximum size of the `POST` request body is `8` megabytes. Increase the value if necessary; keep in mind that file uploads are usually performed via `POST` requests.
- `upload_max_filesize`: Set to `2` megabytes by default, this will need to be increased if you want to allow uploading of large files.
- `date.timezone`: You will get a warning if you leave this blank as it is by default. Refer to `http://php.net/manual/en/timezones.php` to find out the proper value in your situation.

The second aspect of the configuration is the PHP-FPM side. The main `php-fpm.conf` file does not require immediate changes, however, if you haven't done so yet, you will need to create a *configuration pool*: a set of configuration directives that apply to a particular website or application. This allows you to run the PHP processes under a specific user account, and optionally configure a specific network interface for communicating with Nginx.

Create a new pool by declaring its name between brackets:

```
[wordpress]
```

Append the following configuration directives:

```
; Specify user account and group for the pool
; We assume that you created a "wordpress" user and group
user=wordpress
group=wordpress
; Network interface and listening port
; Use 127.0.0.1 if Nginx runs on the same machine
listen=127.0.0.1:9000
; Only allow connections from local computer
; Change this value if Nginx runs on a different machine
allowed_clients=127.0.0.1
```

Optionally, you may enable *chrooting*: specify a root directory for the PHP processes of this pool. For example, if you set the chroot to `/home/wordpress/www`, your PHP scripts will only be able to read files and directories within the specified path (any attempt to read or write a file or directory outside of `/home/wordpress/www` will systematically fail). It is highly recommended you enable this feature: should a security breach be discovered in the WordPress code, attackers would only be able to exploit files within the reach of your PHP process; the rest of your server would not be compromised:

```
chroot /home/wordpress/www;
```

Other configuration directives are documented at length in the default pool file supplied with PHP-FPM; their default values are suitable in most cases.

MySQL configuration

At the time of installing MySQL server, you were asked to set up administrator (`root`) credentials. Since these credentials allow full access to the SQL server, including permissions on all databases, you should never use them in any of your PHP applications. The best practice is to create a separate MySQL user and to assign permissions on the database that will be used by your application. Log in to your local MySQL server with the following command:

```
# mysql -u root -p
```

Create a new SQL database:

```
mysql> CREATE DATABASE wordpress;
```

Create a SQL user and grant all permissions to the `wordpress` database (don't forget to specify a complex enough password):

```
mysql> GRANT ALL PRIVILEGES ON wordpress.* TO 'wordpress'@'localhost'
IDENTIFIED BY 'password';
```

Now, run the `exit` command to leave the MySQL console and try logging in to the server using the newly created account:

```
mysql> exit
# mysql -u wordpress -p
mysql> SHOW DATABASES;
```

You should see the `wordpress` database you created a minute ago.

Downloading and extracting WordPress

The last step is to download the latest version of WordPress and extract it at the location specified earlier; in our example: /home/wordpress/www. The latest version can always be found at https://wordpress.org/latest.tar.gz:

```
/home/wordpress/www# wget https://wordpress.org/latest.tar.gz
/home/wordpress/www# tar xzf latest.tar.gz
/home/wordpress/www# mv ./wordpress/* ./ && rm -r ./wordpress
```

Make sure the user and group are properly set, and give write permissions to the wordpress user over the application files:

```
/home/wordpress/www# chown -R wordpress ./
/home/wordpress/www# chgrp -R wordpress ./
/home/wordpress/www# chmod -R 0644 ./
```

Nginx configuration

Before you can begin setting up WordPress via the user-friendly web installer, you will need to finalize your Nginx server configuration. We will go down to every last detail and suggest a configuration that would be appropriate for relatively low-end server hardware: eight-core Intel C2750 (Avoton) with 8 GB of RAM and a regular HDD. Directive values should be adjusted depending on your own hardware.

HTTP block

We will be going down the blocks starting at the top level: the HTTP blocks, encompassing directives that have an effect on the entire server. This implies that the directives placed here will affect all of the websites served by this instance of Nginx. Open your Nginx main configuration file (nginx.conf) and insert or update the following directives:

```
# Sets the user and group under which the worker processes
# will run. The following values are valid assuming your server
# will only be hosting one website.
user wordpress wordpress;
worker_processes 8; # 1 process per core
pid /var/run/nginx.pid;

events {
# Edit this value depending on your server hardware
    worker_connections 768;
}
```

```
http {
    # Core settings affecting I/O
    sendfile on;
    tcp_nopush on;
    tcp_nodelay on;

    # Default Nginx values
    keepalive_timeout 65;
    types_hash_max_size 2048;
    include /etc/nginx/mime.types;
    default_type application/octet-stream;

    # Set access and error log paths
    access_log /var/log/nginx/access.log;
    error_log /var/log/nginx/error.log;

    # Enable gzipping of files matching the given mime types
    gzip on;
    gzip_disable "msie6"; # Disable gzipping for I.E. 6 users
    gzip_types text/plain text/css application/json application/x-javascript
text/xml application/xml application/xml+rss text/javascript;
    # Include virtual host configuration files;
    # Edit path accordingly
    include /etc/nginx/sites-enabled/*;
}
```

Server block

The following step will require you to create a new file in the directory specified earlier. For example, create a file called `wordpress.conf` in the `/etc/nginx/sites-enabled/` folder. Define your virtual host configuration by inserting or updating the following directives:

```
server {
    # Listen on all network interfaces on port 80
    listen 80;

    # Specify the host name(s) that will match the site
    # The following value allows both www. and no subdomain
    server_name .example.com;
    # Set the path of your WordPress files
    root /home/wordpress/www;

    # Automatically load index.php
    index index.php;
    # Saves client request body into files, cleaning up afterwards
```

```
    client_body_in_file_only clean;
    client_body_buffer_size 32K;

    # Allow uploaded files up to 300 megabytes
    client_max_body_size 300M;
    # Automatically close connections if no data is
    # transmitted to the client for a period of 10 seconds
    send_timeout 10s;
    # The rest of the configuration (location blocks)
    # is found below
    [...]
}
```

Location blocks

Finally, set up your location blocks—directives that apply to specific locations on your site:

```
# The following applies to static files:
# images, CSS, javascript
location ~* ^.+.(jpg|jpeg|png|gif|ico|css|js)$ {
      access_log off; # Disable logging
      # Allow client browsers to cache files
      # for a long period of time
      expires 180d;
}

# The following applies to every request
location / {
   # Try serving the requested URI:
   # - If the file does not exist, append /
   # - If the directory does not exist,
   # redirect to /index.php forwarding the request URI
   # and other request arguments
      try_files $uri $uri/ /index.php?q=$uri&$args;
}
# The following applies to every PHP file
location ~ .php$ {
      # Ensure file really exists
        if (!-e $request_filename) {
              return 404;
        }
        # Pass the request to your PHP-FPM backend
        fastcgi_pass 127.0.0.1:9000;
      fastcgi_index index.php;
      fastcgi_param PATH_INFO $fastcgi_script_name;
```

```
        include fastcgi_params;
    }
```

WordPress configuration

Once your Nginx configuration is finalized and saved, make sure to reload the Nginx configuration, either via `service nginx reload` or `/usr/local/nginx/sbin/nginx -s reload` (or your usual Nginx binary location).

If all goes well, you should be able to run the web-based WordPress installer by visiting `http://example.com/wp-admin/install.php` (replacing `example.com` by your own domain name). You will be prompted for:

- The name of the database you created earlier, in our example: `wordpress`
- The SQL username you created earlier, in our example: `wordpress`
- The password associated to the user: `password`
- The database host: `127.0.0.1`, if your MySQL server is hosted on the same server
- A prefix for all SQL tables created by WordPress: `wp_`

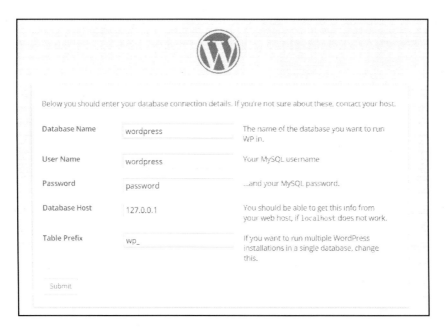

Once the installer completes, you can begin configuring and preparing your WordPress site. In order to enable pretty URLs, you should check the **Settings | Permalinks** section: several URL schemes are offered, such as `http://example.com/post-name/` or `http://example.com/year/month/post-name/`.

Securing communications with HTTPS

Implementing HTTPS support is becoming an increasingly important requirement in the modern web. Visitors no longer trust online stores that don't secure communications; and all of the major players of the industry are slowly eradicating plain-text transmissions. Facebook, Google, and Twitter now all default to HTTPS. Google has even announced that its search engine would promote websites that offered HTTPS support. There isn't any reason left to skip this part, and Nginx makes it particularly easy. We will thus expand on the example in the previous section and enable HTTPS support on our WordPress site; please note however that the guide remains, regardless of the application you are securing.

Self-signed certificates and certificate authorities

In order to enable HTTPS, we have to obtain an SSL certificate, which will contain information pertaining to the domain name we wish to secure. There are two types of certificates that you may set up for your website:

- Self-signed certificates that you can generate all by yourself on your own server
- Certificates signed by a trusted certificate authority, which offer an additional level of security; that is, a third party ascertains the authenticity of your server as your visitors connect to your website

For testing environments or websites that are meant for a restricted amount of visitors, self-signed certificates can be an option; however, bear in mind that web browsers will display a warning message when visitors browse your site:

The site's security certificate is not trusted!

You attempted to reach **192.168.17.129**, but the server presented a certificate issued by an entity that is not trusted by your computer's operating system. This may mean that the server has generated its own security credentials, which Chrome cannot rely on for identity information, or an attacker may be trying to intercept your communications.

You should not proceed, **especially** if you have never seen this warning before for this site.

Proceed anyway   Back to safety

▶Help me understand

In the case of our WordPress example site, the best option is to set up a certificate that is signed by a third party (self-signed certificates are covered further on in the chapter), seeing as we intend for it to be visited by as many people as possible.

In order to obtain a trusted certificate, we can get one issued by the free certificate authority, Let's Encrypt, a non-profit organization designed to help make the web more secure by removing the cost as a barrier. You can find the full details on their website at `https://letsencrypt.org/`.

Obtaining your SSL certificate

In order to generate your certificate, we'll need to provide Let's Encrypt with a few pieces of information, the first of which is a private encryption key that must be kept as safe as possible (any attacker that gets hold of this key would theoretically be able to impersonate your server). This key will be generated with a program called `openssl`, which must be installed on your system. Install it with the following command:

```
# apt-get install openssl
```

Alternatively, for Red Hat-based operating systems:

```
# yum install openssl
```

Run the following command to generate your 2048-bit RSA private key, replacing `example.com` with your actual domain name:

```
# openssl genrsa -out example.com.key 2048
```

A file called `example.com.key` is now present in the current directory. Before you move the file to a secure location, you must generate a certificate-signing-request file, which will be transmitted to the certificate authority. The following command will take care of it:

```
# openssl req -new -key example.com.key -out example.com.csr
```

As you execute this command, you will be prompted to enter details about your company or organization; the most important part is **Common Name** (for example, server FQDN or your name): this is where you should enter your actual domain name, in our example: `example.com`. Once this is done, you are left with a `.csr` file containing the information required by the certificate authority to generate your certificate. Log in to your account on the certificate authority website and upload the `.csr` file (or its contents). Your certificate-signing request will be verified and processed by the **Certificate Authority** (**CA**) and the certificate files will be provided to you immediately or after a short period of time, depending on the certificate authority you selected.

Enabling HTTPS in your Nginx configuration

At this point, you should have received two files from your certificate authority: your site's certificate file (`.crt`), and an additional certificate file containing information relative to the certificate authority itself. These two files must be concatenated into one using the following command:

```
# cat your_site_certificate.crt certificate_authority.crt > example.com.crt
```

The order is important: your site's certificate first, followed by your CA's certificate. Now that this is done, two files are required to finalize your Nginx configuration:

- Your private key file generated during the first step (`example.com.key`)
- The certificate file we generated just now (`example.com.crt`)

Store them in a secure location, but keep in mind Nginx must have read permission in order to function properly. We will now edit your Nginx configuration to enable HTTPS.

Open the existing server block for your domain, and append the following directives after
the `listen 80;` line:

```
# Listen on port 443 using SSL and make it the default server
listen 443 default_server ssl;

# Specify the path of your .crt and .key files
ssl_certificate     /etc/ssl/private/example.com.crt;
ssl_certificate_key /etc/ssl/private/example.com.key;

# Enable session caching, increase session timeout
ssl_session_cache shared:SSL:20m;
ssl_session_timeout 60m;

# Disable SSL in favor of TLS (safer)
ssl_protocols TLSv1 TLSv1.1 TLSv1.2;
```

Save your configuration and reload Nginx. At this point, you are able to browse your site
via HTTPS (while HTTP is still enabled); however, we must inform WordPress that the site
URL has changed. Open your WordPress site control panel; go to **Settings** | **General**, and
update the site address:

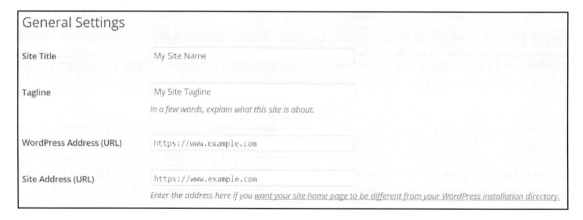

Furthermore, if your custom theme includes elements linked statically, you will want to
update your URLs by replacing `http` with `https` (or better, by removing the protocol
altogether since modern web browsers are clever enough to use the correct one
automatically).

Setting up and testing HTTP/2

As detailed in `Chapter 4`, *Module Configuration*, the HTTP/2 protocol is now supported by Nginx and supersedes the SPDY protocol that was designed by Google, in order to improve page-loading times for visitors through various techniques (data compression, multiplexing of requests, and more). HTTP/2 can be enabled quite simply by making sure the module exists in your Nginx build, and appending a flag to your `listen` configuration directive.

If you are unsure whether you included the HTTP/2 module in your Nginx build, run the `nginx -V` command to find out. If you did not include it, you should rebuild Nginx with the `--with-http_v2_module` command line argument. Once HTTP/2 is available, open up your server block configuration and update the `listen` directive:

```
listen 443 default_server ssl http2;
```

Reload Nginx via the `systemctl reload nginx` command and visit your website again from a web browser that supports HTTP/2 (Google Chrome or Firefox, among others). You may or may not notice speed improvements; if you want to make sure HTTP/2 is correctly enabled, you can use a browser extension that will provide indications. On Google Chrome, you can download an extension called *HTTP/2 and SPDY indicator*, available on the Chrome Web Store free of charge.

Creating your ownCloud drive

By 2018, everyone must have heard of Dropbox and similar services that allow you to store files online and retrieve them easily from all sorts of devices—including mobile phones and tablets. While Dropbox is well known for being easy to use and safe enough to store important files, it comes with a price and limited storage size. The servers your files are stored on don't belong to you and recent events have shown that third parties (that is, government agencies) are sometimes allowed to go through your documents if they can provide valid justification. Parallel to Dropbox and other commercial services, a free open source platform was developed: ownCloud. In this chapter, we will set up ownCloud on your Nginx-powered server, and secure communications with the help of a self-signed certificate.

Getting ownCloud

Before installing ownCloud on your server, you should follow the steps that we covered in the previous section:

1. Make sure your server runs PHP 5.4 or preferably greater, as well as MySQL server, at least in version 5.

2. Update your PHP configuration file accordingly, taking particular care of the directives pertaining to the maximum file-upload size.

3. Create a PHP–FPM pool dedicated to ownCloud. Set up a SQL database and user.

4. Once all of these steps have been covered, you are ready to begin downloading and extracting ownCloud. Head over to `ownCloud.org` and obtain the URL of the latest version, then run the following commands:

```
/home/owncloud/www# wget
https://download.owncloud.org/community/owncloud-10.0.4.zip
/home/owncloud/www# unzip owncloud-10.0.4.zip
/home/owncloud/www# mv ./owncloud/{.[!.],}* ./ && rm -r ./owncloud
```

5. Make sure the user and group are properly set, and give write permissions to the `owncloud` user over the application files:

```
/home/owncloud/www# chown -R owncloud ./
/home/owncloud/www# chgrp -R owncloud ./
/home/owncloud/www# chmod -R 0644 ./
```

Nginx configuration

You are ready to configure Nginx to host your ownCloud drive. This time, the configuration appears slightly more complex due to the nature of the application and its multiple access mechanisms. Initially, we will be accessing our ownCloud instance via HTTP; the final section being dedicated to implementing a self-signed SSL certificate, allowing us to browse our cloud drive over HTTPS.

Begin by creating a new configuration file in our virtual host configuration folder—in our example, `/etc/nginx/sites-enabled/`. Insert the following set of directives (or obtain the default Nginx configuration supplied with ownCloud and edit it to suit your needs):

```
server {
    # For now, we won't be enabling HTTPS
    listen 80;

    # Insert your host name and document root here
    server_name cloud.example.com;
    root /home/owncloud/www;

    # Set the maximum allowed file upload size
    client_max_body_size 42G;

    # Disable gzip to avoid the removal of the ETag header
    gzip off;

    # Rewrite rules for DAV access
    rewrite ^/caldav(.*)$ /remote.php/caldav$1 redirect;
    rewrite ^/carddav(.*)$ /remote.php/carddav$1 redirect;
    rewrite ^/webdav(.*)$ /remote.php/webdav$1 redirect;
    # Set index and error pages
    index index.php;
    error_page 403 /core/templates/403.php;
    error_page 404 /core/templates/404.php;
    # Deny access to the following files and folders
    location ~ ^/(?:.htaccess|data|config|db_structure.xml|README){
        deny all;
    }
    location / {
        # ownCloud rewrite rules
        rewrite ^/.well-known/host-meta /public.php?service=host-meta
last;
        rewrite ^/.well-known/host-meta.json /public.php?service=host-
meta-json last;
        rewrite ^/.well-known/carddav /remote.php/carddav/ redirect;
        rewrite ^/.well-known/caldav /remote.php/caldav/ redirect;
        rewrite ^(/core/doc/[^/]+/)$ $1/index.html;
        # Attempt to serve requested URI
        # or redirect request to index.php
        try_files $uri $uri/ /index.php;
    }
    # The following applies to URIs ending with .php
    location ~ .php(?:$|/) {
        # Prepare URI path info
        fastcgi_split_path_info ^(.+.php)(/.+)$;
```

```
        # Load default FastCGI parameters
        include fastcgi_params;
        fastcgi_param SCRIPT_FILENAME $document_root$fastcgi_script_name;
        fastcgi_param PATH_INFO $fastcgi_path_info;
        # Important: set HTTPS to off for the time being
        fastcgi_param HTTPS off;
        fastcgi_buffers 64 4K;
        fastcgi_pass 127.0.0.1:9000;
    }

    # Allows visitors to cache static files
    location ~* .(?:jpg|jpeg|gif|bmp|ico|png|css|js|swf)$ {
        expires 30d;
        access_log off;
    }
}
```

After saving your configuration and reloading Nginx, open your web browser and load the main ownCloud page—in our example: `http://cloud.example.com`. You should now see a setup page inviting you to create an administrator account and define storage settings:

Proceed with the installation of ownCloud: after the initial setup screen, you will be prompted to enter SQL database information and credentials. Past this point, you should be able to enjoy your online drive straight away; but remember that communications between you and the server aren't secure yet. Proceed to the next step to begin setting up a self-signed certificate:

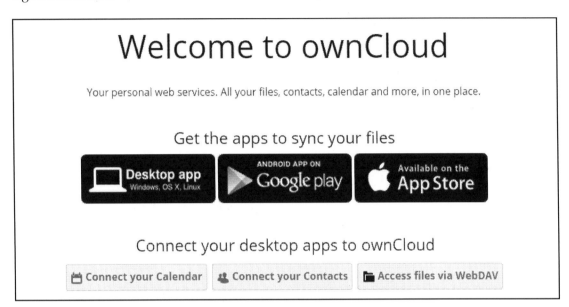

Setting up a self-signed certificate

Since our ownCloud drive is meant for personal use, and for the sake of the example, we will resort to a self-signed certificate: the procedure is relatively hassle-free and it doesn't cost a thing. Run the following commands to generate your certificate:

```
# openssl genrsa -out owncloud.key 2048
# openssl req -new -key owncloud.key -out owncloud.csr
# openssl x509 -req -days 1000 -in owncloud.csr -signkey owncloud.key -out owncloud.crt
```

Now that you have the required files at your disposal, open your virtual host configuration file (containing your server block) and make the following changes:

- Replace `listen 80` with `listen 443 ssl`
- Insert `ssl_certificate /etc/cert/owncloud.crt;` (use your actual certificate file path) after the `listen` directive
- Insert `ssl_certificate_key /root/cert/owncloud.key;` (use your actual private key file) after the previous directive
- Replace `fastcgi_param HTTPS off;` with `fastcgi_param HTTPS on;`

Save your configuration file and reload Nginx. You are now able to browse your ownCloud drive over HTTPS; but since the certificate is self-signed, you will see a warning screen before you can access the application.

Summary

As you may have noticed in the cases we studied in this chapter, the process of setting up a web application can sometimes be long and complex. But when it comes to the part that concerns Nginx, configuration is usually pretty simple and straightforward: a couple of directives in a server block, reload the server, and you're done.

Unfortunately, in some cases, while your initial configuration seems to do the trick, you realize over time that your visitors run into a variety of problems or are presented with unexpected error pages. The next chapter will prepare you to face such issues by exploring several leads, should you ever need to troubleshoot your web server.

11
Troubleshooting

Even if you read every single word of this book with the utmost attention, you are unfortunately not sheltered from all kinds of issues, ranging from simple configuration errors to the occasional unexpected behavior of one module or another. In this chapter, we will attempt to provide solutions for some of the common problems encountered by administrators who are just getting started with Nginx.

The appendix covers the following topics:

- A basic guide containing general tips on Nginx troubleshooting
- How to solve some of the most common install issues
- Dealing with `403 Forbidden` and `400 Bad Request` HTTP errors
- Why your configuration does not appear to apply correctly
- A few words about the `if` block behavior

General tips on Nginx troubleshooting

Before we begin, whenever you run into some kind of problem with Nginx, you should make sure to follow the recommendations given in the following sections, as they are generally a good source of solutions.

Checking access permissions

A lot of errors that Nginx administrators are faced with are caused by invalid access permissions. On two separate occasions, you are offered to specify a user and group for the Nginx worker processes to run:

- When configuring the build with the `configure` command, you are allowed to specify a user and group that will be used by default (refer to `Chapter 1`, *Downloading and Installing Nginx*).
- In the configuration file, the `user` directive allows you to specify a user and group. This directive overrides the value that you may have defined during the `configure` step.

If Nginx is supposed to access files that do not have the correct permissions, in other words, that cannot be read (and by extension, cannot be written for directories that hold temporary files, for example) by the specified user and group, Nginx will not be able to serve files correctly. Additionally, should your web application encounter an error related to file or directory access permissions, the user and group under which your FastCGI or other backend runs should also be investigated.

Testing your configuration

A common mistake is often made by administrators showing a little too much self-confidence: after having modified the configuration file (often without a backup), they reload Nginx to apply the new configuration. If the configuration file contains syntax or semantic errors, the application will refuse to reload. Even worse, if Nginx is stopped (for example, after a complete server reboot) it will refuse to start at all. In either of those cases, remember to follow these recommendations:

- Always keep a backup of your working configuration files in case something goes wrong
- Before reloading or restarting Nginx, test your configuration with a simple command, `nginx -t`, to test your current configuration files, or run `nginx -t -c /path/to/config/file.conf`
- Reload your server instead of restarting it, preferring `service nginx reload` over `service nginx restart` (`nginx -s reload` instead of `nginx -s stop && nginx`), as it will keep existing connections alive, and thus, won't interrupt ongoing file downloads

Have you reloaded the service?

You would be surprised to learn how often this happens: the most complicated situations have the simplest solutions. Before tearing your hair out, before rushing to the forums or IRC asking for help, start with the most simple of verifications.

You just spent two hours creating your virtual host configuration. You've saved the files properly and have fired up your web browser to check the results. But did you remember that one additional step? Nginx, unlike Apache, does not support on-the-fly configuration changes in `.htaccess` files or similar. So take a moment to make sure you did reload Nginx with `service nginx reload`, `/etc/init.d/nginx reload`, or `/usr/local/nginx/sbin/nginx -s reload`, without forgetting to test your configuration beforehand!

Checking logs

There is usually no need to look for the answer to your problems on the internet. Chances are, the answer is already given to you by Nginx in the log files. There are two variations of log files you may want to check. First, check the access logs. These contain information about requests themselves: the request method and URI, the HTTP response code issued by Nginx, and more, depending on the log format you defined:

```
error.log
1  2015/09/12 06:46:19 [error] 10164#0: *221161 open() "/home/example.com/wp-content/plugins/contactformgenerator/documentati
2  2015/09/12 06:46:25 [error] 10164#0: *221162 open() "/home/example.com/wp-content/plugins/seo-interlinking/js/quicksearch.
3  2015/09/12 06:46:25 [error] 10164#0: *221163 open() "/home/example.com/wp-content/plugins/Premium_Gallery_Manager/sprites/
4  2015/09/12 06:46:30 [error] 10164#0: *221164 open() "/home/example.com/wp-content/plugins/rock-form-builder/admin/js/rock-
5  2015/09/12 06:46:30 [error] 10164#0: *221165 open() "/home/example.com/wp-content/plugins/maxbuttons-pro/js/maxbuttons.js"
6  2015/09/12 07:32:23 [error] 10164#0: *221206 open() "/home/example.com/robots.txt" failed (2: No such file or directory),
7  2015/09/12 07:44:08 [error] 10164#0: *221207 open() "/home/example.com/robots.txt" failed (2: No such file or directory),
8  2015/09/12 10:05:14 [error] 10164#0: *221298 open() "/home/example.com/favicon.ico" failed (2: No such file or directory),
```

More importantly, for troubleshooting, the error log is a goldmine of information. Depending on the level you defined (see `error_log` and `debug_connection` directives for more details), Nginx will provide details on its inner functioning. For example, you will be able to see the request URI translated to the actual filesystem path. This can be a great help for debugging rewrite rules. The error log should be located in the `/logs/` directory of your Nginx setup, by default `/usr/local/nginx/logs` or `/var/log/nginx`.

Installing a log parser

While Nginx has great logs, at some of the higher levels of logging, they can also be quite exhaustive in the amount of information they log. A good way to not miss information and get a high level overview of what is going on with Nginx is to install a log parser that can aggregate information and display it in a more approachable format.

 One open source tool we can use for this is called **GoAccess**, and can be found on their website at `https://goaccess.io/`.

The good thing about GoAccess, aside from being free and open source, is that it can be accessed through both the Terminal and your browser. Therefore, it can function as both a monitoring tool that you run in your Terminal and as a reporting tool that generates a kind of dashboard for your stats:

```
Dashboard - Overall Analyzed Requests (01/Dec/2010 - 18/Dec/2010)                          [Active Panel: Visitors]

 Total Requests    248660 Unique Visitors  22953 Unique Files 14666 Referrers 5587
 Valid Requests    248660 Init. Proc. Time 4s       Static Files 10477 Log Size  61.58 MiB
 Failed Requests   0        Excl. IP Hits    0       Unique 404   994   Bandwidth 3.40 GiB
 Log Source        /var/log/apache/access.log

> 1 - Unique visitors per day - Including spiders                                            Total: 18/18

 Hits     h% Vis.   v%    Bandwidth Avg. T.S. Cum. T.S. Max. T.S. Data

15177  6.10% 1138 4.96%   199.02 MiB 333.10 ms   1.40 hr    1.07 mn 18/Dec/2010 ||||||||||||||||||||||||||||||||||||||||||||
13949  5.61% 1245 5.42%   168.14 MiB 285.32 ms   1.11 hr    1.08 mn 17/Dec/2010 ||||||||||||||||||||||||||||||||||||||||
10928  4.39% 1025 4.47%   138.34 MiB 246.56 ms  44.91 mn   31.48  s 16/Dec/2010 |||||||||||||||||||||||||||||||||
 8948  3.60% 1084 4.72%   117.00 MiB 237.29 ms  35.39 mn   43.47  s 15/Dec/2010 |||||||||||||||||||||||||||||
12570  5.06% 1216 5.30%   158.99 MiB 277.96 ms  59.25 mn   45.89  s 14/Dec/2010 |||||||||||||||||||||||||||||||||||||
16111  6.48% 1355 5.90%   202.72 MiB 258.03 ms   1.15 hr   41.93  s 13/Dec/2010 ||||||||||||||||||||||||||||||||||||||||||||||
15415  6.20% 1453 6.33%   214.00 MiB 296.97 ms   1.27 hr    1.26 mn 12/Dec/2010 |||||||||||||||||||||||||||||||||||||||||||

 2 - Requested Files (URLs)                                                                  Total: 366/14666

 Hits     h% Vis.   v%    Bandwidth Avg. T.S. Cum. T.S. Max. T.S. Mtd  Proto    Data

 9723  9.66% 6509 9.72%   34.67 MiB 137.32 ms  22.25 mn   8.29  s GET  HTTP/1.1 /
 4910  4.88%    1 0.00%   19.67 KiB  20.00 us 101.05 ms 531.00 us ---  ---      -
 3804  3.78% 1959 2.93%   11.02 MiB   1.92 ms   7.29  s   2.83  s GET  HTTP/1.1 /captcha.mod.php
 3665  3.64%   37 0.06%   24.04 MiB  55.98 ms   5.42 mn   1.84  s POST HTTP/1.1 /contact.php
 3053  3.03%  295 0.44%  654.73 KiB 757.00 us   2.31  s   6.34 ms HEAD HTTP/1.1 /
 2416  2.40% 2176 3.25%  120.91 MiB 891.83 ms  35.91 mn  40.11  s GET  HTTP/1.1 /mail_interface.html
 1724  1.71%  244 0.36%   27.37 MiB 106.33 ms   3.06 mn   4.86  s GET  HTTP/1.1 /rss.php

 3 - Static Requests                                                                         Total: 366/10477
```

To get started and install GoAccess, you can either check your distribution package manager or download and compile it manually:

```
wget http://tar.goaccess.io/goaccess-1.2.tar.gz
tar -xzvf goaccess-1.2.tar.gz
cd goaccess-1.2/
./configure --enable-utf8 --enable-geoip=legacy
make
make install
```

Once installed, using it is very simple; you can get a Terminal view by running the following command:

```
goaccess /var/log/nginx/access.log --log-format=COMBINED
```

Here, the COMBINED log format refers to the default log format of Nginx, but it is also compatible with Apache HTTPd logs. If you want to get an HTML report that you can view in a browser, or perhaps email to someone for reporting, then run:

```
goaccess /var/log/nginx/access.log -o report.html --log-format=COMBINED
```

A neat feature of GoAccess is that it can also provide a real-time auto-updating HTML page by using the --real-time-html flag. Enabling this will add some WebSocket code to the report that will fetch the latest stats continuously. Create a location block for your report and point it to your report.html to have a report always available online.

Install issues

There are typically four sources of errors when attempting to install Nginx or to run it for the first time:

- Some of the prerequisites are missing or an invalid path to the source was specified. More details about prerequisites can be found in Chapter 1, *Downloading and Installing Nginx*.
- After having installed Nginx correctly, you cannot use the SSL-related directives to host a secure website. Have you made sure to include the SSL module correctly during the configure step? More details in Chapter 1, *Downloading and Installing Nginx*.

- Nginx refuses to start and outputs a message similar to `[emerg] bind() to 0.0.0.0:80 failed (98: Address already in use)`. This error signifies that another application is utilizing the network port `80`. This could either mean that another web server, such as Apache, is already running on the machine, or that you don't have the proper permissions to open a server socket on this port. This can happen if you are running Nginx from an underprivileged system account.

- Nginx refuses to start and outputs a message similar to `[emerg] 3629#0: open() "/path/to/logs/access.log" failed (2: No such file or directory)`. In this case, one of the files that Nginx tries to open, such as a log file, cannot be accessed. This could be caused by invalid access permissions or by an invalid directory path (for example, when specifying log files to be stored in a directory that does not exist on the system).

The 403 forbidden custom error page

If you decide to use `allow` and `deny` directives to allow or deny access, respectively, to a resource on your server, clients who are being denied access will usually fall back on a `403 Forbidden` error page. You carefully set up a custom, user-friendly 403 error page for your clients to understand why they are denied access. Unfortunately, you cannot get that custom page to work, and clients still get the default Nginx 403 error page:

```
server {
    [...]
    allow 192.168.0.0/16;
    deny all;
    error_page 403 /error403.html;
}
```

The problem is simple: Nginx also denies access to your custom 403 error page! In such a case, you need to override the access rules in a `location` block specifically matching your page. You can use the following code to allow access to your custom 403 error page only:

```
server {
    [...]
    location / {
        error_page 403 /error403.html;
        allow 192.168.0.0/16;
        deny all;
    }
    location = /error403.html {
        allow all;
```

```
        }
    }
```

If you are going to have more than just one error page, you could specify a `location` block matching all error page filenames:

```
server {
    [...]
    location / {
        error_page 403 /error403.html;
        error_page 404 /error404.html;
        allow 192.168.0.0/16;
        deny all;
    }
    location ~ "^/error[0-9]{3}.html$" {
        allow all;
    }
}
```

All your visitors are now allowed to view your custom error pages.

400 Bad Request

Occasionally, you may run into a recurring issue with some of your websites: Nginx returns `400 Bad Request` error pages to random visitors, and this only stops happening when visitors clear their cache and cookies. The error is caused by an overly large header field sent by the client. Most of the time, this is when cookie data exceeds a certain size. In order to prevent further trouble, you may simply increase the value of the `large_client_header_buffers` directive in order to allow a larger cookie data size:

```
large_client_header_buffers 4 16k;
```

Truncated or invalid FastCGI responses

When setting up an Nginx frontend for a website that heavily relies on **AJAX** (**Asynchronous JavaScript and XML**), along with a FastCGI backend such as PHP, you may run into different sorts of problems. If your server returns truncated AJAX responses, invalid JSON values, or even empty responses, you may want to check your configuration for the following elements:

- Have you set up a writable directory for FastCGI temporary files? Make sure to do so via the `fastcgi_temp_path` directive.
- If `fastcgi_buffering` is set to `off`, all FastCGI responses are forwarded to the client synchronously, in chunks of a certain size (determined by `fastcgi_buffer_size`).
- In some cases, increasing the size and number of buffers allocated to storing FastCGI responses prevents responses from getting truncated. For example, use `fastcgi_buffers 256 8k;` for 256 buffers of 8 kilobytes each.

Location block priorities

This problem frequently occurs when using multiple location blocks in the same server block: configuration does not apply as you thought it would.

As an example, suppose that you want to define a behavior to be applied to all image files that are requested by clients:

```
location ~* .(gif|jpg|jpeg|png)$ {
    # matches any request for GIF/JPG/JPEG/PNG files
    proxy_pass http://imageserver; # proxy pass to backend
}
```

Later on, you decide to enable automatic indexing of the `/images/` directory. Therefore, you decide to create a new `location` block, matching all requests starting with `/images/`:

```
location ^~ /images/ {
    # matches any request that starts with /images/
    autoindex on;
}
```

With this configuration, when a client requests to download /images/square.gif, Nginx will apply the second location's block only. Why not the first one? The reason is that location blocks are processed in a specific order. For more information about location block priorities, refer to the *Location block* section in Chapter 3, *HTTP Configuration*.

If block issues

In some situations, if not most, you should avoid using if blocks. There are two main issues that occur, regardless of the Nginx build you are using.

Inefficient statements

There are some cases where if is used inappropriately, in a way that risks saturating your storage device with useless checks:

```
location / {
    # Redirect to index.php if the requested file is not found
    if (!-e $request_filename) {
        rewrite ^ index.php last;
    }
}
```

With such a configuration, every single request received by Nginx will trigger a complete verification of the directory tree for the requested filename, thus requiring multiple storage disk access system calls. If you test /usr/local/nginx/html/hello.html, Nginx will check /, /usr, /usr/local, /usr/local/nginx, and so on. In any case, you should avoid resorting to such a statement; for example, by filtering the file type beforehand (for instance, by making such a check only if the requested file matches specific extensions):

```
location / {
    # Filter file extension first
    if ($request_filename !~ ".(gif|jpg|jpeg|png)" {
        break;
    }
    if (!-f $request_filename) {
        rewrite ^ index.php last;
    }
}
```

Unexpected behavior

The if block should ideally be employed for simple situations, as its behavior might be surprising in some cases. Apart from the fact that if statements cannot be nested, the following situations may present issues:

```
# Two consecutive statements with the same condition:
location / {
    if ($uri = "/test.html") {
        add_header X-Test-1 1;
        expires 7;
    }
    if ($uri = "/test.html") {
        add_header X-Test-1 1;
    }
}
```

In this case, the first if block is ignored and only the second one is processed. However, if you insert a *Rewrite module* directive in the first block, such as rewrite, break, or return, the first block will be processed and the second one will be ignored.

There are many other cases where the use of if causes problems:

- Having try_files and if statements in the same location block is not recommended, as the try_files directive will, in most cases, be ignored.
- Some directives are theoretically allowed within the if block, but can create serious issues; for instance, proxy_pass and fastcgi_pass. You should keep those within location blocks.
- You should avoid using if blocks within a location block that captures regular expression patterns from within its modifier.

These issues originate from the fact that while the Nginx configuration is written in what appears to be a declarative language, directives from the Rewrite module, such as if, rewrite, return, or break, make it look like event-based programming. In general, you should try to avoid using directives from other modules within if blocks as much as possible.

Summary

Most of the problems you run into occur during the early configuration stages while you test your server before production. These problems are usually easier to deal with, because you are mentally prepared for the challenge, and more importantly, because Nginx points out syntax or configuration errors on startup. It is, on the other hand, much more difficult to identify the cause of malfunctions while your websites are actually in production stages. But once again, Nginx saves the day: if you properly configure log files (both access and error logs) and take the habit of reading them regularly, you will find that problem solving is made easy.

This concludes our journey with Nginx, during which we have been through a large number of subjects, from basic mechanisms of the HTTP server to web application deployment and troubleshooting. If you are interested in becoming a true Nginx expert, we recommend further reading: *Mastering Nginx* by Dimitri Aivaliotis, and *NGINX High Performance* by Rahul Sharma. You could even develop your own Nginx modules: *Nginx Module Extension* by Usama Dar is an excellent book that will help you get started.

Other Books You May Enjoy

If you enjoyed this book, you may be interested in these other books by Packt:

Mastering NGINX - Second Edition
Dimitri Aivaliotis

ISBN: 978-1-78217-331-1

- Compile the right third-party module to meet your needs
- Write an authentication server to use with the mail proxy module
- Create your own SSL certificates to encrypt connections
- Use try_files to solve your file-existence check problems
- Cache and compress responses to get speedier user interaction
- Integrate popular PHP frameworks with the FastCGI module
- Construct useful logging configurations

NGINX Cookbook
Tim Butler

ISBN: 978-1-78646-617-4

- Practical, real-world examples and recipes on how to use NGINX
- Common CMS deployments such as WordPress, Joomla and more
- NGINX configurations for frameworks such as Ruby on Rails, Django and more
- Detailed SSL recipes, including HTTP/2
- Real world rewrite examples
- Basic web and TCP load balancing configuration
- Bandwidth management and connection limiting
- Detailed NGINX deployment scenarios with Docker
- Performance tuning and monitoring of your NGINX deployments
- OpenResty deployment guides
- Advanced deployments with NGINX Plus features

Leave a review - let other readers know what you think

Please share your thoughts on this book with others by leaving a review on the site that you bought it from. If you purchased the book from Amazon, please leave us an honest review on this book's Amazon page. This is vital so that other potential readers can see and use your unbiased opinion to make purchasing decisions, we can understand what our customers think about our products, and our authors can see your feedback on the title that they have worked with Packt to create. It will only take a few minutes of your time, but is valuable to other potential customers, our authors, and Packt. Thank you!

Index

11442926R00192

Made in the USA
Lexington, KY
12 October 2018